心灵之桥 ——英中友谊和相互理解（英汉双语版）

[英] 孙如意 著

单晓晓 译

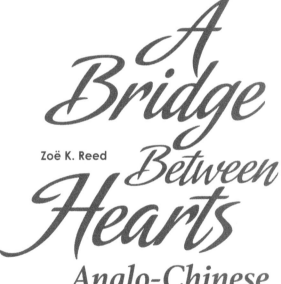

Zoë K. Reed

A Bridge Between Hearts

Anglo-Chinese Friendship and Understanding

北京出版社

Beijing Publishing House

著作权合同登记号

图字：01－2016－5385

图书在版编目（CIP）数据

心灵之桥：英中友谊和相互理解：英汉双语版／（英）孙如意著；单晓晓译. — 北京：北京出版社，2016.9

书名原文：A Bridge Between Hearts：Anglo-Chinese Friendship and Understanding

ISBN 978－7－200－12351－7

Ⅰ. ①心… Ⅱ. ①孙… ②单… Ⅲ. ①孙如意—家族—传记—英、汉 Ⅳ. ①K835.610.9

中国版本图书馆 CIP 数据核字（2016）第 184271 号

心灵之桥
——英中友谊和相互理解
（英汉双语版）
XINLING ZHI QIAO

［英］孙如意 著
单晓晓 译

*

北 京 出 版 社 出 版
（北京北三环中路6号）
邮政编码：100120
网　　址：www.bph.com.cn
北 京 出 版 集 团 公 司 总 发 行
新 华 书 店 经 销
北京京华虎彩印刷有限公司印刷

*

880 毫米×1168 毫米　32 开本　15 印张　360 千字
2016 年 9 月第 1 版　2016 年 9 月第 1 次印刷
ISBN 978－7－200－12351－7
定价：63.00 元
如有印装质量问题，由本社负责调换
质量监督电话：010－58572393

For Kate, Simon and Juanjuan
continuing Anglo-Chinese
understanding

INTRODUCTION

I met my father for the first time on 21st March 1997—
my 46th birthday. I had flown from London to Beijing with
my husband and two children whilst he had travelled rather
more slowly by rail from Lanzhou, the capital of Gansu
Province in the geographical centre of China. With him
were his wife, daughter and son-in-law, and their daughter.
We met at 3 p.m. under the National Flag in Tiananmen
Square.

After that first meeting I made a further five trips to
see him until his death in 2008, shortly before another visit
planned to coincide with the Beijing Olympics. During
that time I was able to piece together something of his
remarkable life. We talked at some length (invariably in
English) during my visits, corresponding frequently, and he
later sent me a series of recollections of the different phases of
his life.

For most of my life prior to our meeting I had no
knowledge of his existence-indeed for many years I was told
that he was dead. He had come to England in 1947 and met
my mother through his involvement with two of the most
significant Westerners in the history of China in the 20th
century—the New Zealander Rewi Alley and the Cambridge

University scholar of Chinese science and civilisation, Joseph Needham. Through these sources I was able to supplement my father's account not only of his time in England but also of his journey with Needham and Alley to the Dunhuang Cave Temples in the remote North West of Gansu in 1943. My mother helped with her personal memories of the brief time that she knew him; she died in 2005.

The following is my father's story told in his own words: a man who made his way in life through conditions that were at times unimaginably harsh, and who kept going through his own determination and intelligence. He got to know two Westerners who had a major influence on China, and developed an affection and admiration for the West and England in particular whilst remaining loyal to, and passionate about, his country. He bridged the divide between East and West, and greatly enriched the lives of those of us fortunate enough to have known him.

Zoë K. Reed

Sun Ruyi

August 2012

Postscript May 2016

I was delighted when the Beijing Publishing Group approached me, through Professor Sun Hua, Peking University, to publish my father's story in both Chinese and English. This was always my ambition to have it properly published in bilingual format. However they said they wanted more material to be included. In the original book my mother's story was only briefly touched on but it was thought that readers would be equally interested in her story of that time. The book would then become a story about what was happening in both China and England over a period that included the 1939-45 War. The publishers were also interested in why I was choosing to spend time, in a voluntary capacity, promoting links between China and the UK as the Chair of the Society for Anglo-Chinese Understanding [SACU]. It was through my involvement with SACU that I had met Sun Hua.

Some additional material has come to light since we wrote my father's story in 2012, which we have used to augment my father's part of this new book.

This new book now tells the story of my mother's life, which was always somewhat of a mystery. She used to "just up and take herself off " , family members say; "she was her own person and very prickly, took offense easily" ; "had so many jobs we couldn't keep track" ; "we all went our separate ways" and this inevitably led to misunderstandings and different perspectives. I am grateful to the many people who have helped me gathering these perspectives together and wanted to especially thank my Aunt Isabel [my mother's younger sister] who is the last remaining family member of that generation. Being somewhat of a family historian she has created a photo album that documents their lives, and has also been a great help in remembering stories and piecing together the past. She also gave me access to the story my grandmother wrote, when she was in her 80s, recalling their time in Africa.

My mother's many conversations with me about her life and the people in it have obviously helped shape this book. In addition she kept all paper documentation including letters and cards from family and friends. When sifting through the boxes of her effects after she had died, I did reflect that future generations whilst not having the burden to sort through such volumes of paper would also not have this rich documenting of our social histories!

After she died I organised a Commemorative Event and sorted out the material into a number of files. I came across all sorts of documents including her nursing examinations, prizes and awards; job offer letters; leaving cards; memberships of the Labour Party and trade unions; Rolling Stones ticket; complaint to the London Transport Executive about the manner of the conductor when you wished to open a window; National Registration Identity Cards; all of which added to the sense of the person and helped clarify dates and places.

Also as part of the Commemorative Event I constructed a timeline and sent people post-it notes asking them to help me populate the timeline by writing their memories of my mother on the small notes. This gave me more perspectives and detail.

I'm grateful to Joseph Needham for also keeping all his correspondence, which I was able to access at the Cambridge University Library where the Joseph Needham Archive is stored.

The Beijing Publishing Group inform me that this book is on the list of "China in the Eyes of International Celebrities" which is a series of books to introduce the aid and relationship between China and its foreign friends. Well, whilst this story does touch on the lives of some "International Celebrities" including Joseph Needham, Rewi Alley, Sir Stafford and Lady Cripps and George Hogg, it is primarily an account of the lives of two people who led fairly extraordinary lives; starting off in two different continents, who met through a series of events in a third and carved out productive lives for themselves through their intelligence and determination—giving me life and a very interesting background! I'm indebted to them both.

I'm also indebted to the Beijing Publishing Group for giving me this opportunity to spend time thinking about the extraordinary people that were my parents; attempting to unravel some of the mysteries in their lives and creating a coherent narrative of my childhood for the first time.

Finally, as with the first book that just covered my

father's story, I am indebted to my family, both English and Chinese, for their help and recollections and to Richard, my husband, and Adam my daughter Kate's partner for all their advice, technical help and support.

Zoë K. Reed
May 2016

Contents

Part one

My Father's Story in His Own Words

K.C. Sun's Story

Part two

My Mother's Story

Susan Eunice

Part three

Zoë's Story

Anglo-Chinese Understanding

Part one

My Father's Story in His Own Words
K.C. Sun's Story

K.C. Sun aged about 18 years*

_____

All photographs are from personal sources unless stated.

Chapter *I*
Happy Early Childhood (1926–1938)

My name is Sun Kuang Chuan and I was born on 17 March 1926 or 4 February by the old Chinese lunar calendar. My parents had twelve children in total but only six survived of whom I was the youngest; I had three brothers and two sisters. Apart from one sister all my siblings were so much older that they were married and had children of their own as I was growing up. As the youngest I was much loved and perhaps inevitably a little spoilt.

My family lived in Henan Province in a village called Ling Gang, near the town of Zhang Shi, now part of the city of Kaifeng. Henan is an eastern central Chinese province with a long history often associated with the Yellow River that flows through the north of the province. Although comprising a population of 99 million in 2007, Henan is one of the least urbanized provinces. In the 1920s it was very much a rural environment and the Sun family like many others made their living through farming and trade.

As a young child I was known as Si Dao (Naughty Number four) and also Yun Cai Ke (Gift from the Clouds). In later life I would be known by English speakers as K.C.— from the initial letters of my forenames. In my early years

I took advantage of the favoured position as youngest child and grew up as an inquisitive and often naughty boy, bold and curious, with a tendency to say whatever came into my head. My mother was often severe in her scolding as I could be fierce in the teasing of my sister, even though she was two years older than me, and my mother would chase me with a stick to try to punish me. I soon learned how to run quickly to get out of trouble, and only when I could no longer hear my mother's voice would I stop running and look for friends with whom to play.

My father was more remote during my childhood. He was generally a serious and quiet man but still made a great impression on me as a growing boy. If I had been particularly mischievous my father would make a rare intervention and although he could get angry this never led to a beating. His name was Sun Peng Ying, known to his children of course as Ba Ba. He was an ambitious man who was determined to work hard so that his family would prosper. I never knew how much he had inherited off his own father but he soon built up a mixed portfolio of small businesses. As was the local custom he began to divide these between his sons during his own lifetime: fathers were responsible for ensuring the livelihood of their sons by arranging marriages and dividing the family resources. Daughters could expect an arranged marriage but no property.

Being much younger than my brothers, I was destined

not to benefit from my father's business sense. My experience was limited to waiting for my father to return from work in his suit (he always liked to be smartly dressed) and watching him dust off his clothes and shoes, wash his face and rest before his meal.

Although we were by and large from agrarian peasant stock, our family was relatively well off compared to many of our neighbours. When my father divided up his property amongst his grown-up sons, he had 1.5 Mu (1,000 square metres) of land, a traditional vegetable oil mill (using man and horse power) and some small houses. My oldest brother (Sun Kuang Yao) ran the oil-milling business; the next eldest (Sun Kuang Ting) was an elementary school teacher; and my third brother (Sun Kuang Zhen) had only studied for a few years at middle school, was married and working with our father and oldest brother.

During the farming season my father led all the family members in our farm work. Out of season those old enough worked in the oil-milling business, extracting oil mostly from peanuts, sesame seeds and cotton seeds.

The businesses went well and in the early 1930s my father was able to buy more than 80 Mu of land and 4 courtyards for his older sons. At that time my brothers were all married; as was my oldest sister, who hired a worker called Wang Duo to feed the mules, horses and cows, and to be responsible for the horse and cart. Brother Wang, as we called him, was popular with all the family and he stayed with us for many years.

Like most of our neighbours my family grew opium plants as part of the crops, but only my father was allowed to keep the harvested extracts and he had sole use of the opium pipes kept in the house. The local custom was that all business was conducted initially over tea and then continued over pipes of opium in a private room, to which nobody else was allowed access. If the negotiations dragged on the smoking could last all day. After customers left my father would clear away all the smoking utensils and nobody, including him, would touch them again until the next customer arrived. He was the only member of the family who ever smoked and despite taking opium with his customers all his life he managed to avoid addiction. He died when he was 55 years old when I was still a young boy but I always kept the memory of my father as a good man who worked hard to ensure his family prospered.

Our village–Ling Gang–comprised 40 to 50 families living in simple houses, surrounded by a wall and a moat. The gates to the village were at the East and West ends with a road running between them. Our family lived in the North East corner. Most of the extended Sun family lived in the Eastern part and tended to be relatively better off and more 'progressive' or 'far-sighted' in their outlook.

We joined together to fund the building of a "modern

school" and invited a teacher to instruct the children. This kind of school was called Yang-Xue-Tang—which means it "followed the western method" . This was reflected in the fact that the school took girls (seen as very modern for a village) and when my sister Sun Lan Fen started I went with her even though I was only 4 or 5 years old. From this point onwards we were to find our lives increasingly linked together.

Given my nature and protected upbringing it was inevitable that I would get into various scrapes at school. As was usual for this type of elementary school there was only one teacher for all the students, he was called Bai Yu Jie. His teaching was based on a system of learning that studied what went on around the children—the heavens, the earth, people themselves. In the other part of the village the instruction was more traditional, based upon the established teachings of the sages Confucius and Mencius.

Teacher Bai did not come from the village: he was given a bedroom at the school and ate with his students' families on a rota basis according to how many children the family had at school. One summer afternoon as I was making my way back to school I heard an uncle calling me from some way off. This uncle was a kindly, well-educated man who had passed the old Imperial examinations that were held by the county. Spotting a local watermelon seller, uncle bought a piece for me and I was delighted to eat it on my way back to school even though I knew this would make me late for my lesson.

Sun Lan Fen had already begun to worry about my absence. She had become very protective of me and was used to taking punishments that should have been mine from Teacher Bai, who was quick to give out beatings. She had developed a technique of allowing her long plait of hair to cushion the blows to her back from the teacher's stick. She told me that although it sounded like quite a blow, in fact she never felt anything. All my life I never really knew whether this was true or not but this behaviour was typical of her never-ending support for me.

When I finally got back to the classroom I was still eating his watermelon and did not notice Teacher Bai, who smacked me round the back of my head so that I fell to the floor. All the watermelon went onto my face and chest; I must have looked a mess and I felt very embarrassed. Of course all my fellow students began to laugh at me, and I started to cry loudly. Teacher Bai joined in the laughter and as I lay on the floor wailing, he told my sister to take me home and clean me up. Sun Lan Fen dutifully did so and whilst she then returned to school I stayed at home for the rest of the afternoon, overcome by embarrassment and shyness.

By chance it was the turn of our family to give Teacher Bai his meal that evening. When I saw my sister arrive home I knew that Teacher Bai would not be far behind. I climbed a tall old persimmon tree just outside the gateway to await my teacher's arrival. My second brother—the one who was a teacher—was with Bai. I shouted out that there were no steam buns for Bai that evening and made some very rude remarks about him.

My brother Sun Kuang Ting looked up and told me to come down. Teacher Bai also raised his head and I noticed with some satisfaction that now he too was embarrassed and flushed all over his face and neck. The meal passed quietly but after the teacher had left I received a heavy smack from my brother. Previously I had only been wary of my father but from then onwards I never trusted my brother again and always found some excuse to leave his presence: I never forgot this experience.

But taking everything into account my early childhood was an idyllic time. I had no worries and, like most children of my age, played freely without any concerns. Young boys and girls often played together in the dusty courtyards— games such as hide-and-seek, or ones that imitated local practices such as marriages or even burials. In the summer the boys would run naked through the village and go swimming in the local pool or catch fish and shrimps in the village moat. There were trees to be climbed, nestling birds to be caught, frogs to be found in the ponds, grasshoppers and crickets to be captured in the yards. During summer and autumn, most houses had cages that were filled with birds, especially sparrows, and grasshoppers. Young birds were taken from their nests and put into cages so that we children could see them grow as the parent birds came with worms and other food, which they poked through the wire of the cage. There was a great deal of different bird song both day and night.

Many of the local children were from the extended Sun family—indeed one of my best friends was Sun Kuang Quin, who was about the same age and confusingly had the same local nickname. Some were near relatives (by which was meant having the same grandfather) and some further removed. Most of the other children were slightly older than me but this did not stop us all playing together.

Our play was usually focused on what was happening around us children but with no real planning-ahead as to what we should do or who should be involved. One day I met up with my friend Sun Xiao Hai and the two of us walked out to a nearby field. Suddenly we came across a snake—it had a green body, black dots, a white belly and we knew that it was not poisonous. We overpowered and killed the snake, which I carried home. At the village gate we met my sister as I held the dead snake behind my back. I would often try to frighten my sister by pretending to have a snake when all I really was holding were clumps of grass, so this time she just assumed it was another joke when I asked her if she was afraid of snakes. She laughed away the two of us saying of course she wasn't afraid of snakes. But before the words were out of her mouth

I placed the dead snake around her neck and she immediately went very pale and started crying hysterically. She ran straight back home, lay on her bed under the quilt and cried so much that she actually made herself ill. The fun had got out of hand, and both she and I would remember the episode for many years.

The relative calm and happiness of my early childhood was broken by the death of my father, but a few years later in 1937 (when I was aged 11 years) the escalation of a series of "incidents" into the War of Resistance against Japan was to transform my life forever.

On the Move

Within a few months a full-scale Japanese invasion of China was well under way and Henan Province was in the firing line as the invading forces advanced on the strategically important city of Wuhan in neighbouring Hubei Province.

There were a number of clashes involving people from nearby villages and Japanese soldiers. There was also trouble with a few local people who went over to the side of the invaders. Our village was already angry and tense as a result of rumours of a number of rapes in neighbouring villages. So when we heard that there was a small band of soldiers and sympathisers in the countryside near the village, local people gathered together what weapons they could lay hands on and sought them out. All the men from our village went after the small group, whom they heavily outnumbered although lacking their weaponry. For me, at my young age, it was a time of great excitement and local camaraderie in defence of our country. We had the same high spirits as when a crowd would chase after a rat that had been spotted in the village street. But the euphoria did not last long: that same afternoon other local sympathisers said that the Japanese would return in numbers to kill the villagers and burn our houses.

However, our family and the rest of the village did not have time to worry about revenge attacks, for that night, without warning, the protective dykes of the Yellow River at nearby Huayuankou were blown up as the Government tried to prevent the Japanese advancing. My home became part of a vast lake: I saw the sky link with the waters and the waters with the sky as effectively the river changed direction from west/east to north/south. All our fields were flooded and the village houses collapsed under the pressure of the murky waters. We never knew how many people died as a direct or indirect consequence but there were undoubtedly many casualties, as well as many more local people who became homeless.

Our family had to respond to this situation. My eldest brother was now head of the family, and he followed the old adage: if you just sit idle and eat, your whole fortune will soon be used up. After a few days he took a decision—the family had to move away. We were not afraid of the Japanese but there was simply no way of earning a living—no crops, no business, no trading. So a few days later, the first group including my sister Sun Lan Fen and me left home by a wooden boat heading for the south of Henan province. The group also included my mother and second eldest brother Sun Kuang Ting with his wife and 3 children, the eldest of whom was 10 years and the youngest still a baby.

The group made our way precariously to Xuchang in the middle of the province where we were accepted as refugees by the local authorities, and given some food and temporary accommodation. Of course, there were many other people in the same situation, fleeing the floods and the Japanese. Our family group was amongst about 100 people directed to Xinyang district about 300km away in the south east of Henan. The plan was that we would then be individually allocated to accommodation in a small town or village or even in a landlord's home, which was the case with our family.

Our group made slow progress to Xinyang. There was no transport of any kind, everybody had to walk carrying what possessions we could: pans, bowls, gourds, basins and clothes. Those with more possessions pushed them in wheelbarrows or pulled them in carts; those with less carried them on their backs. There were families and single people, men and women, boys and girls, young and old, people with various disabilities. Some children were too young to walk and there were even those still at their mother's breast. I was struck by the number of women with bound feet (in the old style), for whom walking even the shortest distance must have been very hard.

It took nearly 20 days for us to complete the trek. In the circumstances the organisation on the route was good: the refugees were given food at designated halts, if the weather was bad we were accommodated in temples and classrooms. Otherwise we slept in the open, perhaps under some trees, leaning on one another for comfort and support.

My family was a relatively large group of eight in total and we had more possessions to carry than others. My brother was not very strong so we used a wheelbarrow to take his family's possessions and the two younger children. I tied a rope to the front of the wheelbarrow and pulled, whilst my brother pushed from the back. Unfortunately this was the first time for both of us and the wheelbarrow kept turning over. So we took advice from others in the group and soon learned the art of keeping an upright wheelbarrow: being in front, I had to avoid all the obstacles on the road and my brother pushing from behind had to stay flexible to ensure the balance of the wheelbarrow. I also had to kick away obstacles that included stones and dried animal droppings—so much that my shoes were soon worn out.

We walked through the day and rested at night. The refugees wrote a song about the journey and in a strange way enjoyed talking, laughing and crying together over the twenty-day journey. I felt quite happy and the journey passed quickly as everybody helped one another along the way.

When the family arrived at our designated house we found it ready for us, although the landlord who owned it had left because the Japanese were threatening the local area around Xinyang. But everybody was now exhausted by the 20 day march and decided to stay at least for a while. The abandoned farm had wheat crops and peas that were ready for gathering, so there was enough to eat even if it was very basic. However, before too long the local tenant peasants also began to harvest the crops, which meant that they would not last long. My brother gave out tasks to the rest of the family: he would go to town to try to get some temporary work; our sister would look after the two young children; his eldest son and I would look around for firewood, water and fish; my mother and his wife would go out and beg for food. This was very hard for them to do because our family were landlords, not basic peasants, and not used to seeking assistance.

This sort of life was too much for our by now demoralized family group and it was decided to move to a nearby small town called Yuantai to consider what to do next. But events were about to overtake me. After a few days we heard about a visiting teacher called Mr. Li who had just arrived from neighbouring Shaanxi Province (west of Henan). He came from an orphanage there and his brief was to gather children from the areas occupied by the Japanese. It was agreed by the family that my sister Sun Lan Fen, eldest nephew Xiaozhong and I should sign up for the orphanage. After a few days Mr. Li had about 20 volunteers and so it was time to leave.

We said our farewells and walked to Luoyang railway station where we took a train to Tong Guan, on the banks of the Yellow River in Shaanxi Province. The railway line ran close by an area where Japanese troops were known to be positioned (on the opposite bank of the river) so the train had to travel at night, unlit and with little steam. The railway cut through a pass on the route to Tong Guan: the train was known as the "*Rush Through Train*" but this stretch of the line was now generally considered too risky except for the most brave.

Mr. Li therefore decided that us children should leave the train and walk through the pass. The older children had to look after the younger ones. Most of us had very little luggage so walking was not a problem. My sister, nephew and I only had one change of clothes each to carry; she also had a small wooden box containing a mirror, wooden comb and knitting wool to do up her hair. Our group of children walked by night through the pass mostly following the railway line and hiding under bushes to avoid being seen. Just as we left one of the tunnels on the line and emerged into the fresh air again an alarm suddenly sounded and we hurried into a nearby air raid shelter. As we reached it a bombardment started. There was a great deal of noise in the shelter, with lots of shouting and crying; some people were praying. I felt calm and was not at all frightened.

When we emerged from the shelter I looked around and noticed a man had been killed, his leg now hanging in a tree. We moved on and arrived at our destination, the orphanage at Feng-Xiang Wang fort in Shaanxi Province, to the west of the provincial capital Xian.

Chapter II
Life in the Orphanage (1938–1942)

I was now 12 years of age and from 1938 I was to spend over 3 years at the orphanage. It was large, accommodating nearly a thousand children. My sister also stayed there but in 1941 she had the opportunity to move not too far away to the recently opened Baoji Girls Vocational School. However, my nephew was soon collected by his father and taken back to live with him and the rest of the family. I was able to maintain some occasional links with them all including my mother, but I never returned to them—the orphanage was my place of safety even though conditions were fairly harsh and I was now on my own.

The orphanage was organised on military lines. The children were grouped into "squads" of 10, each with a leader, and five "squads" formed a "squadron" which had a commander. At meals each squad settled down around their bowl of vegetables, and each squadron had two buckets of porridge for the 50 children. The team leader was responsible for making sure the porridge got safely from the bucket to each bowl. When the commander was satisfied that all the bowls had porridge he blew a whistle to show that eating could begin. When the whistle blew the only sound was like that of a pack of hungry wolves eating because those who were quick might get a little more.

The food was really quite poor: meat was only occasionally available and meals were mostly steamed breads, maize or wheat porridge, boiled beans or bean sprouts with salt and oil. As a result the children were vulnerable to all kinds of diseases and infections due to malnutrition. Many developed scabies that could easily become life threatening. I did not entirely escape these ailments during my time at the orphanage, but I did manage to keep going.

The children were generally also poorly clothed. The orphanage relied on small grants coming from the authorities to buy material, but there were often delays in receiving the grants. By the time our winter padded clothes were ready there was usually snow on the ground, and we then had to wear them well into the summer before the unlined ones were finished. All the clothes were made by the refugees themselves including the children in grade 5 and above.

Schooling

An important part of the orphanage was the school— I was by now especially determined to further my education to progress to a better life. I was a keen learner and had been doing well at my village school before the flooding. From talking to the other students when I arrived, I reckoned I should be able to get into grade 3 or even 4—allocation to a class was based on ability rather than age.

When it came to allocating the new classes all the other newcomers had been told which grades to attend and I found myself left out, so I went to the grade 4 classroom and reported to the teacher there. She set me a calculation problem on the blackboard to see how much I knew about arithmetic. But I did not understand any of the Arabic symbols for plus, minus and so on that the teacher was using so she sent me off to the grade 3 classroom. Here exactly the same thing happened: I had become adept at using the abacus but had no idea how to address these calculations without it. I remained silent and the teacher, who was called Gao, became irritated by this and marched me by the hand to the grade 2 classroom. I was by now distraught and cried with the shame of what I saw as my ignorance.

Fortunately for me the grade 2 teacher was Mr. Li, who had been part of our group that had travelled from Henan province. He was a kind and virtuous man whom everybody respected. He had told us children various traditional stories on the journey, such as the Monkey King, Bao Gong's Legal Cases, Xue Ren'gui's Campaigns of War, and (my favourite) the King of Tang's Dream. Teacher Gao told Mr. Li that I did not know anything about arithmetic and so she would leave me with him, and with that she left.

Teacher Li looked at me and told me to stop crying; he found a seat for me and said he understood that I had only learnt the abacus and not how to calculate sums. But he would now help me learn and that I should stop feeling sorry for myself. But I felt very ashamed—I had lost face in front of all the others. My sister, despite being older, was also in this grade and now she was the only one not looking at me. She lowered her head and kept still; she knew that my Chinese language proficiency was good enough for grade 3 or 4, but not my arithmetic.

There was no grade 1 class at the orphanage so all the low achievers were also part of grade 2. The classroom was set up in the hall. There were no desks or stools so the children used tied-up sorghum (a type of grass) stalks as benches. Each student had a notebook, a pencil and a wooden board (on which the notebook rested). There was a blackboard in front of the class and everything had to be written down on it because only the teacher had a textbook. We had to copy everything into our notebooks, which became like small encyclopaedias.

The amount of writing down was especially difficult in the winter months, which were often harsh, with heavy snow and temperatures below -10 degrees centigrade. There was no heating at all in the classroom or in the bedroom, not even a stove. Like most poor people's homes, the orphanage had basic brick-built sleeping platforms called kangs: these were designed to retain the warmth of the fires within their cavity during the night, but at the orphanage they were never heated and we slept on them in the cold. Often in the winter my hands and feet suffered so that I found it difficult to hold my pencil because my fingers had swollen so that they looked like baby carrots. But I remained determined to learn, and hungered for knowledge.

After six months in grade 2, with the help of my teacher and classmates, I moved up into grade 3, where I worked hard through the year. The rule at the orphanage school was that in the summer each student could decide which exams to take depending on how well our studies had gone. So when I finished grade 3 I sat for grade 5 exams and got through. This meant that I spent the next two years in grades 5 and 6, and completed my higher primary school education in 1941. I was then ready to move on to the next grades in middle school.

Living Conditions

All this time living conditions had been getting worse, nothing like what the refugees had been promised by the authorities who had overseen our move. Our food and clothing were poor; even the basic maize porridge was hard to come by and everybody looked pale and emaciated. My stomach constantly rumbled for lack of food—I was hungry during the day and could not sleep well at night.

In the summer months fleas were all over the dormitories, which each had two large kangs where around

15 children slept. Anybody who had to get up in the night (generally to use the bucket in the middle of the room) found their legs covered with fleas. I would sit on the edge of the kang and quickly brush them off before getting back under the quilt. Here I could still expect to find more fleas, lice and sometimes scorpions, centipedes, big spiders and lizards all trying to keep me awake. One night it was my turn to be stung by a scorpion—it was really painful and I cried all night. Some of the other children told me that it was acceptable to cry but that I should not call out for my mother or it would make matters worse: this was because of the legend that female scorpions always die after giving birth, meaning all scorpions are motherless.

My tattered quilt weighed no more than 1.5 kg; it was blood stained, shiny with dirt, smelt terrible, and was never washed in all the time that I used it. Originally the quilt had weighed 2 kg to 2.5 kg but because of the lice munching their way through and my smashing it with a brick to get rid of the lice, it just disintegrated. Instead of a mattress I had some wheat straw under a wheat mat in the winter and just the mat in the summer. For a pillow I had my cotton padded clothes in the winter and in the summer a stone. The quilt and clothing were my only possessions.

Under such hard and difficult conditions nutrition was poor and hygiene basic. Although there was a clinic and a doctor there was very little medicine or medical treatment.

If the scabies got too serious maybe some sulphur cream would be provided; anything more serious often led to death. Remedies such as pork liver boiled in water as soup sometimes worked as a cure but as time went on more and more children died from illnesses.

At first deaths were properly acknowledged: the local leaders would put on their best clothes and provide a wooden box for burial, whilst the headmaster would make a speech with sympathetic words and tears. But as the deaths grew in number the ceremonies became more and more basic: the dead child would be buried in their own clothes (if they had any), rolled up in a straw mat and tied with a piece of rope; two boys would carry the body off to the graveyard, dig a pit and then bury it. Sometimes they could use the previous burial pit as bodies were often eaten by dogs. Most local families kept large dogs to keep off the wolves, which I heard were sometimes responsible for eating babies also. These dogs would be present at the burials and then fight to get at the pickings. Nobody liked to go to the burials at first, but that changed when a payment of two steamed breads was made for assisting in the proceedings. We were desperate for food and bread meant life: it became an important currency in its own right. I took part in the burial of several of my unfortunate friends and received two steam breads each time in return.

Getting Water

The orphanage was located at altitude in rather dreary rural terrain. Getting hold of drinking water was very difficult: the village only had one well and the water was 50/60 metres underground. The diameter of the well was around 2 metres— from the top the water looked like a rice bowl. My friends and I would drop a stone down the well so that it bounced off the walls giving out different sounds until eventually it hit the water. The well was about one kilometre from the orphanage and consisted of a frame with a winch mounted at the top of the hole. There was a long rope attached to the winch and a bucket at each end of the rope. Two people operated the handle so that as the empty bucket went down the well a full one was hauled up. When the full bucket reached the surface the water was poured into another bucket ready for two children to carry it back to the orphanage kitchen. Whatever the season or the weather all children in grade 4 and above had to take their turn to carry the essential water from the well.

The water was rationed to make sure everybody benefited: every morning ten of us would share a half basin of water for washing. It was difficult to keep my hands and face clean, never mind the quilt. I never had a bath all the time that I was at the orphanage. But there was a small pit nearby that would fill with rainwater in the summer and I would often slip away with friends to swim and wash. In the winter, face, hands and feet were exposed to the elements and we often suffered badly with blisters and worse. But no matter how difficult it was to walk we still had to take our turn getting water from the well. I had to walk barefoot through the snow when my shoes had fallen apart. My feet would swell up and I would go immediately to the dormitory and put them into the quilt until the swelling went down. My feet got so cold they went numb, and when the swelling went down the pain took over, preventing me from walking.

A Lesson for Life

During my time at the orphanage I received not only important basic education but also some firm moral grounding on which I based the rest of my life. Despite the hardships I was grateful for what the orphanage taught me, even if I did not always appreciate it at the time.

One morning in late spring a friend and I were returning to the school with a full bucket of water from the well. We came upon some of the villagers harvesting alfalfa, a plant usually grown as feed for animals. The villagers would gather the plants, boil them and then dry them in the sun; they would store them for eating in the winter instead of vegetables. It was still early morning when we passed by and as I hadn't had any breakfast I put down the bucket and grabbed a handful of half dried alfalfa. I devoured it greedily like a hungry wolf eating meat. Before moving on I grabbed another handful and chewed it on the way back to the school. At the front gate I met my teacher Mr. Liu, who asked me what I was eating. When he realised it was alfalfa from the fields he slapped me across the face several times until it became quite sore. He was clearly angry and I now felt ashamed:

"What have I taught you? No matter how hard your life is you should never steal. You should starve to death before you steal other people' s food. You must be an honest and upright person. I want you to remember from now onwards, always do what is right. What do you say: am I right or wrong to hit you so hard?"

I replied that of course he was right. I thought my punishment was justified and accepted it; and I remembered this incident for the rest of my life. It helped me to make the right decisions and to avoid the wrong paths. I was determined to understand fully the importance of following the right principles and values.

Moving On

In 1941 I was 15 years old and ready to move on to middle school or to a polytechnic school, so that I could go on to earn a living. I wanted to leave the orphanage but the rules were such that I needed a good reason as well as somewhere to stay. Any runaway who was caught and brought back was confined to a locked and darkened room for three days, and was also likely to receive a beating. So I had to carefully consider my options before trying to leave.

I had a classmate called Li Min Xue; our sisters now attended the same school. This school had been set up by the New Zealander Rewi Alley as part of the Chinese Industrial Cooperative movement in order to produce trained technicians and managers, and was supported by the Communist Party. It was located not far away in the west of Baoji County. In terms of both education and accommodation the girls' school was much better than the orphanage. Li Min Xue and I made a plan to run off to our sisters' school.

So one Sunday morning in early summer of 1941, with a breeze blowing on our faces, we distracted the attention of the boy at the gate to the orphanage and made our way on to the main road leading westwards. The distance to the school was about 25 kilometres. As we left we looked around us—none of our classmates were in sight so we began to walk quickly, and then broke into a run from time to time. So in only just over half a day we were able to meet up with our sisters.

We stayed with them for three days, talking about our futures—what were we going to do? Where should we go? But before we could reach any conclusions a man arrived from the orphanage to take us back. He was one of the older students and was quite a kind person. My sister pleaded with him to say some good words on our behalf to the officers of the orphanage—not to let them hit us or put us in the darkened room. He told the girls not to worry, that he would say we had been missing our sisters and hadn't really intended to run away. When we got back to the orphanage he kept his promise—we were not punished but instead received some flour to make a good meal of noodles.

So my first attempt to leave the orphanage ended in failure. But I was still restless there and decided to follow the proverb "failure is the mother of success" . I reckoned that if I stayed at the orphanage the future was hopeless for me; I would be dependent on what the authorities arranged for me. Success would be like finding a needle in a haystack. So for a second time I began to make plans to run away.

I had another friend, Gao Wen Jiang, an older boy, who knew the master of a small cotton weaving mill. The two of us made a plan to go to his mill with the aim of becoming apprentices. Having made the decision to leave we began to collect steam bread for the journey, helped by the contributions of other boys. After a few months we reckoned we had hoarded enough bread for the journey, which would take up to ten days walking but less if we were able to take a train.

We left the orphanage during the 1941 Spring Festival (Chinese New Year) holiday—I had lived and studied there for nearly 4 years. We walked to nearby Gui Zhen railway station and took a train to Xian Yang. We had no money between us and so could not afford to buy tickets for the train;

we relied upon meeting kindly ticket collectors who would let us travel for free. The cotton weaving mill was in Bei Tong Guan. This was a coal mining area so we were able to take a coal freight train, which meant that we were less likely to get caught. When we arrived at the mill only a watchman was around, he told us that the mill master was on holiday and he did not know when he would return. This was a problem, especially as our steam bread rations were almost exhausted.

My friend Gao Wen Jiang took control: he had an aunt who lived back at Xian-Yang with her son who was about 12 years old. Their home was by the road near to the railway station, a grass hut just big enough for the two of them that barely kept out the wind and rain. Gao Wen Jiang introduced me to his aunt, saying I was his very good friend and like a brother to him. He explained that we were looking for work at the mill and that he would now return there to continue the search. If he found some he would then return for me. He told me to regard his aunt as my own, to do what she said and to work with her son, and then he left.

Their lives were really very poor and tough, only a little better than beggars'. Their main income came from the aunt washing, sewing and mending clothes for other people. The son would go to the nearby railway station to collect pieces of coal from the locomotives, which would be used for cooking meals.

Fortunately there was an army barracks nearby and the

aunt arranged for me to sleep there. I ate a single bowl of noodles each day at lunchtime with the aunt and most days went to the railway station to see if I could see my friend. I was very concerned that she could not afford to look after me and insisted on also going to collect coal. But she would not let me go, saying I was welcome to stay as long as I liked; she told me she could tell that I was a "learning person" . She was very kind to me and in effect saved my life, for which I was always very grateful. I waited several weeks for Wen Jiang to return but I never saw or heard from him again.

Reunion with My Sister

One day, after I had been staying with the aunt for about a month, I got up early as usual and went to the station. It was a lively, noisy scene with the usual crowd of people entering and leaving the station, and traders selling food and drinks from stalls along the road. I felt very hungry and thirsty: what would I give for just a bowl of oil tea, or fine bean mash, or a sesame seed cake with deep-fried twisted dough sticks. But as ever I had no money and could only watch and listen.

As the day dragged on, the crowd thinned out and I was nearly the last to leave the station. Just outside I noticed an obviously well-to-do woman walking in front of me wearing a blue skirt and carrying a little boy. He looked as though he was asleep but I saw that he held a banknote in his hand. Suddenly the note fell out of his hand onto the ground right in front of me. The woman did not notice and carried on walking. When I reached the banknote I looked around and saw nobody. I put my foot on the note as my heart began to beat faster, like a rabbit in my chest. The rich woman had disappeared and there was still nobody else about. I reckoned that it was now safe to pick up the money, which I did. As my priority was to get back in touch with my sister I decided to use the small windfall on writing paper, an envelope and a stamp: I wrote a letter telling her of my predicament in Xian Yang. With the change I had just enough to buy a sesame seed cake, which tasted so sweet to me. I reckoned that my need for the money was greater than that of the rich woman and that she probably would not notice that her child had dropped the note.

At this time I was a regular visitor to the Xian Yang railway station waiting room, usually once or twice a day. It was just after the Spring Festival and there were still more people travelling as workers and students returned after their break. Rather than being afraid of the crowd I actually enjoyed being part of it; the jostling mass of people helped to keep me warm. Suddenly I was overjoyed to see somebody I knew, a girl called Li Zi Huai, who had been at the orphanage with me and now studied at the same school as my sister. I called out to her and once she got over the shock of seeing me she asked what I was doing at the railway station. I related the story of how I had run away from the orphanage and was now staying with Gao Wen Jiang's aunt and really did not know what to do next. I asked if she could help me meet up with my sister, to which she immediately agreed. She explained that she was spending the night with a school friend and then would return to their school in Baoji the following day. She invited me to travel with her, and she promised that I would see my sister. She told me to bid farewell to my new aunt and bring my things with me.

So I ran nearly all the way back to the barracks where I rolled up my small pack of luggage, thanked the guard who had allowed me to stay, made the short journey to the aunt's hut and explained to her that I had the chance to join up with my sister in Baoji. I bowed deeply in gratitude to her, and she watched tearfully as I left.

Zi Huai was where I had left her in the station waiting room. She looked at me with surprise: "Is that really all the luggage that you have?" she asked. I put my pack beside her bench and sat on it. We chatted for a while, with me occasionally having a furtive scratch as the scabies I had contracted, whilst getting better, had not fully departed. Zi Huai had a number of both large and small bags with her, including some with food. I gathered that her father was a doctor working in the army, and so her standard of living was better than most. The time passed quickly as we chatted away. As the evening wore on she took a small and thin pastry out of one of her bags. I looked at it and thought I could easily eat four or five like that one. Instead I took the half that she broke off for me and told her that was quite enough.

Eventually the train arrived and we set off for Mao Ling where Zi Huai's friend lived, just one stop down the line. We made our way through the village in the direction of her friend's home, with me now carrying all the bags. It was a lovely moonlit night with twinkling stars, the quiet only broken by a howling sound not far away. I told Zi Huai not to worry, that it was only some dogs. Suddenly Zi Huai stopped and told me that she had forgotten how to get to the house. She said we had to find a villager and ask for directions. So we turned back to the village and found a house where a lamp was burning. Zi Huai burst in quickly to find 4 or 5 men inside gambling. This was quite common in villages during the Spring Festival as the farm workers took some time off before returning to work the land. As it was only a temporary occurrence the authorities generally turned a blind eye. But the men were too occupied to listen to the request for directions. Once outside again the howling sound had stopped and surprisingly Zi Huai quickly found her way to her friend's house. She banged on the door and was relieved to be let in.

Zi Huai explained that we were late because she knew that it was a wolf that we had heard howling nearby. She had become afraid and so she pretended to be lost so that we had had to go into the village. She had then regained her courage and so had run all the way to the house, imagining the wolf at her heels. I remained calm as the family all laughed at the tale from the breathless Zi Huai. She then calmed down and introduced me to the family as Sun Lan Fen's younger brother. When we were offered a meal I quickly accepted before Zi Huai had the chance to offer a polite refusal. I was presented with a large black bowl of fine dried noodles and two fried eggs, which I proceeded to finish off without looking up from the bowl. The friend's mother watched me eat and became tearful, realizing that I had not eaten properly for a long time.

After the meal I had a really good night's sleep and the following morning we left for the station and the train for Baoji. I climbed on to the luggage rack and hid from the ticket collector behind some bags. I fell asleep again and woke up as we reached our destination. Since I did not have a ticket I decided to carry all Zi Huai's luggage past the ticket collectors, pretending that I was a hired porter. Without any further mishap we arrived at the girls' school, where my sister and I had a tearful reunion. She had been very worried about me and explained that it was only when she received the letter I had managed to send from Xian Yang that she knew for certain I was still alive.

Chapter III
Life in the Bailie Schools (1942–1946)

At School with My Sister

I knew that I would not be able to stay with my sister for very long. After all she was still a student with no income or accommodation of her own, but she was soon able to find a job for me in a small weaving mill at Shi Li Pu, a small town only 5km from her school.

The mill had four hand-driven weaving looms producing cotton fabric. Each loom had one weaver and there were two apprentices to supply the weft to the weavers—I became one of these apprentices. It was hard work and there was no payment other than two meals a day. The proprietor was impressed

K.C. and sister Sun Lan Fen taken in 1942 or 1943

by my alertness and willingness to work and promised to make me a new pair of shoes. Despite not receiving any wage I much preferred working at the mill to roaming the streets and in addition I was now able to eat proper meals. I slept on a high, narrow shelf at the mill: this was fine so long as I did not turn over in my sleep. One night I dreamt that I was sleeping in a big double bed and of course ended up falling on the floor.

The workers at the mill seemed to like my being there probably because I just got on with my work—spraying water on the floor of the mill, carrying the yarn, fetching water, sweeping the floor, buying foodstuffs. I quickly became quite skilled at the basic technical aspects of weaving that meant that I could give some help to the weavers themselves. At first my arms ached a good deal from turning the wheel quickly enough so that the weavers could get on with their production work. But my general enthusiasm for the work meant that I was usually spared the feelings off (and worse) that other apprentices received because of making mistakes. One of the weavers promised to teach me to weave as soon as I was tall enough to work the loom, which meant that I would be able to earn some money.

One morning as I was getting on with my work the proprietor called me out to the yard. My sister was there: she told the mill proprietor that someone had come to take me home. She thanked him for looking after me and said that I would have to leave immediately. I was puzzled—I was enjoying my time at the mill and knew that I was never going to go back home. When we had left the mill I asked my sister what was going on. She laughed and explained that she needed a reason to get me away from the mill. In fact someone had offered to recommend me to another school—the Bailie School at Shuangshipu (now Fengxian). When I heard this I was very excited, also because my old friend from the orphanage Li Min Xue was also being recommended.

Our supporter was a friend of Sun Lan Fen and of Li Min Xue's sister; he was something of a local poet and in love with Li Min Xue's sister. However, when we went to collect the promised letter of introduction a problem arose because it seemed that the recommendation for me was somewhat lukewarm. If there was only one place on offer the school was advised to take in Li Min Xue. My sister and I were both very angry at this apparent favouritism as I had now given up my work at the mill. We felt that it would be wrong for me to present myself at the new school with such an introduction so my sister and her friends went to their school master and asked for help. His response was a novel one: he agreed that the girls' school should, for the time being at least, enrol me as a single male pupil as a special favour.

I took my place in the school: the arrangement was that I should be the last to go to bed in the dormitory and the first to get up in the morning. It was at this point in 1942 that my life really began to take a turn for the better. The school was distinctive in that it had a training room with wooden looms operated by foot pedals and handles, usually with four or five students at a time. I was able to busy myself helping to keep the looms supplied with weft yarn. When anything went wrong with any of the looms the school brought in a technician from a local cooperative. I was intrigued by the technical aspects of the machinery and soon picked up how to make running repairs: I became known as "the little technician" . Until this time my life ambition had been to become a machine operative, but now I became more interested in the workings of the machinery and my ambition grew to designing new and more efficient machines. For the first time I heard mention of the term "engineer" and from then on this was what I aspired to become.

This school was especially suitable for me because it offered both academic and practical skills training. It was one of a growing number known as Bailie schools that were being set up in China by a man from New Zealand called Rewi Alley, who also had the role of honorary headmaster. Later I would get to know Rewi Alley quite well but I always maintained a respectful attitude toward him as he was nearly 30 years my senior. I always called him Mr. Alley, never Rewi.

Born in New Zealand in 1897 Mr. Alley had arrived in

China in 1927. He worked as an inspector, initially for the local Fire Service in Shanghai and then for the local Council's factory inspectorate. He saw at first hand the destruction wreaked on the city by the Japanese and especially the impact on the industrial sector.

He had long supported the developing Chinese Communist Party. With others he founded the Chinese Industrial Cooperative (C.I.C.) movement that was also known as Gung Ho (Working Together). With other prominent foreigners he supported Chinese resistance against the invading Japanese forces. In 1940 he opened the first Bailie School with the aim of setting up a network of schools to educate and train Chinese young people to become future leaders in the industrial development of their country. The education they received was a mix of academic learning and training in technical skills and knowledge. By 1942 Mr. Alley was already an influential figure with strong connections with the Communist Party: he had had meetings with Mao Zedong and was later to be on friendly terms with Chou Enlai, Deng Xiaoping and other senior leaders.

Meeting Mr. Alley

I first met Mr. Alley not long after I joined the Baoji School when my sister introduced me to him. This introduction was a major moment in my life. We got into conversation and I clearly made an impression on him with my knowledge and enthusiasm so that he decided to accept me as a Bailie school student in my own right. He told me that I would now definitely be moving to the Shuangshipu School and would shortly be collected by my new headmaster.

My sister and I were both overjoyed at this news, as I could not really stay at the girls' school indefinitely. I was now 16 years old and on the brink of adulthood: my life so far had been nomadic and focused on survival. Now I was to be given a chance to prove myself and set the course for the rest of my life. I was eternally grateful to Mr. Alley and stayed in touch with him for a further 45 years until his death in Beijing in 1987.

The schools were named in-part after Joseph Bailie, an American missionary friend of Mr. Alley's. This was partly to attract sympathetic foreign funding but also because Mr. Alley was careful not to draw unnecessary attention to himself and the activities of the Gung Ho movement. The invading Japanese forces that had driven my family and me from our home were still something of a threat in this more remote western area of Shaanxi Province. The name Bailie is also a play on words, being close to the Chinese phonetic Pei-Li which translates as "training" and "day break" : Mr. Alley explained to me that this referred to training technicians for the new China whilst the old China still waited in the dark for day break.

Shuangshipu and on to Lanzhou

A few days after my meeting with Mr. Alley I was collected by my new headmaster George Hogg, a young Englishman who had first met Mr. Alley in 1938, shortly after his arrival in China. The two shared a commitment to the co-operative movement as a means to support the development of China. Mr. Hogg arrived at Baoji with apprentices whom he had already gathered from other cooperative schools in the area.

We all trekked to the school at Shuangshipu, which was now establishing itself under Mr. Hogg's leadership as the most successful of the Bailie Schools in the area despite the impoverished conditions under which Mr. Hogg and the other staff had to work. Like me, most of the students were refugees from Henan Province. By this time in 1942 Mr. Hogg had been able to build up the numbers from around 12 to 60. This involved some personal sacrifice (his own accommodation was in a cave) and an emphasis on ensuring that living conditions improved for us students.

Mr. Alley and Mr. Hogg had by this time lost some confidence in the parent Chinese Industrial Cooperative movement, which was dominated by the reactionary forces of the Nationalist Kuomintang Government, and they both wanted to commit to a more individualistic system of education that would benefit the local people. They saw the outlying North West of China as the most propitious area for this, and began to make plans.

I had heard about another school even further to the west at Lanzhou in neighbouring Gansu Province. After about a month at Shuangshipu, I spoke with Mr. Hogg about the possibility of my moving on to that school. I was happy at Shuangshipu but was still concerned to keep moving as far as I could from the Japanese armies and the areas where fighting was taking place.

Some days later (toward the end of 1942) five of us boys travelled in the school truck to Lanzhou and I joined my new school. Here I settled down to some hard studying: I was now 16 years old and had matured from a rather disruptive boy into a respectful and open character who was generally popular with both my teachers and fellow students. Mr. Alley continued to follow my progress and always made a point of seeking me out on his frequent visits to the Lanzhou school. I spent some four years at the school from the end of 1942 and made Lanzhou my home for the rest of my life. I settled down quickly at the school and gained a reputation as a good student.

To the Dunhuang Cave Temples with Dr. Joseph Needham

In September 1943 I was fortunate enough to be chosen to accompany the eminent English academic Dr. Joseph Needham on an expedition from Lanzhou to the North West of Gansu Province.

Dr. Needham had been seconded from Cambridge University to be Director of the Sino-British Science Cooperation Office based in Chongqing, the temporary capital as the Government sought safer territory further from the advancing Japanese.

His brief was to seek out areas of Chinese industrial and technical development where British aid might usefully be deployed, as part of an effort to improve overall relations between the two countries. Dr. Needham's early career was as a biochemist but he became fascinated by China and was to go on to be arguably the greatest Western analyst of Chinese science and civilisation in the 20th century.

Dr. Needham had set out from Chongqing on an expedition to visit the Yumen oilfields in North West Gansu. He was travelling in an unreliable Chevrolet truck that halted in Shuangshipu (where I had been at school) for repairs. He met up with Mr. Alley who was attracted by the prospect of joining the expedition north-

On the journey to Dunhuang, 1943 — photo taken by Joseph Needham

westwards as he was on the lookout for an alternative site for the school. He gladly accepted Dr. Needham's offer to join his small party.

Dr. Needham had some calls to make in Lanzhou, the capital of Gansu Province, located on the Yellow River. The party decided that they wanted two students to travel with them as assistants, and from all the Bailie School students Mr. Alley chose me and my friend Wang Wensheng to join the expedition. We left Lanzhou on September 18th: for me the journey was yet another step into the unknown but this time as part of an organised group with specific objectives. But we were to meet many difficulties on the way and our problems began almost immediately: the travelling mechanic was perhaps the busiest of the group as the trucks broke down several times.

This was something completely new for me and a massive addition to my education and general life experience; meeting Dr. Needham as well as Mr. Alley would affect the rest of my life in ways I could not predict. But for the moment I took in the sights around me on the journey: I saw columns of soldiers marching along the road, many of them not much older than myself. From Dr. Needham I heard how Gansu was rich in resources, especially wool—if only local people had the capacity to turn the raw material into finished products. When we were 450 km out of Lanzhou we came across a place called Shandan; compared to the rather basic towns and

On the way to Dunhuang. Photograph by Joseph Needham, reproduced courtesy of the Needham Research Institute

villages we had seen before, this was a veritable oasis. It was an old walled town described by Dr. Needham as the "loveliest, spacious place, beautiful old architecture" [1]. Mr. Alley saw it as the new location for the Shuangshipu Bailie School.

We eventually reached Dunhuang on 30 September and then moved on to the cave temples at Chienfotung 24 km away. The intention was to spend a day or so inspecting and photographing the caves before beginning the return journey. The walls and ceilings of the caves were covered in plaster and paintings, and were reckoned by Dr. Needham to be China's greatest art museum. We ended up staying for around 3 weeks, due to the truck breaking down again and having to wait for parts to arrive. Whilst Dr. Needham filled his notebook with details and sketches Wang and I

[1]   Science Outpost, Papers of the Sino-British Cooperation Office 1942-46, The Pilot Press, London1948.

busied ourselves obtaining supplies and doing the cooking. We also had time to learn the delights of English Morris Dancing, this being but one of Dr. Needham's many and varied interests.

Wang and I made several journeys by donkey to the nearby town to collect provisions, as well as visiting the cave temples with Dr. Needham and Mr. Alley. The food was quite simple but it was plentiful enough: Moslem bread rolls, a huge cartwheel loaf, a bit of mutton; but mostly fruit, especially melons, pears and quinces; also potatoes and other vegetables. We often made what Dr. Needham told us was Irish stew.

One particular day Dr. Needham and Mr. Alley became concerned when Wang and I had not returned from Dunhuang by the agreed time: the two men had a nagging fear throughout their stay of armed Kazaks who were rumoured to be in the vicinity and looking for trouble. They went out into the desert to meet us, and made little fires from the crude salt in the ground to keep off any wild animals. The sun was setting when they spotted us in the distance: we were each carrying a long stick to frighten off wolves and other animals. When we saw Dr. Needham and Mr. Alley waiting for us Wang and I raised our sticks and increased the pace of our donkeys. Unfortunately, with the sun behind us casting long shadows, to Dr. Needham and Mr. Alley we appeared as hostile horsemen—they turned and ran back toward the camp. It

With Joseph Needham (left) the painter Wu Zuoren and Wang (far right) in the desert near Crescent Moon Lake near Dunhuang. Photograph by Joseph Needham, reproduced courtesy of the Needham Research Institute

K.C. and truck on the journey to Dunhuang. Photograph by Joseph Needham, reproduced courtesy of the Needham Research Institute

was only when they heard our voices that they realised their mistake and laughingly turned to greet us warmly. We had indeed seen both Kazaks and wolves on our journey into the town but our late arrival home was in fact caused by a queue at the bank.

The cave temples (of which there were around a thousand) made a very beautiful sight in the autumn light. The leaves of the trees were beginning to turn orange and the scene looked to me like an oil painting. Surrounded by desert, the caves seemed like an oasis complete with a stream and surrounding trees. Mushrooms grew in the woods and with nobody to pick them they grew big and tall, reminding me of a chicken's leg with a big round head. They were white and tender, and delicious to eat when washed and properly cooked. Dr. Needham provided the recipes and Wang and I did the cooking and other tasks around the camp.

One day, after returning from another food shopping trip to Dunhuang (which had required an overnight stay), we found both Dr. Needham and Mr. Alley in some discomfort. It turned out that they had eaten a mushroom meal that they had cooked themselves and this had made them unwell; we pointed out to our two renowned travelling companions that washing the sand from the mushrooms was an essential part of the food preparation. We all had a good laugh at this rather basic omission on their part.

En route To Dunhuang 1943. Photograph by Joseph Needham, reproduced courtesy of the Needham Research Institute

At Dunhuang with Wang 1943—K.C. on the right. Photograph by Joseph Needham, reproduced courtesy of the Needham Research Institute

After an enjoyable return journey we arrived back in Lanzhou where the party dispersed at the Yellow River Bridge. Wang and I returned with Mr. Alley to the Bailie School whilst Dr. Needham went to stay with friends elsewhere in the city. But my friendship with the eminent English academic had only just begun.

Back at Lanzhou

With communications difficult I did not see much of Dr. Needham at first. At this time Lanzhou had no cars or buses, only horse drawn carriages and donkeys. There was only one bridge across the Yellow River, otherwise crossings were by sheepskin raft. So Dr. Needham decided to move from the city centre to stay with us at the Bailie School itself, where Mr. Alley had his own traditionally built hut.

The school was on the north side of the river some 10 kilometres from the city centre. It was built on a slope with the front part higher than the back. All the classrooms and training rooms (textiles, machinery, chemistry and so on) were at the front together with the playground. At the back, about 3 metres lower and near to the river, were the accommodation and other communal areas.

Mr. Alley's hut was generally locked but when he was due to visit it was opened up and given a clean. It was surrounded by flower beds and to get to the door visitors had to pass through what seemed like a tunnel of various flowers that blossomed in spring, summer and autumn, including peonies, chrysanthemums, read-peas and morning glories. I really enjoyed the effect of the different flowers and the array of colour produced at different times: red, blue, yellow, white and green. I thought that approaching Mr. Alley's room was like walking under a dragon made of flowers, leaping up to the sky. I helped with the garden and in due course was able to grow my own grape vine, whose produce was much appreciated by Mr. Alley and his guests.

One afternoon late in 1943 the school held a small celebration to mark Dr. Needham's successful journey to the Dunhuang cave temples. Desks and chairs were placed on part of the basketball playground. On the desks were refreshments for the guests and teachers: teapots, cups, watermelon seeds, sunflower seeds, broad beans, winter pears and other fruits. Wang and I, with all the other students, were sitting on the ground; several of them performed scenes from traditional operas, related the history of the cooperative movement, and told stories or jokes. Dr. Needham had two interpreters—Dr. H.T. Huang, who was then his secretary, and Liao Hong Jing, who taught chemistry at the school. This was a very warm and friendly occasion; for me it felt just like a family reunion.

Mr. Alley joined in the festivities with a New Zealand Maori dance and demonstrated the traditional Maori greeting of bumping noses. Not to be outdone Dr. Needham responded with a traditional English folk dance and despite it being early November he finished his dance in quite a sweat to warm applause from his audience. My contribution to the proceedings was to speak some words of what I called "false English" (in fact just making voice sounds) which a classmate then "translated" into Chinese. This performance went down well with everybody but especially with Dr. Needham and Mr. Alley who seemed to find it very amusing. For me the performance gave me the idea of really learning to speak English and of going on to become an interpreter.

Not many weeks after I returned to school and lessons I received some amazing news. I had just finished playing basketball in the playground when senior teacher Madam Wang approached me and asked if I had enjoyed the game. I replied that I had but that I didn't really play basketball very well and just made up the numbers. Madam Wang asked me to come to her office. I followed her, trying to work out what this might be about as I hadn't been in any sort of trouble recently. When we got to the office I saw that Mr. Alley was already there. I was invited to sit down, but as I was still expecting some sort of bad news I said I'd rather stand up. Mr. Alley smiled at me and encouraged me to sit down.

Madam Wang spoke: she told me they had all decided that I should be given the opportunity of travelling to the West with Dr. Needham and Mr. Alley. Apparently they had been impressed with my hard work and attitude both at school and on the expedition to Dunhuang. Their original idea had been that I should go to England immediately for about a month, but then they thought that both the school and I would benefit more if the trip were delayed until I had finished my schooling. This would be in four years time when I would be older and more equipped to get to grips with English. Meanwhile Dr. Needham would be responsible for setting up my further education in England. My friend Wang Wansheng from the Dunhuang expedition would also make the trip to England.

I was both excited and overwhelmed at this news, and for once was lost for words, thinking that I was imagining what I had heard. I bowed deeply in thanks to Madam Wang and Mr. Alley, who patted my head and told me that I should now study even harder and keep in good health so that I could be a credit to my country. Madam Wang supported this view and said that she would tell the rest of the school at the next Monday assembly. As soon as the news was released Wang and I inevitably became the subject of various conversations. The news even reached the other Bailie Schools where some people were very pleased for us, and others less so.

Life at Lanzhou

It had been my good fortune to come into contact with the Bailie school system firstly through my sister's school at Baoji. Now I was a senior student and had made some amazing contacts. The whole school regime at Lanzhou was like paradise for me compared to the poverty of my childhood and my hazardous escape from the Japanese. In addition, I now had the journey to England to look forward to.

I had enough to eat, proper clothes to wear in summer and winter, a bed to sleep in; there was no need for me to hide or be in fear for my life. I was part of a collective effort that transformed a small old leather factory on the outskirts of Lanzhou into a smart new technical school where standards matched those of the West.

Inside, the rooms were clean and painted in white; kitchen, dining room, bedrooms, classrooms, machinery rooms, chemistry laboratories and sewing rooms. The area around the school was cleaned up so that it looked attractive: roads were cobbled and gardens laid out with colourful flowers and a number of apple trees—a gift from USA Vice President Henry A. Wallace. The school also grew our own vegetables such as cabbage, tomatoes, and chilli. I developed a deep lifelong appreciation of the Bailie School system and its values.

The school followed the new educational policy, based on using hand and brain, practice and theory, a method that encouraged rigorous and independent thinking. Student numbers soon increased and like me the new students mostly came from those areas occupied by the Japanese, from co-operatives and from poor families.

Initially there was one mixed class, with no specialities

being pursued but the single class soon evolved into three classes—High, Middle and Low. The subjects taught covered a range of theory and practice: maths, physics, chemistry, Chinese, English, geography, history and natural science, textiles, machinery, surveying and drawing, machine drawing, accountancy, cooperation, and so on. The facilities at the school also developed until it had a textile shop, dyeing and carpet-making area, machinery shop (with lathe, vice, plane, forging cast) and chemistry workshop. The regular pattern was theory lessons in the morning and practice in the afternoon, where technical support teachers helped the students to develop their skills and try out new ways of doing things.

I spent the next four years until 1947 at the Lanzhou Bailie School. At first my special technical subject was civil engineering survey drawing but after a year I changed to mechanical engineering, which I studied for three years.

At the end of 1943 a new teacher called Mr. Li joined the school—he was an "overseas Chinese" (born outside China) who had moved to Lanzhou from the South East of China. Despite his poor command of Mandarin Mr. Li made an immediate impression on me because of his technical drawing skills. He was a straightforward and strict teacher who was unpopular with some of the less keen students. I learned how to use the simplest measuring equipment to produce accurate drawings, including a diagram of the school. Despite pressure from many of my fellow students, I worked well with Mr. Li and refused to join in the general criticism of his strict teaching manner.

I was determined to take advantage of the educational opportunity that had come my way. I still felt a great desire not to return to the harsh sort of life that I had very recently left behind. But my classmates held a

K.C. in 1945 aged 19—a photo sent to his mother (whom he had not seen for 10 years) before he left for England

secret meeting at which they planned to physically attack Mr. Li. Whilst I refused to join in this action I also decided not to inform the school authorities of the plan. I was trying not to offend anybody: at the meeting I kept my head down and did not speak. Next morning, a few minutes into the class, one of the older students stood up and called on the class to attack the teacher, who quickly escaped from the classroom. I remained in my seat the whole time. As a result of this incident several students were expelled and Mr. Li left the school. It was as a result of his leaving that I changed my specialist course from survey drawing to mechanical engineering.

As part of my mechanical engineering course I had to learn about the diesel engine. The school only had one example from which everybody had to learn. This engine had just arrived from Shanghai and the school had not yet decided how to make best use of it. So when it was time for the lesson the engine did not yet have its foundation base and was still on the floor within the frame in which it had arrived. Teacher Chang gave the class full details on how to start the engine and we each took it in turns to try and start it.

Nobody had yet been able to get it going properly when I went back to the classroom during the lunch break to take my turn (as I was so keen to get it started). I decided to light up the blowtorch and heat the cylinder in order to get the oil to a decent temperature first. As the temperature rose I picked up the starting handle and had only given it a few turns when there was a loud noise and black smoke started to come from the engine's exhaust. This had never happened before. I jumped on to the engine frame to give it more oil: the engine began to start up, slowly at first and then it began to jump around on the ground. Although it was still lunchtime, quite a few students as well as teachers had gathered around to see what was going on. I was squatting on the engine trying to keep it under control as it jumped up and down. Teacher Chang now appeared on the scene and shouted to me to stop the engine, and that I had already gained full marks for my practical work. The engine was now at a high velocity and I was getting rather flustered at what to do next; I was relieved to hear that I could turn everything off and leave the engine. This was one of my most important lessons in integrating theory with practice and after this episode I was given special responsibilities at school for the gas lamps and generator.

When the school grew in size and was divided into three classes I was one of 10 or 12 in the top class. That number was soon reduced to seven as some left for various reasons. We called ourselves the "Seven Heroes" , who were the Chinese legendary equivalents of Robin Hood and his Merry Men or the Three Musketeers. Like me, my classmates were keen students and used their learning well in their later lives.

Whilst I was becoming even more interested in, and committed to, both the theoretical and practical aspects of my education, I never developed any expertise or interest in sport (or music for that matter). The only sports that I ever took to were swimming, fishing and table tennis (which I only really took up later on in England). I had always managed a basic sort of swimming since my childhood days by the Yellow River, and it was to this same river that we would now go in Lanzhou. In truth this exercise was as much about the importance of cleanliness as it was about learning to swim properly. Later in life I did manage to learn front crawl and backstroke when I went to a modern swimming pool. Fishing had always been an important pastime (and, of course, source of sustenance) and this interest stayed with me all my life.

Inevitably Physical Education played a part in the school regime so I could not escape some involvement in what we knew as "big ball sports" . But I was always one of those students who just made up the numbers, certainly in any competitive game. My only advantage on these few occasions was that I understood the various calls made by the other players because these were always in English, in which I was now interested from my time with Dr. Needham. My only game of any importance came against the teachers' union team and I was drafted in because the school basketball team was a player short. I ran about the court and passed the ball as quickly as I could whenever it came to me. As soon as the missing player arrived I was substituted and that was the end of my involvement in basketball.

I saw a good deal of Mr. Alley in Lanzhou and had determined from my early meetings with him to learn as much as I could. In particular I took to heart one of Mr. Alley's pet phrases: "no trousers, no socks, no money, no can do." I learned the importance of work as the only means to earn money and therefore the way to have a decent life. If each individual worked hard not only would they benefit, but others would too. Another favourite phrase was: "each for all, all for each". I took this philosophy as a guide for the rest of my life. I saw it as an encouragement to go out and achieve rather than accept a destiny of poverty as many Chinese people then grew up to believe was their lot.

In the winter of 1943/44 I briefly met up again with George Hogg, who was passing through Lanzhou as he marched his 60 students from Shuangshipu to their new school that Mr. Alley had indeed located at Shandan, on the way to Dunhuang. Tragically, Mr. Hogg died of tetanus in July 1945 after stubbing his toe whilst playing basketball with the students. From that time onward Mr. Alley spent more time at Shandan and less at Lanzhou. But he had by now made a firm impression on me and I was looking forward to completing my education in 1946 and then the promised journey to England.

Before he left for Shandan, Mr. Alley had a meal with me and he reminded me of the responsibilities that I would have as a Bailie School graduate and as a young Chinese man in England. He explained that Dr. Needham was making all the necessary arrangements for my continuing education there the following year (1947).

I was excited but understandably nervous about the prospect: this was still a period of relative isolation for China and very few people had the opportunity to spend time abroad, never mind people from my background. Mr. Alley reassured me that all would be well, that I was now sufficiently grown-up to cope with the demands of life in the West and that I should steer clear of prostitutes and their sexually transmitted diseases. This was the first time that I had received anything approaching sex education—it was simply not addressed at schools in China where the custom was that fathers talked to sons and mothers to daughters. Effectively without a father, I had missed out and Mr. Alley was the nearest that I had known to a father figure during my adolescence. We parted with a fond embrace.

Chapter IV
Going to England (1946–1947)

Back in England, Dr. Needham, further inspired by what he had seen at Dunhuang, was embarking on his monumental series of works entitled Science and Civilisation in China that was to radically affect the way the West saw China. He did not neglect his promise to Mr. Alley to support the continuing education of Bailie School graduates so that they could be better equipped to lead the industrial and technical development of the emerging nation. The aim was also to demonstrate the effectiveness of the Bailie School system and the wider co-operative movement which both Dr. Needham and Mr. Alley supported. Working with the London-based British charity United Aid to China, he ensured that the necessary funding was in place and began to put together a study programme.

As the time to leave approached and I began to prepare for my big adventure I was aware of developments in China. At this time, the summer of 1946, the civil war of liberation between the Nationalists and the Communists was just starting. Mr. Alley was a long-time supporter of the Chinese Communist Party and considered the Kuomintang Nationalists rooted in the past and generally inefficient and corrupt. Dr. Needham's role in China had been part of tentative steps by

Britain and other Western countries to determine the extent to which they could work with the Communists, who had offered sterner resistance to the Japanese.

In this climate, travelling overland was much slower than normal. Wang and I set off in October for Shanghai to sort out passports and other necessary documentation. The journey took us six weeks, initially by truck and then by train, until we finally reached Nanjing by boat. Here we presented ourselves at the British Embassy in order to get our visas sorted. After staying a few days we then left for nearby Shanghai where we were looked after by the local office of the Chinese Industrial Co-operatives (C.I.C.), who also arranged for us to receive a course of English lessons. This intensive study was a new experience for me although I had picked up a few words from Dr. Needham and Mr. Alley. For some time I struggled to get to grips with a language that was so fundamentally different to Chinese.

The C.I.C. was responsible for Wang and me in Shanghai, and for getting us to England: they put us up at a hostel where we got three decent meals a day and were able to make use of a swimming pool, where at last I learned how to dive properly. An Englishman called Peter Townsend was our main contact at the C.I.C. where he worked as English Publicity Secretary; he was later to become an influential contemporary arts writer and editor. He took care of all our requirements so that I had no idea how much our stay in Shanghai was costing.

Altogether it took six months until we eventually obtained our passports in March 1947, and we were finally able to leave Shanghai by boat for Hong Kong. When we docked we were met by Chen Yimin, who was an old friend of Mr. Alley's. He worked as an accountant, was well known locally and quite well off. He was also very kind to us at this first stage of our great journey and treated us to dinner at his home. I gained an insight into a different way of life as attentive waitresses refilled my plate and cleared away the crumbs of a meal that not long ago I could only have dreamed about.

We had been allocated a ground floor room in a small hotel for a few days. Although it was only March the weather in Hong Kong was already very humid, so we kept the windows open day and night. One morning we awoke to find that all the washed clothes we had left to dry by the window had disappeared. I phoned the hotel manager, who told me not to worry and that he would get the clothes back. Soon afterwards that morning a man came to our room carrying a big cloth-wrapped bundle. He put it on the floor and opened it—it was full of different types of clothing. Eventually we were able to find every item that we had lost. Amazed, I asked the hotel manager what had happened and he explained that a thief had used a long bamboo rod with a hook to reel in the clothes through the open window. The manager had phoned the Police and explained that we were from mainland China and were about to travel abroad, and that the hotel was responsible for them. He also explained to us that the Police and the local thieves were often like one family—so it was not long before the thief was caught and the clothes returned.

After a couple of days, as we arrived back from a session relaxing at a nearby beach, we received a telephone call from Chen Yimin saying he would pick us up at 6 o'clock for supper at his house. When we arrived we were introduced to an Englishman called Bob Porteous who was about to return home and who had agreed to keep an eye on us on the voyage.

The ship we sailed on was the SS Chompollion, a French passenger liner being used primarily as a troop ship, with little on-board comforts. Like everybody else I was given a makeshift hammock to pitch where I could. I was terribly seasick for much of the voyage, even in the slightest swell, and the hammock was of some consolation on these occasions. I had some respite as the ship called in at several ports, usually every 4 or 5 days. In the particularly rough seas I found it impossible to eat anything and became quite despondent.

When the ship docked in Bombay I was so fed up that I seriously thought I should abandon the voyage. But once the ship had anchored I had a swim in the sea and then went for a walk around the city, and even managed something to eat. Feeling a little better I determined to continue and from that time it was only the really big storms that upset me. On the month-long voyage I was able to continue to practise my English in conversation with Bob. Although I spoke no French I did manage a few words of English with some of the French soldiers (returning from the war in Indo China) and soon picked up some basic French. I also learned how to play chess and even managed to win a game against the soldier who taught me.

Once I had found my sea legs I liked to take a walk on deck surrounded by the vastness of the ocean. I got to appreciate sights that I had never properly observed before, especially the rising and setting of the sun against the horizon. The red setting sun was like a burning ball for me, until it slipped gently into the water only to burst forth again the following morning like an old friend. There were other sights too: flying fish leaping across the waves, sharks roaming around the ship looking for anything edible, a whale spouting a fountain of water into the air, seagulls following and sometimes settling on the ship. One morning, as I set off for breakfast after watching the sunrise, a sparrow fell down in front of me. I crouched down and picked it up in both hands. There was very little sign of life and soon it was clear that the small bird was dead: I wondered how it had got there, where had it come from, and where was it trying to get to?

It was quite a landmark when the ship passed through the Suez Canal. I could clearly make out life going on as the banks of the canal were so close. The ship tied up in Port Said for two days so I had the opportunity to sample a little of Egyptian life. The streets struck me as narrow and the buildings mostly low rise; I thought that many of the local people looked unhealthy, perhaps due to the obvious lack of sanitation.

After Port Said the ship made for Marseille, where Wang and I again stayed in a hotel for a few days. Bob was still with us and the three of us set off to explore the city. There was still a lot of war damage evident and there were few goods on display in the shop windows. I wondered if this sort of damage and poverty was what I had to look forward to in England. The scene made quite an impact on me as I took in my first impressions of Europe. At one stage as we strolled around the port I realised we were being followed by three young women and was puzzled. I asked Bob if he knew what they wanted: Bob pointed out that the women were prostitutes and were offering their services. I remembered Mr. Alley's advice and we quickly moved on.

On the afternoon of our fourth day in Marseille we caught an aeroplane to Paris, where Bob said farewell to Wang and me. We had an overnight stop before our connecting flight to London. By this time I had recovered all my original enthusiasm and more, and was impatient to set off again. After breakfast the next day, the hotel receptionist called a taxi for us and we set off on the last leg of our journey to London. As we passed the Eiffel Tower the taxi came to a halt and the driver struggled to get it started again, much to our frustration, as the time was slipping by. Once we had walked round and admired the Tower, I had had enough and despite speaking hardly any French, persuaded the sweating taxi driver to stop another taxi. So we finally completed our journey to the airport and caught the flight to London just in time.

Chapter V
Life in the UK (1947–1950)

Mr. Alley had written to British United Aid to China (BUAC) in London confirming that "the two Shandan Bailie boys" (as we were incorrectly known throughout our stay in the UK) were at last on their way. A meeting had been held in May to plan our welcome: the intention was to accommodate us in London for a few days before going to the Stanford Hall Cooperative College in Nottinghamshire where we would have accommodation and take some general lessons. We had also been enrolled on a textiles course at a nearby college. At this time the cooperative movement was prominent in both China and the UK.

Wang and I arrived in London on 12 June. We had not been able to confirm our time of arrival and so when we landed at the recently opened Heathrow Airport there was nobody to meet us. We obtained the help of a friendly taxi driver for the final part of our journey and arrived in the centre of London, where we met the awaiting committee members gathered at their offices in Mayfair.

The committee greeted us formally and gave us tea, after which Wang and I were taken first to our hotel at nearby Holland Park and then out to eat at a Chinese Restaurant in Central London. The BUAC committee members assumed that then we would have done enough for our first day in England. But we were so excited to be in London that we wanted to see more and so we were taken to Wembley Stadium in North London for a motorcycle speedway meeting. We travelled

Photo from BUAC Monthly Review July 1947

by the Underground and rather belatedly joined 60,000 other spectators and were entertained by a representative of the stadium. We finally got back to our hotel and then enjoyed a few days in London settling in to life in England.

Everybody was very kind and pleased to see us. And we both tried hard to make a good impression as we had been coached by Mr. Alley. After this short stay in London we were taken north to Stanford Hall College where we immediately began our studies. Stanford Hall was the British Cooperative Union's residential college and a former stately home, set in the Nottinghamshire countryside. It was situated in beautiful grounds with a lake, and made a stark contrast to what I had been used to at home in Lanzhou. Wang and I were the only Chinese students but there were others from all over the world.

When we arrived at the College it was, of course, during the summer vacation and formal classes were not due to start until October. So for about 3 months we spent a very interesting and instructive time working at the Nottingham Cooperative Society transport machine shop. We also spent a good deal of time in the College swimming pool and the lovely grounds, as well as trying to improve our very poor English.

In October 1947 our training began in earnest. The basic working pattern was that we went off to Nottingham Technical College (30 minutes by bus) four days a week to learn about different aspects of textiles (Fabric Analysis, Raw Material, Textile Testing, Applied Design and Textile Mechanics). The course consisted of practical work in the laboratories and machine shops as well as some lectures; in the machine shop we worked on hand and power looms. For the other weekday and Saturday Wang and I remained at Stanford doing English lessons and learning more about the cooperative movement (Sunday was a day off). I also went on various visits that were organised both for training purposes, such as a bakery in Nottingham, and sightseeing in places like Edinburgh.

My main problem was getting to grips with the language. I had already picked up some good conversational English but this was not enough for the more technical aspects of our lessons and so, like Wang, I found the studying rather heavy-going. Meanwhile, back in China, it turned out that Mr. Alley was having reservations about the whole venture, which he expressed in a letter to Dr. Needham: perhaps we should have stayed at Lanzhou or gone to Shandan Bailie School and continued our studies there.

Dr. Needham himself had tried to contact us, even sending two postcards from Mexico, where he was on UNESCO business. But it was not until December 1947, six months after our arrival, that we managed to make contact with him and arranged to spend some time in Cambridge with Dr. Needham and his wife Dorothy. We also visited Sheffield to study first-hand some examples of Cooperation and to help with some fundraising for BUAC's efforts to support development in China.

I was beginning to get to grips with the technical demands of the language but it was clear that neither of us would be able to make much progress in our learning by the end of the original planned 12-month stay. The key aspect of our trip was to learn from how things got done in the textile industry in the UK and to take this knowledge back to China for the benefit of industrial development there. With this in mind, between them, the BUAC Office, Mr. Alley in China, and Dr. Needham in Cambridge ensured additional funding so that Wang and I could remain in England for a further year through to summer 1949.

So in 1948 I was able to continue my studies at Stanford Hall and Nottingham but was also able to get more practical experience by spending some time at a textile mill (Marling and Evans) in Gloucestershire in the west of England. This gave us practical experience in all applications—carding, spinning, weaving, dyeing and finishing—of woollen textile operations. We stayed with a local family who were very kind to us and I kept in touch with them for a time afterwards. We paid a second visit to Dr. Needham in Cambridge in the spring of 1949, and we all agreed that we were now making good progress in our studies.

Our courses at both Nottingham Technical College and the Cooperative College came to an end in April 1949. After a short Easter break we rounded off our experiences with some factory visits organised by Dr. Needham and by Mrs Moore of BUAC. We spent a few days at the Garnet factory near Leeds, where they specialise in making machinery for reconditioning the waste products of textile mills. This was of special interest to us from China where there was always a shortage of new raw materials and so a need to make use of all available products. We also visited a small factory at Haslemere in Surrey, where they assemble spinning sets, which we were able to reproduce back at Shandan. We also spent a short time at Courtaulds factory in Essex where we saw many interesting processes in the manufacture of silk and rayon.

Meanwhile I had also been making progress in another direction. At Stanford Hall I had met and fallen in love with one of the very small number of young women studying at the college. She was Eunice Reed, known to most people as Susan. There were other women on the campus but they were involved in catering, administration and domestic tasks. Susan arrived early in 1949; she had paid a shilling to enter an essay-writing competition organised by the Cooperative Society. She won the first prize, a year's course in business studies at Stanford Hall.

Perhaps appropriately we first met saw one another during one of the International Cooperation classes. Our relationship quickly took off, and soon our fellow students were teasing us for our obvious mutual infatuation.

Having been convinced of our English language skills, Dr. Needham was now ensuring that Wang and I were able to take full advantage of our stay in England. He arranged visits to textile works for us and showed us some of the material that he had collected during his studies of China's textile industry. He was also concerned that we should further extend our education by getting some practical experience of working in a textile mill on the more advanced machinery that was now in use in the UK. He began to look for practical work placements. I was very appreciative of his efforts, not least because it would extend my time with Susan.

During my time in England I noticed that the changing of the seasons was much more significant than in China and I particularly enjoyed the coming of Spring, and the manner in which flowers bloomed and the leaves turned green. This was a time of year for people to enjoy themselves, so for the Easter holidays of 1949 Susan and I took a short holiday together in London, staying at a friend's flat. In order to be able to do this I had told the BUAC office that I was going off by myself on a walking holiday.

This was a memorable week for me, experiencing life in the capital and being in love. I especially liked walking through the parks, observing other people and just engaging Susan in conversation about life. I visited London Zoo at a time when the BBC was running a campaign to encourage people to send in bamboo shoots for the sick panda Lien Ho. These were the beginnings of panda diplomacy as the BBC wondered whether liberated China would send another panda to Britain. In another visit that also reminded me of life back home, I saw the tomb of Karl Marx with its impressive bust of the founder of Communism.

Susan took me to many other places across London, including Kew Gardens where I marvelled at the different varieties of flowers and grasses. I saw bananas growing in the hothouse, and stared up at the palm trees reaching upwards. The botanical garden struck me as the most complete and satisfying type of garden in the world.

After we looked around the Gardens Susan and I found a large grassy space and lay down to chat about what we had seen that day. We were about to return to the flat when some young people (girls and boys) invited us to join a ball game with them. We happily agreed and I was soon soaked in sweat from running around. Suddenly I realised that I needed to pee, and Susan pointed out a nearby public toilet. I ran across to the building, and by this time was so desperate that I dashed into the Ladies and caused a good deal of laughter.

Susan also introduced me to more cultural pursuits: we went to the opera, paid several visits to the cinema and twice went to hear Paul Robeson. These experiences in London were a far cry from the life that I had led back in China and again served to broaden my view of the world and what it might offer me.

Whilst Dr. Needham continued to use all of his contacts in search of more work experience for Wang and me, the BUAC office was concerned both at our apparent lack of progress and at our diminishing funds. It was really only through Dr. Needham's efforts that BUAC had provided funding in the first place; normally their scholarships were intended for older students who had more experience. So BUAC began to make

K.C. in Holywell, North Wales, 1949

arrangements for our return to China.

At the eleventh hour, Dr. Needham found an interested mill owner, Thomas Waterhouse at Holywell in North Wales. Mr. Waterhouse wrote to Dr. Needham on 12 May 1949, just two days after Dr. Needham had heard from BUAC that they had in fact booked return tickets for Wang and me. He quickly got on the phone and the bookings were cancelled. Mr. Waterhouse had agreed to take us on for 12 months as paid weavers, having been assured that we would have no difficulty using the power looms at his mill.

Dr. Needham's personal support for our continuing education went as far as agreeing to stand as financial guarantor should anything go amiss at Holywell. I wrote to Dr. Needham expressing my great thanks for all his efforts, noting that he had done this when everybody else seemed to have given up (I also mentioned that Susan too sent her thanks!) On 19 May 1949 Wang and I took the train to Holywell.

At Holywell with Wang, August 1949

The mill (known as Waterhouse Top Mill) had been built in 1777 during the Industrial Revolution, its location being due to the water supply in the Greenfield Valley. At its peak in the 19th century it employed up to 1,000 workers including orphan children from workhouses. The mill went into gradual decline until it was rescued by Thomas Waterhouse and became successful as the Holywell Textile Mills in the 1940s and 50s. The site of the mill is now part of an industrial heritage area.

Life at Holywell was very different to the rural tranquillity and relative luxury of Stanford Hall. Wang and I had been found a room very close to the mill above a local café. The room was very small, there was rarely any hot water and the food was poor, but work was more enjoyable and I quickly picked-up how to operate the power looms. I was also impressed by the quality of the machinery, which although some years old, worked like new.

I was working a full five-day week as well as finding time to do some studying and reading. A few weeks after I started at Holywell, Susan visited and we spent a night at the seaside resort of Llandudno just along the coast. Shortly afterwards she obtained a job as a housemother at a nearby children's home. Together we made trips to Chester, Rhyl and other local places of interest. Susan also helped me when I was called upon to make a speech to a local Women's Institute in Gloucestershire, where I was visiting another textile mill: she typed out what I had to say so that I could read it more easily.

As autumn replaced summer, the coastal breezes blowing up the little valley where the mill was located became much cooler. I began to miss my winter padded jacket from my Bailie schooldays, but on our wages there was no way that Wang and I could afford to buy more clothes. Stuart Waterhouse (the owner's son and manager of the mill) wrote to BUAC explaining the situation and asked them to loan us some funds. The response was distinctly frosty: the General Secretary of BUAC replied saying that her husband's factory workers just had to save the money if they needed to buy clothes. But again Dr. Needham intervened to help us: his action in quickly agreeing to make us a loan so impressed Stuart Waterhouse that he immediately matched it from company funds.

He reported to Dr. Needham that they were very satisfied with our progress and found both of us intelligent as well as likeable. He had ideas about further extending our practical education before we left the following May. By this time life had become more comfortable for Wang and me as we had moved to better lodgings. Dr. Needham paid us a visit and was happy with what he found. He was also able to report back to BUAC that we were not unhappy at the prospect of returning to China in the summer, contrary to what BUAC had heard. We did not follow the line of other Chinese students at the time who accepted support for their education and then concentrated on improving their own positions. I had always felt a responsibility to take my new skills back home in order to benefit others. Mr. Alley had already written to Dr. Needham indicating that he wanted us both to return to teach at Shandan Bailie School, which had now replaced the school at Lanzhou.

By the summer of 1950 I had spent 3 years in England and Wales and had learned a good deal. I now knew much more about the practical operation of machine powered equipment and I knew more about life in general, for which I had my teachers but also Susan to thank. I had also spent short holidays with some kind friends including Dr. Needham and Miss Lester, aunt of George Hogg the late teacher at the Bailie School. My command of English had improved significantly, so much that I never lost my fluency for the rest of my life.

When I had set out on the journey to England I had seen myself as a representative of my country at an important time, when few people in the UK would have met anybody from China. I was aware that some Chinese students had acquired a poor reputation at home for spending most of their time abroad learning social skills and equipping themselves to make money at home. I was never driven by financial gain and was always rather suspicious of those who were able to buy large houses. I was proud of the fact that I came back from the West still not knowing how to dance, which I think showed that I had not been wasting my time.

The UK then was still in a period of post war austerity, but the country's woollen industry remained at the forefront of world developments. My education in China had mostly been based on manually operated machinery and I had very limited experience of automated equipment. My experiences and learning in England and Wales opened my eyes to the new possibilities of faster and higher quality woollen production processes. My training had covered all aspects of the textile industry (including use of fabrics) but it was the machinery that particularly interested me and I worked hard on memorizing the detail of the equipment. If anything I found my training too traditional and on one occasion bought a nylon hairbrush so that I could study its fabric.

My appetite had been whetted for the opportunity to not only put the learning into practice, but to try out new ideas that had begun to gather in my head. My earlier graduation project in England was the manufacture of a woollen scarf from raw materials to finished product. I took it back with me to Lanzhou where eventually it ended up with my sister who had helped me so much. I also took home a sleeveless Fair Isle sweater knitted for me by Susan and gave her a sample of my weaving. I remained grateful all my life to the many people who helped me and kept a fondness for the UK and the West in general.

I continued working at Holywell until shortly before

Wang and I finally sailed back to Shanghai in November 1950. I also continued to see Susan throughout this period although by now I was looking forward to getting home, and soon stopped any thoughts she might have had of accompanying me. Wang and I paid a final visit to Dr. Needham and his wife in Cambridge where we spent a few days at the end of October before getting the train to London, shortly before Dr. Needham became President of the Britain-China Friendship Association. On 7 November Wang and I sailed from London on the SS Chusan, a new P & O liner built in Barrow-in-Furness specifically for the recently established Far Eastern route.

Chapter VI
Back in China (1951–1988)

Working as a Teacher (1951—56)

By early 1951 both Wang and I had been enrolled as teachers at Mr. Alley's Shandan Bailie School. Of course, much had changed in China since I had left in 1947. In 1949 the Communist Party's Mao Zedong had proclaimed the Chinese People's Republic with himself as Chairman of the Party and Zhou Enlai Premier of the State Administrative Council. For Mr. Alley and the Bailie Schools this represented a positive step: Mr. Alley knew both men, especially Zhou Enlai, and could look forward to greater personal influence as well as a more dynamic Chinese state.

But for me on my return to China the situation was less sure. From the moment I disembarked in Shanghai I realised that I now stood out in a crowd: I was still wearing the Western clothes that I had bought in England, whilst everybody at the dockside was in the plain traditional suit that Mao was popularizing as the uniform for the Chinese proletariat. In 1951 the Korean War was in full flow and relations between China and the Western Powers were in decline. Realizing that I was attracting attention, and anxious not to stand out, I changed my clothes as soon as I could.

Despite some official efforts to persuade me to stay and work in Shanghai I was keen to return to Lanzhou. I knew that the school had closed but its main building had become the home of the former part time schoolmaster Chang Guan-lian and his wife Wang Xianlien and their family. I was already well known to them and they invited me to stay with them as one of their family. I stayed there for about two weeks until Mr. Alley arrived in the school truck from Shandan. He explained that there was a room ready for me at Shandan so I could begin my teaching duties, once I had constructed the carding machine and spinning frame that were awaiting me. Mr. Alley noticed that I had managed to get myself some appropriate clothing but reckoned it would not be warm enough with winter approaching, so he handed over his own patched-up felt boots and darned camel hair stockings, which were to keep me warm for many years ahead.

Meanwhile, my friend and fellow traveller Wang stayed behind in Shanghai and then went on to Beijing. Here he tried without success to get into university before he too returned to Lanzhou. He then moved on to teach at a Technical School near Xian, after which he and I drifted apart. Whereas I had sought to further both my general and technical education in England and at home, Wang had always been more interested in a general education: he learned how to operate machines but he was not interested in how they worked or what they might achieve in the way that I was. Despite being probably less skilled in English than me he went on to become an English teacher.

I moved to Shandan and stayed there setting up new equipment and acting as a technical assistant—paying back what I considered I owed. I was happy enough to teach others but my real aim was to pass on my skills by practical example in the textile mills. The Chinese Government planned to double the number of cotton mills in the country in 1951. Already the number of spindles for textile production had nearly doubled between 1947 and 1951. For a young man with my skills and drive the time was right: one of my first jobs at the school was to restore an old engine that had been bought from Canada, making direct use of the knowledge that I had acquired in the UK.

In 1952 the now well-established school moved again, at the Government's insistence, back to Lanzhou, where it became the Bailie Oil Technical School. From 1953 Mr. Alley had less of a hands-on role and was mostly based in Beijing. Here he stayed in a hotel until 1958 when the government provided him with a large residence where he remained for the rest of his life. In 1954 an earthquake flattened most of Shandan: a former student returned to lead the rebuilding but I never went back. I taught at the Technical School until 1956 when it achieved university status, spending time during this period interpreting and translating to and from Chinese and English. I was generally regarded as a good teacher and something of a technical expert but I was getting frustrated; what I really wanted to be was an engineer.

In early 1953, when I was 27 years old, I got married to Zhang Fengyun, whose father was a teacher at the Bailie School. He had got to know and like me over a number of years and introduced us. She was nine years younger than me and still a student at the school. Her first impression of me was simply that I was on the short side, but I worked hard to win her over. She reckoned that anybody who had travelled abroad and learned from the experience must have something to offer. After she left school she qualified as a nurse and then went on to spend most of her working life at the Lanzhou No.1 People's Hospital, where she became a senior nurse in the Obstetrics Department until she retired in 1990.

K.C. and Fengyun 1976

At Last an Engineer (1956 — 88)

In 1956 I was able to persuade the Lanzhou City Council that I should join the new project to build up No.1 Woollen and Worsted Textile Mill in the city. Ever since my return from England I was convinced that I had something to contribute to the development of the local textile industry. I spent two years involved in planning and design work at the factory before production started. At its peak the mill had 5000 spindles and over 2000 workers; I worked there for 10 years as Technical Director until 1966, a position that took me to different parts of the country seeking out the best equipment.

In 1958 I was in Beijing on business when I spotted Mr. Alley walking along the street; we had not seen each other for some years and Mr. Alley invited me to supper. This reunion enabled us to resume our friendship, and we met again at regular intervals in both Beijing and Lanzhou, with me often providing him with his favourite Gansu pears. I had apparently become something of a model product of the Bailie School philosophy and justified Mr. Alley's and Dr. Needham's choice for the trip to England. I had always maintained a respectful attitude toward Mr. Alley. First and foremost for me he was a consistently kind and encouraging mentor, correcting me whenever necessary but never in a harsh manner. He mixed with powerful people from around the world as well as China's new leaders Mao Zedong, Zhou Enlai and Deng Xiaoping, yet for me and many of his fellow students he remained an easy-going man that we all found approachable. From him I learned a respect for my fellow man and woman as well as a love for my country, whilst having a window to the rest of the world.

Over the years several of his students and also many of his Chinese friends wondered and often asked Mr. Alley why he had never married. Later it became generally acknowledged that he was gay, but in those days he would mostly give a gentle smile and say nothing, or perhaps shake his head whilst peering through his thick-rimmed glasses. I once questioned Mr. Alley myself: I wanted to know how to answer the various people, including my foreign friends, who asked me why he had never married. Mr. Alley reflected for a while: *"From now on"*, he replied, *"if anybody asks you again tell them that after you get married you have a home, if you have a home you become selfish."* I went on to have a successful marriage and happy family life of my own but I always recalled with great fondness the conversations and time that I spent with Mr. Alley.

From 1966 the Cultural Revolution made its impact on me as it did on the whole of China. I knew that my position of seniority at the mill was the cause of envy amongst some of my neighbours and work colleagues, some of whom also remembered that I had spent time in the West. I felt somewhat vulnerable and nervous about my position and decided to get rid of any papers and other material at home that showed English connections or indeed that showed my relatively higher education.

I was quite relaxed when the local party authorities instructed me to leave No.1 Woollen and Worsted Textile Mill and move to the Lanzhou Cotton, Printing and Dyeing Mill at Xi Gu, 15 kilometres away on the outskirts of the city. The mill needed an engineer to build up a new department for the printing and dyeing of cotton. I spent two years here getting the right machines in place and ensuring that their settings were correct. This was a period for me to keep my head down and put on hold my plans for further making my mark. My skills and experience were in demand so although it was a difficult time I managed to survive. I had to be adaptable and wear ordinary workers' clothes rather than any that might draw attention to my status at the mill, and although I worked as an engineer I no longer retained this title. I made sure I got on well with all the workers on the floor of the mill, where I made many friends.

It was certainly not a time to talk about my stay in England or my knowledge of the language, which I kept in my head and never spoke for many years. But my past even pursued me to the new mill at Xi Gu: some of my former Lanzhou workmates went there and put up posters proclaiming my former links with the West and showing me being led by a sheep, in a play on the Chinese homonyms for West and Sheep. I often felt anxious and on at least one occasion even considered ending it all as a way to free my family from any possible retribution.

For all of this period my family life was most important to me. Between 1966 and 1984 our home was an apartment on the hospital site, which Fengyun was eventually able to buy. In 1984 we moved into a new apartment on the site of the new Top Mill, near to the Yellow River.

Our first child was born in 1956, a son, Sun Chung, followed by two more boys in 1959 and 1964 (Sun Yu and Sun Long) as well as a daughter Sun Kun in 1962. I tried hard to be a caring father and got on well with all my children, although my wife inevitably took most of the domestic responsibilities (especially when I was working away from home). The children especially looked forward to special treats when I got home, such as boating, swimming and fishing adventures in the nearby Yellow River, with a tasty picnic of local produce, and with our neighbours' children often joining us.

Later Years at Work

I worked busily in the Cotton, Printing and Dyeing Mill until 1982, often travelling around the country on business matters. My skills were such that other jobs were offered to me but my manager would not let me go.

However, in 1982 my wife Fengyun became unwell: she had remained in Lanzhou whilst I worked at Xi Gu, commuting except for the evenings when I worked overtime. I was now concerned that we should not spend any days apart and also worried that the pollution at Xi Gu was even worse than Lanzhou's, so I looked for opportunities to return. The Government had started a programme of building eight so-called Top Mills in the major cities of China, one of which was in Lanzhou. I joined the Top Mill to set up the wool-washing and scouring machines. There were brand new types of machines made in Shanghai that had to be installed: in some places this had to be done by the manufacturers themselves but I was confident that I could do it myself. I completed the job in two months with the help of three technicians, and received high praise for doing so. The mill was on the banks of the Yellow River and near to the hospital where my wife worked. I worked at Top Mill and lived in an apartment block on the factory site until my retirement in 1988 at the age of 62 years. As is the practice in China, Fengyun and I were then able to carry on living in the same apartment. I was eventually able to buy this flat and one in a neighbouring block for use by members of my family. Despite the difficulties of the Cultural Revolution years I had a successful career and financially had achieved above average earnings (which also provided me with a relatively good pension for the rest of my life). Fengyun had also worked as a senior nurse for much of this time, adding to the family's financial stability and buying her own flat, which is now inhabited by our son Sun Long.

In 1985 I visited the Wool Research Organisation of New Zealand, where I worked for six months on a trip part-funded by Mr. Alley, with travel costs met by the Mill. During this visit I was also able to pay a visit to Mr. Alley's younger sister who was 80 years old at the time. I arrived in Christchurch in April and stayed at Lincoln University. It was my first trip abroad since returning from England in 1950, and also the first time in nearly 35 years that I had been able to practise my English.

At first I found it difficult to follow what was being said and had to postpone my initial meeting with the head of the Research Organisation (this also gave me the chance to recover from my first long plane journey). Two days later I felt much better and met the Organisation's Dr. Ross, who was to look after me during my stay and arrange various visits. We talked about the current development work being done and decided that I should spend some time looking at how raw wool was treated, as this was a particular problem for the mill at Lanzhou.

During my tour of the Organisation's different departments I was introduced to a man called Ian, whom Dr.

Ross described as a special person because he reared 500 pigs in his spare time. I was amazed to hear that Ian and his wife were able to do this without any other labour. Ian was taken by my interest and arranged for me to visit one evening after work. The smallholding, 20 minutes drive away in the countryside, comprised a 3 bedroom single story house, a small stand-alone shed that was only used for changing into and out of clothes, and a large garage that was more like a tool shed. About 100 metres away from the house was the pigsty. Ian showed me how he had put together various pieces of equipment that stored the barley (the basic ingredient of the pigs' food) and then distributed it to the different pens where pigs of different ages were kept, with various nutrients automatically added to the blend during the process.

In New Zealand 1985

I ended up spending most weekends with Ian and his wife, working on different aspects of the farm: driving the tractor, weighing the pigs, helping to take them to market, and so on. I was impressed by the clean and healthy conditions for the pigs: they were fed twice a day and cleaned through every day. Ian and his wife both had very clear roles around the place, and his wife was able to change quickly from being a very clean and tidy woman to one who had no hesitation about assisting at the birth of piglets and looking after them.

Six years later, back in Lanzhou after my retirement, whilst I was out fishing I bumped into an acquaintance who owned some land and turned out to be interested in joining me in rearing pigs. We signed an agreement to work together and to share the responsibilities, with me meeting the initial costs and putting the equipment in place. We started with four piglets and became quite successful in breeding from these until we had about 60 pigs and piglets. I copied the practice that I had learned from Ian of feeding twice a day and cleaning thoroughly every day so the neighbouring small farmers joked that our pigpens were cleaner than their own houses.

Gradually though, my business partner became less enthusiastic in his work and the neighbours began to get a little resentful of our success. In fact, the pigs were never as well fed as the New Zealand ones had been and therefore were less healthy and so less profitable. My wife and I later got involved in feeding the pigs and piglets, but eventually I decided it was too much work for a man of my age and sold all the pigs at the time of the Spring Festival. The venture had just about broken even financially but my one attempt to become an ethical businessman had come to an end.

Everywhere I went in New Zealand I was aware of sheep—it was a country dominated by sheep for wool and for food—and by the sheer number of animals to be seen in the countryside. I thought that in some ways New Zealanders took on some of the characteristics of sheep, being gentle and dogged. Once, when out driving with one of my hosts, I playfully suggested that he might feel lonely because we hadn't seen any sheep for a few minutes. "It's true", he replied, "they make us rich, keep us healthy and taste delicious."

When I had nearly finished my stay in New Zealand I met up with Courtney Archer, who had worked for a time at

Shandan Bailie School and was a good friend of Mr. Alley. Mr. Archer's family owned a flourmill and he had returned home out of a Confucian sense of filial piety to run it on the death of his father. I made some pancakes from the Archer family's famous flour that seemed to go down well; together with pickles and typically delicious local lamb this was one of my last meals in New Zealand and served as a strong lasting memory.

I was always on the lookout for new equipment and would try to understand how it worked, and consider how it could benefit the Mill in Lanzhou. In New Zealand I saw some special non-twisted yarn that had just been rolled and still acquired the necessary strength: I wasn't allowed to see any drawings but I remembered in detail what I had seen and later the following year managed to reproduce a series of samples using the same sort of yarn that was both very soft and long lasting. I believe that I was responsible for introducing this technique into China although I never received any financial benefit. The Bailie school method of learning had again proved invaluable: once I understood the basic theory of how something worked I was able to put it into practice.

Whilst I was in New Zealand I felt safe enough to write a letter to Dr. Needham for the first time since my return from England in 1950. The political climate, especially during the Cultural Revolution, had meant that previously the personal risk was too great. I had regularly been warned by Mr. Alley not to try to contact anybody in England. But now Dr. Needham replied promptly saying that he had never forgotten Wang and me, and the wonderful expedition we had made to Dunhuang in 1943. Dr. Needham was pleased to hear that I was using my experience in woollen textile engineering to help New Zealanders and that I too was learning from them. He invited me to visit the UK, where the Needham Research Institute at Cambridge University was taking shape.

I returned from New Zealand with a number of new ideas as well as many different kinds of wool specimens, but I found it difficult to persuade colleagues in Lanzhou to take up my ideas or to look at the "new wool" that I had brought back. In 1987 I became involved in a research project looking at the use of the particular spinning technique that I had learned in New Zealand. My partner in the venture, however, was only interested in making money, so the project did not progress. I set up a similar venture to help plan a carpet factory in Tibet with patents that I had taken out, but this also came to a dead end.

My knowledge of English had been a distinct disadvantage ever since I had returned to China but from the end of the Cultural Revolution it started to become quite useful. At the mills I was able to interpret and to translate texts from the English originals. I was also able to teach English locally as it began to replace Russian as the preferred second language for Chinese school children. This became a useful second job for me that I was able to continue after my retirement. Following my trip to New Zealand in 1985 I was able to buy for the first time a colour TV, fridge and camera. I had always been wary of chasing money for its own sake and distrusted the new "big potatoes" then becoming more evident in China. I preferred to live what I regarded as a clean life relying on my own skill and knowledge and not on the patronage of others.

In 1987 I was appointed the official English language interpreter for a Lanzhou textile industry visit to West Germany. My final trip abroad was in November 1994 when the Gansu Provincial Government arranged for a group of 27 people to visit New Zealand, Australia, Singapore and Hong Kong. These visits led to my forming various friendships with foreigners and there were several occasions when my family and I would entertain visitors for days in Lanzhou.

Visiting Cologne in 1987

Chapter VII
Family Matters: East and West

Although our four children all received a good basic education, none of them went on to university. It was, of course, known that I had been to England and together with my position as a mill manager this meant that the children to some extent had an uncomfortable time during the Cultural Revolution. Certainly, the eldest, Sun Chung, struggled to get a job when he left school because of my background. To some extent all our children responded for a time at least by becoming anti-intellectual supporters of Chairman Mao.

I worked hard to ensure that the children had good opportunities in life, often working overtime to bring in more money on top of what was a relatively decent salary. My business trips away from home usually meant presents for the children when I got back. Despite my career advancement and my modest achievements I was concerned to continue to live a simple and principled life, and so to my children I appeared as a decent-enough father who looked after them—but nothing out of the ordinary. Of my four children, three in due course got married and three granddaughters subsequently enriched the lives of Fengyun and myself.

I had not forgotten that Dr. Needham had written to

me when I was in New Zealand inviting me to visit him in England. Of course, I had another reason to want to resume my links with England. Despite my happy family life I often thought of Susan and wondered what had become of her. Although we remained close until my departure for China the relationship had begun to cool a little towards the end. What I did not know was that when I left England Susan was then about 4 months pregnant. During the Cultural Revolution time a stranger gave F.Y. my wife a small black and white photograph of a little girl that clearly looked possibly Indian or Chinese rather than European. There was no explanation or indication of who the child might be, merely what I thought was a strange question asking if I recognized her.

In Tibet in 1990

For some reason I took great care of the photo, despite not knowing who the child was, although years later when I came to look for it I could not find it and assumed it must have been destroyed because during the Cultural Revolution it frequently happened that people would search your house and confiscate property.

Letter from Juanjuan to her grandfather K.C.Sun May 2016:

Dear Grandfather:

This year's Tomb Sweeping Day is coming soon. It has been eight years since I was holding the chrysanthemum so as to see you again. During those past years I have finished my postgraduate learning and got a nice job. And I married a man who loves both life and books, just as you did. We have a beautiful little girl now. You have always been in my mind whenever I am low-spirited or faced with setbacks in my life. You seem to come into my heart and talk to me gently and peacefully: "Life is always full of sweetness and bitterness and no matter what it gives you love life and keep fighting. Finally, beautiful life is sure to unfold itself ahead of you".

It was always interesting and full of fun to be with you. We came out together to enjoy the fantastic nature. In the spring, we would step on the green grass in the park nearby and closely observe the blossoming of colorful flowers. And in the summer time, fishing was the best choice for us and you would teach me to wait patiently. In autumn, we could feel the joy of a big harvest in the field. In the winter time, snowballing and making snowmen were our favourite option and we were completely involved in that happy time. You told me that life can be both tasteless and tasty but it all depends on you.

Every morning, when I am still sleepy in my warm bed, I can smell the delicious breakfast coming out of the kitchen. It must be the amazing British breakfast cooked by you. These are all my favourites: sausage, bacon, baked beans, scrambled eggs, toast, cereal and milk. And at 4 o'clock in the afternoon, you would bring out cakes and dessert, together with milk or coffee. Then we would enjoy the wonderful afternoon tea. So an ordinary day was full of expectation and fun because of the amazing food from your magic hands. Due to the love surrounding our family, I am learning to find the simple and special love, and to enjoy the happy hour with my family. Today from our well-prepared food, I am able to understand the fun in cooking. The food you would cook with your heart for our family was more than sitting together and eating, it was your whole devotion to all your family members.

From my primary school until middle school, I would stay with you every holiday season both summer and winter. You taught me to learn English and other subjects. You always asked me to keep on learning when I was tired of studying all day long. You set me a good example in studying. It is still in my memory that when you were in your 80's you were eager to continue to learn English even in your hospital bed. I was puzzled why you were acting like that at the crucial moment of your life. Learning is never something easy to do, is it? You told me that there is no end to learning; it can be life-long. And I joked that you were going to pursue your Ph.D. Today there is an old and torn English dictionary on my bookshelf, which is like a beacon encouraging me to persist and keep battling all the time.

Since you passed away I have always been writing to you. But the address of the letters is not easy to put down. And remembrance of you is embedded in the letters. As time passes by my schedule is full of different things so letters to you are fewer than before. Even this short letter is finished during my daughter's nap. In the past eight years you have often been in my dreams. Every time something happy happens in my life I would share it with you. And if difficulty comes you would come into my life showing me the way forward.

Dear Grandfather, I wish you peace in paradise.

Yours, Juanjuan

May 2016

Part two

My Mother's Story
Susan Eunice

Susan Eunice David Reed in her early 20s

Chapter *I*
Happy Early Childhood (1926–1935)

My mother too had a happy early childhood. She was born Eunice Elizabeth David Reed on 6th June 1926 in Kota Kota, a small village on the shores of Lake Malawi, as it is now known. Malawi was then called Nyasaland, part of the British Empire in central East Africa. Eunice's parents were Agnes and Ernest; she had an older sister, Lavena and younger twin siblings, Isabel and Ernest.

My mother's father Lance Corporal Ernest Reed MM Royal Engineers was very badly wounded during the 1914–18 Great War (and indeed carried 30 pieces of shrapnel in his body until his death years later when he was 63 years old). After the war he applied for a job in Nyasaland because the warm weather was considered good for his health. He obtained a job with the British Central Africa Company as an accountant. The Company had taken over several European-owned firms engaged in general wholesale and retail trading. The largest of these was Mandala, which, in addition to its main urban stores, had opened a chain of around 50 rural retail stores. My grandfather's job was to involve going around these rural stores, doing the accounts and collecting the money. By the time he moved to Africa to take up his job

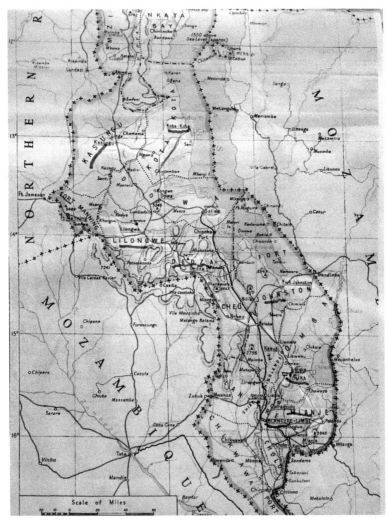

Map of Nyasaland, Kota Kota on the shores of the lake and the other main
towns that the family visited

he had married Agnes Jane David in April 1920.

My grandmother, tells in her account of her life how they met, and how my grandfather had sustained his war injuries:

I came back to Chatham in 1916, and joined the Army Pay Office of the Royal Engineers. Here I did clerical work in the Records Office, passing top in the examination in 1918; I could have gone on to Whitehall on transfer, to a better post. But here, at this time, a change came into my life. I was then 25 years old, and was going on a visit to nearby Maidstone, on the River Medway, with a friend. The story of my life could be called "Met in a Tea-Shop"! We were having tea in Maidstone that afternoon, and so were two wounded soldiers, the "Boys in Blue" , —my life was completely changed; instead of going to Whitehall, I fell in love with the tallest of the "Boys in Blue" [Ernest Reed]. He had been badly wounded in France in 1917, aged only 22. He had captured a German machine gun, and lay beside it for a few days, believed killed, but was found, and taken with the German wounded to a German camp. When they discovered he was English, he was returned to the English lines and thence to England, where he spent eighteen months in various hospitals. He was awarded the Military Medal for bravery in the field of battle, and was finally discharged in November 1918, as unfit for further service. (He had as a young man been employed with W.H.Smith and Sons, but aged nineteen years and four months, in September 1914, he had joined the Army and was

Grandmother Agnes and Grandfather Ernest on their wedding
day 1920

posted to the Royal Engineers, going over to France early in 1915, and remaining there until wounded, in April 1917.)

After leaving hospital (refusing to have his leg off at the groin and so being confined to a wheelchair for the rest of his life), he was told by his doctors that his health was very poor, he must not stay in England, he must go abroad where the sun shines; so he chose Africa. But first he must needs go back to the City of London College to "brush up his education" , he said — so would I wait for him? Which I was pleased to do. So after he sat the examination for entrance into the College, we were married, in April 1920; that was a wonderful day for us both.

Shortly after the wedding, my grandfather obtained a passage to travel to the British Protectorate of Nyasaland, now called Malawi. No passages could be got for women at that time so he had to travel alone; my grandmother remained behind with the promise that the company would get her over to join her husband as soon as a berth became available on any ship going to South Africa. My grandmother recounts the situation:

This happens to many wives. I just had to hope and hope... .what a joy it was to me, at last to get a chance of a berth on Dec.4th 1920, on the SS Braemar Castle, for Durban. I had never travelled so far alone before, and going on that ship was very worrying. My parents saw me off from Tilbury, and I shared a cabin with two ladies. It was a full ship indeed. Soon I was called to the Purser's Office to be told that a senior official of the Company, who also had five other young officials with him, was escorting me all the way out. I was pleased to find that all arrangements had been made for me, from London to Blantyre, so I had no more worries, and could just take things in my stride.

Having never travelled far in all my twenty-six years, I was now at sea on a journey of some 9,000 odd miles. I felt daily that I was getting nearer and nearer to my Beloved, as we steamed down the English Channel through to the Bay of Biscay. On to our first call, which was the island of Madeira, where we stayed for a few hours, then on to Tenerife. We had time for a few hours onshore at each, and went on a small boat to see the shops and visit some cathedrals and other sights. Then we went on to the island of Ascension; this was only a Cable and Wireless Station, so we were not allowed on shore here, only some C&W officials, and supplies—and the funniest thing was seeing some cattle being swung ashore, along with bundles of hay for their feed. And so on again to the island of St Helena, where Napoleon was exiled. Here was a beautiful island, so old-world. You either walked round up a long incline, or got a taxi, which several of us shared, or you could if energetic walk up the 365 steep steps—a foot each—to the top of the island, where the British Government HQ were.

Now we were away once more to Cape Town, and arrived here on Dec.31st, 1920. We had a wonderful view of Table Mountain and stayed only two days, so we could not explore Cape Town much, but what a thrill to think we were on Africa's shoreline, and heard the church bells and ships' sirens going off at midnight, peeling in the New Year. We stopped at Port Elizabeth and East London, and then reached Durban on Jan.10th 1921. Here we had to disembark and go to a hotel, to wait for three weeks, until our next ship arrived to take us to Beira in Mozambique, on the East Africa coast. Staying two nights in Lorengo Margues, we arrived at Beira in due course.

Here we had to wait again for two weeks, until the small coastal steamer came to take us on to a small port named Chinde, a small British Concession at the mouth of the great River Zambezi. Beira was a small place then with no roads, only sandy tracks. There was a sort of trolley bus you could hire to take you around, which ran on tramcar lines and was pushed by two Africans, who were very steady. There were very few shops here, and only two hotels. We were now in February 1921, and I was very anxious to get on, as my husband was telegraphing me all the time about when I could be expected.

At last we were off on a still smaller steamer for Chinde. But the cabins were below deck, and were alive with very large black cockroaches—ugh! I couldn't sleep in that cabin, nor did any others of the forty or so passengers care to sleep below. It seemed we were carrying a cargo of sugar, hence the *cockroaches. So we all slept on deck.*

We reached Chinde the following morning. Here now was a difficulty! We could not tie up, but had to stand out in what was termed the "Roads". We all had to be taken ashore in a rowing boat, but then there were more difficulties; we could go no further, and yet had another ten yards to go before reaching some planks forming a landing jetty. Everyone else was being carried ashore, and I had to follow suit, very nervous, as two burly Africans got me to sit on their crossed hands with my arms round their necks and carried me to one of the planks. This was my way of entering into East Africa. One had to walk up the planks up to the several houses in the "Concession", as the sand was too hot to walk on. It was said one could cook an egg on the hot sands!

This was a nerve-racking experience, but easily over, as the Africans were so kind and soon had me ashore, up to our Agent's bungalow by the sea. I was then taken on board the little river steamer, very like the paddle steamers that run on the Mississippi in the USA—very tiny, with cargo boats lashed to each side. It was most comic indeed; for some reason, all the other passengers, about twenty of them, slept ashore somewhere. I alone was put on the little paddle steamer, where I dined, and being tired after an exciting day, turned in early. I was awakened at 4 a.m., in brilliant sunshine, by the noise of banging going on. Owing to the heat (it was now February), Africans always started their work—called a "task" —early, in the cool of the day, as much as possible, and so would be done with the task by about 10 a.m. .

Soon the other passengers came on board, and we set off on our five days' sail up the River Zambesi. It was all most interesting, but it was very hot, and the flies and mosquitos were very trying. We stopped at dusk, at what was called a "wooding station" , where there were supplies of wood for the engine fires, fruit, vegetables and so on. Any African passengers too would board, if they could find a perch on the cargo boats to the next stopping point. One of them was a place called Shupanga, where we saw the grave of David Livingstone's wife. She had been buried there in 1870, and lay there in lonely state, in a little railed-off cemetery all by herself. She had died of malaria fever, so poor David Livingstone had to leave her there and trek on alone.

After five days, we got to our last journey by sea, and reached Chindio, the railhead for Blantyre. After two days and a night on the train, we reached Blantyre at dusk on the second day, to find a crowd of Europeans and Africans awaiting the arrival of the weekly train, which in those days caused great excitement. People were eager to see who had arrived, to meet old friends returning from leave home, and so on. You can guess I soon spotted my Beloved, who had been so anxiously waiting for me.

Here now were no limousines, Daimlers, or Buicks to carry one on; the last mile and a half of a journey of over

9,000 miles must be done on foot, so I walked up a hilly road to my first married home. I was amazed. I had been given to understand in Durban that homes in Central Africa werc mostly petrol boxes covered with fancy calico. To see a nice carpet on the floor and a suite of furniture astonished me. My Husband had busied himself in his spare time making a nice place for me, and the double bed with framework overhead, and mosquito curtains around, were lovely. It was a very large bungalow, with a sitting room, dining room, and two bedrooms, a bathroom and dressing room, and a verandah all round outside, overlooking a beautiful garden. To think that I had at last arrived, halfway round the world, to be with my beloved Husband, in February 1921.

Life for my grandparents was certainly extraordinary for the times and a far cry from what they might have experienced as W.H.Smith accountant and Records Office clerk based in Chatham, Kent in England. My grandmother describes the life:

Blantyre was a nice place, very spacious, but there were no roads, as we know them now, just plain earth tracks, very dusty in the long Dry Season. We had three seasons, the "Hot", the "Dry", and the "Wet" seasons. When it rained it was a deluge, leaving the roads full of ruts, over which one had to pick one's way when out on a walk [as snakes and small animals used to sleep in the ruts!].

There was no English Church. Once a month a priest

from the upcountry mission of the University Missions to Central Africa came and gave us a service, in a room at the back of a one-time saloon bar—now turned into a general store. There was a very nice Scottish church, beautifully built under the direction of David Livingstone and Dr. Heatherwick, in the 1870s. We went there sometimes, when there was no English service. There were several nice shops, a club, a cinema, and lots of sports arranged at the club, so we had some amusement.

Visitors began to call on me, and I returned the calls. Every lady had her set day in the month to receive callers. So life was not in any way dull—and yet all so different from the life we had led in the United Kingdom. We had no car; there were hardly any about, so my Husband acquired a "Garetta" for me (a small type of Chinese rickshaw), so I could get

Agnes and daughter Lavena being transported in a Garetta

about more.

I must mention that we had no electricity or gas lamps, only paraffin wall-lamps, and hurricane lamps for the kitchen. The kitchen was a brick room, away from the bungalow. The stove was only a sheet of corrugated iron fixed over a platform of bricks. Here the cook boy broiled and boiled foods, and baked the breads and scones in the hot ashes. On my request to make some cakes and tarts myself, being a new bride, just arrived, the cook boy, in a polite tone, in broken English, said "You a Dona [madam], you not work", at which I was greatly amused.

No water was laid on. It was carried from the river two miles away, heated in a petrol tin, and carried into the bathroom to fill an ordinary bathtub, daily. There was no sanitation either, only an arrangement of a brick shed down the garden, but my Husband made a commode for me in the bathroom to save me going down the garden in all weathers.

And so this was my first year in Blantyre. Dysentery and malaria (picked up at Beira) attacked me, but happily we had a good doctor at the Government Hospital, who helped me a lot.

In January 1922 my mother's older sister Lavena was born. By all accounts she was a bright child who picked up African words initially and did not begin to speak English properly until she was three. By this stage my grandmother had also decided that she should pick up the African language too and she felt that her grasp of the language helped her to get on better with the African staff and enabled her to retain the same servants for many years.

In 1925 they left Blantyre and my grandmother describes it:

In 1925, my Husband was transferred to Kota Kota, on the shores of Lake Nyasa. We went part of the way by lorry, and the rest by machillas. Down the hills we travelled into Kota Kota, sleeping in tents each night, as our machilla teams of African men walked only about 15 miles a day. We used to camp by the native villages. Here the chief would come forward with his counsellors, and exclaim at a white child running about and talking to them, at the age of four, talking to them in their own lingo. He kindly presented us with eggs and chickens. My little Pomeranian dog amazed them also; they called it a "nkulani" (lion), as it was a yellowy brown colour.

Sleeping in tents on the journey to Kota Kota

Here in Kota Kota my second daughter, Eunice, was

born at home [in our mud hut], in June 1926, with the help of the Government doctor and the Mission nurse [from the Mission 74 miles away—our nearest neighbours]. And what an astonishment she was to the village chief, as no African had ever seen a white baby before. This chief was very old; he really was a good man. He had been to London, he said, in 1897, to see Dona Queen Victoria at her Diamond Jubilee. He would call often to see the baby, and bring a present of eggs, bananas, and the most beautiful white rice I have ever tasted, grown there in the local swamplands. He would also bring a large sized medicine bottle, empty. On my enquiring of my Husband what this was for, "Oh, you fill that with paraffin, and that will be a present for him in return." So you see the exchange of barter we always maintained.

Mud hut in Kota Kota where Eunice was born 1926

The greatest concern at first—and yet a thrill it turned out to be—was when my new baby was a week old; the compound was full of Africans sitting down. "What do they want?" I enquired. "Oh, "was to see the white baby." So my Husband had to bring the baby out, and show it to them all. Great shouts and clapping went on, and the chief's special present to her was a bull and cow in calf, for the milk. We had had no milk for four months, owing to the drought that persisted that year. [He lent us an African child to look after the cow, too.] I had been allowed a cup of milk for my eldest child from the Mission, as well as a cup of goat's milk; for ourselves we had none, until that kind chief's present of the loan of a cow in calf. Now we had basins of milk, and any extra I returned to the village people. I had also read how to make Swiss condensed milk, by boiling 1 cup of sugar to 4 cups of milk. This made excellent condensed milk for my Husband's "Ulendos" (meaning a journey).

At the birth of my second child [Eunice], I had been left with her at three weeks old, as my Husband and all the other Europeans had gone up country on Ulendo for three weeks. I got into trouble, and had a frightful haemorrhage. What to do now? Out came my medical book, which said 'Stay in bed' ; so there I stayed for three weeks, alone, being nursed by my native servants. They brought in a basin of water and towels, so my baby was washed on my lap in bed, all that time. So she had a poor start in life. But my staff were very good. They brought us food, and looked after my eldest child also. The doctor returned during the second week, when my Boys called him—he was young, but trained, and a kind man; however, he would not come in, just advised me through the wired off window, to stay in bed for the rest of the three weeks.

As well as looking after two small children, my grandmother seemed to have other duties:

I was sometimes left alone with the whole village, when all were out on Ulendo—the doctor, the District Commissioner, the Agricultural Officer, my Husband, and the four missionaries. So I had to hold the fort myself, so to speak, with my family, and treat all sick villagers, who thought it great that with the aid of Black's Medical Dictionary I was able to read up what could be done for this or that trouble. The villagers' commonest troubles were stomach problems; a tablespoon of paraffin and a little sugar did the trick and soothed the pains of many, and when I gave the old chief his dose, mixed with liquid quinine (we always carried our medicine chest with us), he went away chuckling to think I could be able to help him.

No telephones were to hand in those days, so I was unable to know where my husband was or when he would return. If we heard shouting and singing in the distance, this was a signal that up in the hills the Bwana (master) was coming. So my hearing became well trained always to be on the alert, which has stood me in good stead. The slightest noise would awaken me many times. While I was on my own, boys (Africans) would arrive with bags of money. I was unable to get along the khonde (verandah) to put it in the safe, so I had to put it under the mattress and sleep on hundreds of pounds until the morning, never fearing that I would be attacked or robbed, and when counted, the cash would never be even a halfpenny short. (When my husband counted the coins, there was over £ 5,000!)

I really liked Kota Kota, and its lovely views of the vast inland sea, which stretched as far as the eye could see. It was now getting on to our "Hot Season", so it was pleasantly dry and warm. But the Doctor, now being "At Home", decreed that it was now time I went up into the hills above Kota Kota, to where it was cooler. I did not want to leave, as I liked it there and the family were well; I felt we should stay, but he was insistent. At the same time, my husband received orders to be transferred to North Nyasaland, some 300 miles away. So go we must. The old chief gave us a hearty send-off, and a reluctant goodbye, with the usual exchange of presents.

So we set off by machillas, on our nine-day journey, sleeping each night in native villages. Eunice can say she must be about the only baby to be fed at the roadside at feeding time, on nature's milk. As we went further north, my children were the only white children ever seen in those parts, in 1926/27; there were exclamations of surprise at every village, to see a white child running about, aged five, and a small baby in its cot-cum-machilla. We had with us a small portable gramophone, so daily was the request from all to see the "Mwana Ayera" (white baby) and hear the "Mbale's apiano" (gramophone records playing). This gave great pleasure.

On our journey we passed through two government "Bomas" (settlements) and two Dutch Reform mission stations, manned by Europeans [the men wore long white gowns, and had long beards], where we were received most kindly, and asked to stay overnight. There were few Europeans in that country then, so all were friendly, whatever their religion. And the service from the Africans was enormous—in fact, they thought it an honour, it seemed to me, to carry the little white children.

Eunice being carried across Rukuru River 1926

We had many adventures as we went along. On another occasion we slept in a mud hut; my husband heard heavy breathing—he thought it was an African come to steal the money. He just opened his eyes a little and did not move. Just as well! There was a lion in the hut looking at him. He kept still, but opened his eyes wide, and stared into the eyes of a Nkulani, without moving. The lion turned and walked out— a little later an African came rushing in, shouting 'Bwana, Nkulani is chasing a carrier!' my husband got his gun and shot the lion. We had its dewclaw set in African gold.

Lion killed by Ernest because it was chasing a local African man 1930

The lion's dewclaw set in African gold is photographed below with the shell of the pet tortoise that had belonged to my mother whilst she was in Africa. It died shortly before she came to UK and she brought the shell with her and kept it all

Shell of Eunice's pet tortoise and dewclaw from lion shot by Ernest

her life.

And so we got to my husband's new station, Mzimba, where a two-roomed brick bungalow with a grass roof had been hastily put up for us, and so we could unpack and settle in. At this place a District Officer and Assistant Officer and their wives were living, so it was good to meet up with Europeans again, and their children met ours. All such places were called stations, not hamlets, although there was no railway; in fact we were far from the railway at Limbe and Blantyre some 400 miles away.

In deciding on a name for my mother, her father chose Eunice because of a promise he had given in the war. He had been injured when the train he was travelling on was bombed and the nurse that tended him refused to leave his side until transport arrived to take him to hospital. Her name was Eunice and he promised the nurse that if he ever had a daughter he would give her that name. This was a name that was the cause of concerns for my mother later in life!

My mother had, in many ways, an idyllic life in Nyasaland—playing with her sisters and brother and the local African children. They participated in many of the local activities and Isabel, my aunt, remembers vividly going hunting for food! The local children would rattle the wire netting on the outside of their windows [put there to protect against the lions] to wake them up at 6 a.m. in the morning so that they could go with them as they followed the men of the village on the trail of animals to catch. She explained that you learned very quickly to do exactly as you were told— for example if you were told to stop, you did so instantly as it probably meant there was a lion ahead and silence was essential

Eunice on konde [verandah] of their house 1927 wearing shoes made by her father

Thomas and his wife

to survival!

The family had a number of servants who helped with the cooking, cleaning and other domestic duties in the house. The children particularly remember Thomas and John who looked after them. They came from the local village and so were able to join the Reed children in the local activities.

The children all spoke the local African language Chinyanja with Thomas and John and the local children that they played with. Chinyanja [the language of the Lake] is, according to a book called "A Practical Approach to Chinyanja" by T.D.Thomson, one of the family of Bantu Languages. It was spoken then in various dialects and was the official language of Nyasaland. The introductory notes say the book is intended to provide a practical guide to the newcomer whether they be planter, missionary, civil servant, business man or housewife: this gives an idea of the sort of people visiting Nyasaland at that

Eunice, Ernest and Isabel the twins and
Lavena 1929

time.

The children's parents also spoke Chinyanja well
as they used it to communicate with the farm workers,
servants and people looking after the children. They
also used it with the children and to this day some family
members still use a number of phrases in daily language

Zomba 1933—Agnes in the Ladies Rifle Club

that were learnt by the Reeds when they were in Africa. My mother and her sisters and brother had little recollection of their parents looking after them—with their father in a job which involved long trips away travelling across Africa and their mother busy with her many duties and the Ladies Rifle Club, sewing and knitting and Bridge parties in Zomba.

Despite this, my mother had a happy, early childhood, running free with the local children in African rural settings, speaking the local language and not attending any schooling. She was by all accounts bright, awkward and rebellious which would not stand her in good stead for the next stage of her life's journey.

Chapter *II*
Life in the Boarding School (1935–1939)

Every two years the company paid for the whole family to journey to England. This was a long journey of about 6 weeks that remained vivid in their memories. When they arrived in England they would stay with relatives for a few months in various places in Kent, South East England—Chatham, Upchurch and Rochester. In 1933 when Eunice was 7 the family made one of these visits to England and stayed with my mother's Auntie Doris. She clearly made a strong impression on her because I remember as a child that my mother would quote "as Auntie Doris says" to me when seeking to enforce some behaviour or other!

They would also visit other relatives in South Wales and take holidays. The photo of the 4 children standing on a gate with their

Eunice aged 7 years

The 4 children and their father on holiday in South Wales 1933

father at their side was taken during a caravan holiday at the seaside.

The sea crossings between Africa and England were also treated as a holiday with activities arranged on board as well as the general adventure of being at sea. My Aunt Isabel recalls the time she and her twin brother Ernest were tied to the ship's railing for safekeeping and left by their mother when she had to take the older two children to the toilet. When my grandmother returned they were nowhere to be seen. They had gone through the railings and were to be seen "paddling" in the sea! Sailors pulled them safely aboard and Isabel, always seen as the ringleader in their adventures, got slapped for putting Ernest's life at risk!

In 1935 the family came to England again and this time it was Eunice's turn to be left behind. Lavena had remained

Photo of Eunice [far left] with a group of other children on board

in 1930 to attend an English school and now my mother was to follow suit. Both were left in England for their education at about the age of 9. My grandmother recounts that in fact this was quite old for them to be back to England. The children of civil servants based in Africa were returned to UK at the age of 5 or 6 years as the hot climate was considered bad for their health and it was deemed a good age to start their education.

Family memories are that when one of them was left in England, whilst their father showed some emotion, their mother showed none at all—they felt she seemed glad to be rid of them as they were seen as a nuisance! This is not my grandmother's recollection, who felt it was hard for them as parents and that it was even harder for the child left behind. Nevertheless their experience was one of lack of emotional engagement, which must have had an impact on their lives.

Eunice was left in the charge of her Auntie Cath and went to University School, Rochester. This was a small privately run boarding school, with Mr. Morgan as the headmaster. It was a traumatic time by all accounts not least because my mother arrived into this restrictive environment after the freedoms of Africa, without the basic level of education that was expected of a 9 year old. She vividly recalled the occasion when Mr. Morgan sent her out of the classroom into the hallway to look at the grandfather clock and to come back and tell the class the time. She remembered the sensation of standing in front of the clock and not knowing how to tell the time and then having to return to the class and tell them all she did not know what time it was. That shame and humiliation caused by this headmaster—a male figure of power—stayed with her throughout her adult life and was to shape her experience in many settings.

In 1938, it was the turn of Isabel and Ernest to be left in England. Isabel recalled that they were much more familiar with speaking Chinhanja than English and they, like my mother, had not attended any schools whilst in Africa. Her description of it was that whilst they notionally could read some English books it in fact was rote learning with no real understanding of the English language.

In 1938 Isabel and Ernest joined University School, Rochester, which meant that then all 4 children were then in attendance. Lavena, 4 years older than Eunice, had the advantage of attending school in Blantyre before leaving Africa, and therefore had a better start into school life in England. Isabel's recollection was that Eunice was too bright for Mr. Morgan and would disagree and correct him. She described my mother as very bright but awkward and this would lead her into arguments with Mr. Morgan. So whilst Isabel loved school, and described Mr. Morgan as being fond of both Lavena and herself, Eunice hated school because of him.

The one good thing which Mr. Morgan did do, in Eunice's eyes, was to confirm the correct pronunciation of her name—Eunice. As Peter Morgan, one of his sons who was also educated at the school recalls, fellow students used to call her "You-Niss" but his father, relying on his classical education, immediately addressed her [correctly] as "You-Knee-See" and the whole school soon adopted the correct form. The incorrect pronunciation of her name continued to be a great annoyance to her throughout her life. And by the time she met my father, my mother had all but abandoned Eunice as her name and adopted a more pronounceable one: Susan.

Chapter III
Life in the Evacuated School, Wales (1939–1944)

In 1939 the University School, Rochester, with all its pupils, was evacuated to Llandingat House, Llandovery, Wales. The Headmaster had been able to rent the building and transfer the school as a boarding school to that location for the duration of the War. Throughout the 1939–45 War years my mother's parents stayed in Africa so the children were left in the care of the School. My grandmother recalls that she and her husband were booked to return in 1940 but the intervention of the War meant that they could not return until 1944.

My mother had a small circle of friends some of whom she knew from her time living in Africa. One of these was Valerie who knew Eunice from when she was about 5 in Kota Kota and they lived opposite each other; she could recall playing with her on the long veranda of their house. Years later they both attended University School, Rochester and were together there, when just before War broke out the whole school was evacuated to Llandovery, Wales. When they arrived at the new school premises they shared a dormitory. Valerie says my mother was a great reader and was known as the "sober-sides". One night the other girls in the dormitory decided to play a trick on her which included taking a little picture that she had above her bed. However Eunice returned from the bathroom before the trick was finished and so Valerie hastily hid the picture under her pillow. The girls then tried to disguise the fact that they had been planning a trick and Valerie forgot about the picture and promptly stood on the pillow and broke the glass of the picture frame! Valerie said this was a disaster! What could they tell the matron and then the headmaster! However it was Eunice she recalls that came to the rescue and cooked up a story that a bat had flown in the window and knocked the picture off the wall! They got away with it but Valerie thinks Matron found it hard to believe.

Margaret Dunn was also at the school in Llandingat House, Llandovery, Wales. She was my mother's cousin and remembers the lovely garden and that my mother taught her about birds and even the difference between a nuthatch and a tree creeper.

Her brother David Dunn was also at the school and mainly remembers his contact with Eunice during their time there from 1941 to 1944. His most vivid memory was of her teaching him how to knit. The girls were engaged in knitting comforts for the troops and David says he was bullied by Eunice, her sister Isabel and his sister Margaret into being the only boy in the school to help. He says he was not trusted with anything difficult like socks or balaclava helmets that required turns and a variety of stitches. Eunice, David said, would cast on about 20 stitches onto the needles the thickness of pencils and he would knit plain stiches back and forth row by row until the scarf had reached the required length when Eunice would cast off that scarf and cast on the next one for him to knit! David says it was like a treadmill but he can still remember how to do plain knitting all these years later!

My mother's sewing and knitting skills, honed during those early days at school, were to stand her in good stead years later. David sent me a photo of an entry in his autograph book from my mother, which was signed and dated 1942, which shows that Eunice also had drawing skills!

Drawing done by Eunice in 1942

Another pupil at school was Frank and my mother spoke fondly of their time at school together. Frank was the proud possessor of a Mahjong set and taught Eunice and her siblings to play. He and his mother Marjory were to feature later in my mother's and my own life.

My mother was very much the loner in the family setting —describing Lavena as the bright one, Isabel as the pretty one and Ernest as the boy. She would simply "take herself off" if she didn't like the social situation. Isabel's view is that Eunice disliked the twins because they got to go back to Africa when she was left behind in England. Whatever the reasons for her style she became seen as a rebellious outspoken person at the school and Peter Morgan, recalls the 'acute expression on her face as she confronted me in conversation' and says that in those days he believed her to be a socialist.

Reed children at Llandingat House

Chapter *IV*
Going into Adulthood (1944–1948)

Ernest remembers that in 1944 the remaining Reed children left school and went to their colleges. Their father, just back from Africa, had arranged the places for them with the help of Kent County Council. Eunice's was Swanley Horticultural College and Ernest's was HMS Worcester, Naval Training College. Eunice went with him and their father to get his uniform. She said to Ernest that she was proud that her brother had joined up to take part in the War.

Isabel says that Eunice got the grant to attend Swanley College although she hadn't even weeded a garden—the first of many examples of my mother entering a career without prior experience. At Swanley College my mother met Madeline: Lanny, as I always called her, remained my mother's friend throughout her life and was to become my most significant informal foster mother. At Swanley College they were thrown together because they both refused to attend the daily Church of England service. Lanny says they had to sit in a room adjacent to the Church so that they could hear the whole service even if they refused to participate! The students had to undertake various gardening projects, which was part of their course, including at the Royal Horticultural

Society Wisley Gardens, Woking, Surrey.

Lanny recalls Eunice introducing her to Marjory and some of her friends whilst they were at college. They were based in London living in the Victoria area and seemed to be Communists. Lanny felt unable to embrace what she saw as their rather narrow political views. However she did give support to the Party in their quest to release unoccupied dwellings for the many local residents and continental refugees who were living in overcrowded, sub-standard accommodation in Victoria.

Eunice and Lanny continued to make trips to London, not only to visit my mother's friends but also to go to the theatre. Lanny recalls that Eunice introduced her to the Unity Theatre, near Euston, which was a popular venue for political plays. There they saw the acclaimed Irish play Juno and the Paycock of which, Lanny says, she understood very little. The theatre was cold, with hard seats and access to it was very difficult. Lanny did not attend again but she knows that my mother did.

After Swanley Horticultural College Eunice and Lanny shared an assortment of lodging houses for several years. One had a particular notable history—Gatwick Hall Hotel, near Crawley, which is now demolished. At the Hotel also lived the notorious "Acid Bath Murderer" George Haig. Lanny recalls that he drew their attention because he "owned" an unhappy red setter dog. It was later found that this dog in fact belonged to two of his victims. He seemed to them a dapper, vain man with little to say for himself, and it was quite a revelation when they realised the identity of their recent neighbour!

After their time at Swanley College both Lanny and my mother obtained jobs working for FW Berk and Co. Ltd, Horticultural Research Station, Tilgate, near Crawley, Sussex and she worked there from November 1945 to July 1946. Lanny says she was not sure why Eunice left working at FW Berk's but thought that probably, like Lanny had, she found the man in charge a bad-tempered so-and-so!

During 1946/47 Lanny and Eunice took various gardening jobs in the local area so that they could afford to pay the rent. In October 1947 Eunice got a job at the Pelican Bookshop, in Redhill, Surrey. Lanny recalls that my mother enjoyed life working in the bookshop and found Mr. Pizzey a good boss to work for.

It was during her time working at the Pelican Bookshop that my mother went into the local Cooperative Society store and found a leaflet inviting people to enter an essay competition. The essay title was about International Cooperation and Eunice wrote the essay and sent it off to be judged. She told me the story about how one day some time afterwards Mr. Pizzey called her into the office and said there was a telephone call for her. This of course was an extremely rare event in those days and so she picked up the phone with some nervousness. The phone call was from the Cooperative Society to say her essay had won first prize! Her prize was to attend the Cooperative College, Stanford Hall, for a residential year and to undertake a number of courses. My mother was delighted at this new opportunity and Mr.Pizzey was very supportive of her and encouraged her to make the best of the year at the Cooperative College.

Eunice was given to making clean breaks and fresh starts in her life, and used to describe to me the many occasions when she would simply leave one setting and start afresh. The opportunity presented by winning this prize was something she leapt at. In doing so she left behind her friends just as she had already largely lost touch with her family. In talking with Isabel it seems the siblings had very little connection with her after school and apart from the occasional meeting didn't really keep up with developments in her life.

Chapter V
Life with K.C. Sun (1949–1950)

My mother and father met at the Cooperative College in Stanford Hall in 1949.

The Cooperative College was established in 1919 by the Cooperative Union and was based in Holyoake House, Manchester; and in 1943 it became a charitable trust.

In 1945, Holyoake House was damage by bombing, and the Cooperative College was forced to relocate to Stanford Hall where it spent almost fifty years. During the years that the College spent in Stanford Hall, it ran residential courses in social/economic subjects for adult learners and a wide range of retail and management courses for Cooperative employees. In 1946, Dr. Robert Marshall, OBE, MA, became the Principal and Chief Executive Officer and built up the reputation of the College as a national and international institution.

Stanford Hall is a listed 18th-century English country house in Nottinghamshire, England, in Stanford on Soar just north of Loughborough. It is a large red brick building, two storeys high and with a 7 bay frontage. It was beautifully maintained and had a number of facilities including lovely gardens, a lake, a swimming pool and a theatre.

K.C. beside swimming pool in England

From the description of the programmes that the Cooperative College was running at the time it seems likely that Eunice had won a place to join in business studies courses being run for staff of the Cooperative Society who worked in retail settings. She mentioned the International Cooperation classes which she enjoyed and where she met students from all over the world. My mother spoke of the beautiful gardens, in which she and K.C. used to walk and of the views from the lounge/conservatory across to the lake. She and K.C. would return from their walks and, since neither were big people, would sit in one large armchair together and look over the lake. She remembered that their fellow students would sing words from *I'd Like to Get You On a Slow Boat to China*, which was a popular song by Frank Loesser that was published the year that they met.

They clearly enjoyed an idyllic year at Stanford Hall

together. For my mother this was another opportunity for another 'new beginning' , something she did quite often during her life, and one at which there was very little competition for the boys! This was in contrast to her previous experience where she always felt in competition with her sisters—Lavena she saw as cleverer than her and Isabel was prettier and both were blond and curly haired whereas she had straight brown hair! She told the tale that there were a hundred male students and only a few women so she felt able to enjoy meeting fellow students who were from all over the world. Certainly the 1949 Cooperative College Year Book photo, which is included in my father's section of this book and also here, would support the fact that the vast majority of students were men. Lanny remembers her speaking about an Icelandic boy, for example, but it was my father to whom she was most drawn and they quickly became an inseparable couple.

Cooperative College Stanford Hall Class photograph: K.C. is 3rd from left in back row; Susan is 2nd from left on front row.

When my mother passed away in September 2005, I sent people who knew her blank 'post-its' notes, inviting them to write their recollections on the post-it notes and return them to me. I then compiled a commemorative book documenting my mother's life with photos and the post it notes. K.C. responded to my request and sent in a few memories [written in Chinese and English] for inclusion. They informed the section of this book about my father which was originally printed in August 2012 however I have included some of the detailed stories that he sent below as I think they give an insight into the character of my mother and the nature of their relationship. I have copied the stories exactly as my father wrote them on the post it notes because I think that gives a better sense of his feelings for my mother—he wrote these with much thought and knew they were for inclusion in the commemorative album which everyone at the event would read. So clearly they were significant stories which he wanted us to know about how he thought about my mother.

Three stories from their time together when based in Stanford Hall:

The first chat we were in the living room at the Cooperative College during the half term of spring in 1949. Most local students back to their home. Some other foreigners went to other places for their holidays, only a few of us left. One evening I was sat in a long sofa read some newspapers. Susan came in and said "May I sit here?"   "Sure."   "My name is Susan" and ... oh "K.C." We shook hands. Susan [苏三] this name is very familiar to me because it's a very popular Chinese opera so it gave it to me a deeply and nicely impress, since then we meet each other more and more. The next afternoon Susan asked me take a walk, we walk along on a pathway the woods and grass fields to the lake, the lake is not very big but it has a pair of lovely and beautiful white very big swan. I often come here to feed them. Around the lake they are very grassy. We started hand in hand walk around the lake. What I was feeling—happy or strange, I couldn't say so we held hands gradually tighter and tighter, when we arrived a place of nice green grass we lay down and hug and kissed ...

K.C. in Lanzhou
Nov. 7th, 2005

In a summer holiday in London (1949)

In this summer holiday, the college didn't arrange anything for the first two weeks, so I've two weeks free. So I asked Susan took me to London for a week, she agreed. We were staying in her friend's house in London. Her friend been away for her holidays. One night, she took me to a very famous singer (he's a negro American) Paul Robeson's concert. The first time, sat the last row, too far away from the singer can't see and hear clear, makes her so unhappy. The next night she bought another two tickets in the middle of the *first row, we can even touch the singer and the violinist. At that moment a strong thought suddenly came to my mind, she's a strong willed girl, she's great!*

K.C. in Lanzhou
Nov.8th, 2005

In autumn holidays in 1949, I got a letter from Mr and Mrs Stephens, they invited me to their home for a week, also want me make a speech to their Women's Federation. I got complicated, it is too difficult for me. But I can't refuse them, because they were so kind to me, when I stay with them, what can I do? Suddenly call to mind my "teacher" Susan. She's my girl, also, she is my good, kind "teacher", she teaches me English all the time, in my eyes and mind she's very clever, wise, kind-hearted and a helpful mate. I told her, they want me talk about Chinese Communist, so she read a book, which was called "the Red Star over China" eventually she did a very well speech and typed it down for me. When I got to the meeting, I just read it. Since then, we meet each other more and more, I really admire her very much.

K.C. in Lanzhou
Nov.9th, 2005

Two stories from their time together after K.C. got his job in Holywell, North Wales:

In Holywell, Susan found a temporary job at a clinic;

sometimes she works in the day, sometimes at night. She stay here about a week so we meet every day or night. In the last evening she said "shall we go for a hiking?" "What 'hiking' mean?" "Well, we just walk and walk, no time, no place, when we feel tired, just have a rest, no matter where we are, sit or lie." "That's will be wonderful." At about 6 o'clock we met outside a fish and chips shop, we bought two bags of chips, as usually put some salt and vinegar on them. I love the vinegar smells. We started our hike, walk along a road, which is to Chester. When we cross a bridge, we found under the bridge there is a beach. She said "shall we go down have a look?" "O.K." I said. We stay under the bridge a whole night, the next morning we felt time past too quickly for us, our feelings exactly the same, time is too short—cannot bear to part.

K.C. in Lanzhou
Nov.9th, 2005

In the mid of 1950, I was doing my weaving practice Holywell, Wales, about June or July Susan came to see me, it was in a weekend. She took me to Rhyl's swimming pool. From Holywell to Rhyl about 12 to 10 miles away. We went there on a bus. The road seem not very far to the sea, along the road there are many beautiful sceneries, she often pointed out to me; that's the sea, that's the ... , we were sat very close, talking and laughing all the way. When we got to the

swimming pool's gate, found there are full of people. Why
so many people here today? She answered "there is a diving
show" (a great variety of figures diving) although I took many
photos, but there is only one left, which is there are two divers
on the diving tower (the diving tower is very high, about 15
meters) one jump down the other one follow at once and with
his two hands held the first one's two feet, they are one by
one got into the water, it's great, but it's danger. I thought it's
very dangerous. We watched, till they're finished, and then I
swam a while. When we back on the bus I asked her "How
did you know the diving show?" "From the newspaper,
I know you like it, I often watch you're swimming in the
swimming pool at the Cooperative College swimming pool,
you like dive too, that's why I came" "Thank you very much,
you're too kind to me. I love you." "Me too."

K.C. in Lanzhou
Nov. 9th, 2005

Lanny told me that she well recalled meeting with the
gorgeous student that Eunice had met at the Cooperative
College who then became my father! She said she also
remembers her disappointment at being lumbered with K.C.'s
friend whom she considered had considerably less attractions.
Both my uncle Ernest and aunt Isabel also met him briefly
during this visit to London but that was the only occasion
he met any family members. She continued to keep her life
private and to enjoy this special relationship.

In her later life my mother would talk to me about the things that had happened to her earlier in her life including the time with K.C. . My impression was that towards the end of their time together he was looking forward to returning to China and she was rather hoping that they would build a life together—accepting that it would not be immediately but thinking somehow eventually they would get together. However she understood this was not what he wanted. She said that their last meeting was on Crewe Station some time before K.C. sailed. For her part I think at that stage that she would have followed him to China to start a new life and she always spoke passionately about the way to solve the conflicts in the world was for a whole generation of children to be born who were of mixed heritage "a world full of coffee-coloured people" .

In November 1950 K.C. left England for China never to return. By that time my mother was about 5 months pregnant with me.

Chapter VI
Working Life as a Single Mother (1950–1951)

Pregnant and unmarried: seeking help from Joseph Needham (1950 — 51)

As was customary in those days, once my mother's pregnancy became obvious she lost her job as a senior housemother working for Flintshire County Council Children's Home, Upper Downing, Whitford near Holywell. She told me that the matron called her into the office one day and said "there's something wrong with your tummy dear" and, looking meaningfully at her stomach, told her she had to leave.

Again as was customary for unmarried mothers in those days my mother headed for London, not knowing what to do but without a job or a roof over her head she had to do something. She told me about her arrival at Euston Station late at night unsure what to do next. She sat on a bench and eventually a policeman came and offered to help her find accommodation for the night. My mother ended up in a hostel for girls in need of a home. From early January until 29th January 1951 she lived there in the National Council for Unmarried Mothers home at 5 Roxborough Avenue, Harrow-on-the-Hill, Middlesex.

Being a resourceful person my mother also decided at this stage to write to Joseph Needham and seek his help. My father, who called himself in his later years K.C. Sun but is referred to as Kuang-Chün (a misspelling) by my mother in letters, had frequently spoken of and visited Joseph Needham during his time in UK. I have been able to date where my mother lived and for what duration by the dates and addresses of her letters to Joseph Needham, which I discovered when my husband, Richard and I researched his archive in Cambridge University Library on 1st June 2004. We looked through the catalogue of Needham files and papers held in the Library and asked to view three of them—one entitled *"The Boys"*, one entitled *"Reid (sic) Z.K."* and one entitled *"The Adoption Case"*. It was only on reading these files that I discovered, again as was customary for women who found themselves unwed and pregnant, that my mother had considered having me adopted.

Eunice's first letter to Joseph Needham was dated January 17th 1951 and was from the Harrow-on-the-Hill home. The letter sets out the predicament she was in and what she was asking of Joseph Needham.

Dear Dr. Needham

I wonder if you can or would help me? You do not of course know me, but by way of introduction I can say that I am that Susan Reed that Sun Kuang-Chün talked of marrying a couple of years ago. Needless to say we both thought better of it, but now I find myself in the quite terrible situation of going to have his child in March. I understand from Mrs. Atherton of Holywell that he has returned to China, although I have not seen Kuang-Chün for some four months at least. I had been working since June in a Children's Home very near to Holywell.

I would not have bothered you now, as I realise that all this has come about entirely through my own fault, were it not for the fact that I have run into considerably more trouble than I had bargained for.

I applied to the National Council for Unmarried Mothers in the firm conviction that they would find me a job until the baby is born. But! I find myself bitterly disillusioned; nobody it seems will take the responsibility of employing a so nearly expectant mother. The best they or a Welfare Worker could do for me is to put me in the hostel for girls in need of a home. There it appears that I stay until six weeks before the birth when I am transferred to a Mother and Child Home where one is allowed to stay until six weeks after the birth.

The whole point is that I badly need a job from a pecuniary angle as well as my own peace of mind. And this is where I wondered if you would help. I am strong, healthy, very adaptable and intelligent. I can do most things—sew, cook, type and anything else I am willing to learn. If I have to remain idle for all these months with nothing to do but think I

shall go demented. Please help me if you can—there must be
some job I can do, and I don't care what part of the country I
go to. I will if necessary work only for keep.

Also there is one other point I should like to raise with
you. It is that I don't want the baby and I am told that because
it will be half-caste no English family will want to adopt it.
Kuang-Chün has said that he would very much like the baby
to bring it up in Shandan. This of course would be the best
solution but the Government will not allow us to 'export'
babies! Could you find out for me if there are any Chinese of
Chinese-Anglo families who would like the baby for adoption
or to "foster". I will if necessary contribute towards its
keep. I want to train for S.R.N. after this is over so it is quite
impossible for me to keep the child.

I wish it were possible for me to meet you to discuss
it all with you, but please in any case will you be so kind as
to write to me as soon as possible and let me know if there
is anything you can do to help. I am quite desperate with
frustration and worry and I know how much you thought of
Sun Kuang-Chün.

Yours sincerely

Eunice David Reed
(Susan Reed)

Clearly the Needhams responded very quickly to this cry
for help because the next letter is dated January 30th 1951 and

is addressed to both Dr. and Mrs Needham, thanking them for sending a £1 and accepting their invitation to visit them in Cambridge. The letter also includes a change of address saying that she had persuaded the powers that be to give her a job and she was now a kitchen maid at the new address Amherst Lodge, 47, Amherst Road, Ealing, London W13 where she would be able to remain for a month.

On February 26th 1951 she wrote to Dr. and Mrs Needham letting them know she had been transferred to a British Red Cross Society Hostel at 16 The Park, Golders Green, London NW11 to await the birth of her baby. In the letter she says that as she has not heard from them she assumes they have had no results to report re their efforts regarding the adoption of her infant. She then goes on to say that she hopes her time will come sooner than planned as the hostel is not good *"All the nurses are petty tyrants; most of the other girls are silly and empty headed; there is absolutely no privacy and to cap it all we never get enough to eat!"* She finishes the letter by saying that girls in her position can expect no better it seems so there is little point in complaining.

There is then a brief letter dated March 6th 1951, thanking the Needhams for the welcome and unexpected food parcel they had sent. Eunice then goes on to say that she had written to Kuang-Chün using the addressed envelope. She asked that when Dr. Joseph had time could he kindly address some more envelopes for her, as she wanted to let Kuang-

Chün know when the baby is born.

The next letter in the file is from the National Children Adoption Association, 71 Knights bridge, London SW1 dated March 6th 1951. It is addressed to Joseph Needham at Gonville and Cauis College, Cambridge and thanks him for his letter. They say that they very much regret that they are unable to help his acquaintance as they have no adopters who are willing to consider a child of Chinese parentage. They suggest he approach the League of Coloured Peoples.

The National Adoption Society, 4 Baker Street, London W1 sent a reply dated 7th March 1951. They think it would be unlikely that they would be able to place a half Chinese child but would be willing to try to assist however success would depend on a suitable family of 'mixed' origin coming forward.

A doctor acquaintance of Joseph Needham wrote on Royal National Orthopaedic Hospital, Stanmore, Middlesex headed paper on 27th March 1951 to say that he does not know of anyone who would wish to adopt the child and *"those now returning from China are extremely hard up"*. He asked whether an advert in the New Statesman might help and also that he was willing to ask the Institute of Almoners if they would help.

The next letter on file was dated 29th March 1951 and was from the League of Coloured Peoples, 19 Old Queen Street, London SW1. They responded saying that there was little hope that they could do anything to help as they had great difficulty in placing their children and had a large waiting list. They said of course they would keep the case in mind in the event that something unforeseen and favourable turned up.

From these letters it is clear that Joseph Needham had gone to great efforts to try to find an adoption route but that

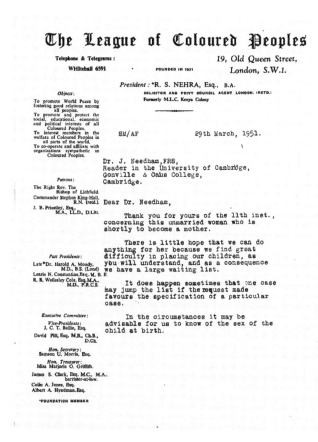

Letter from League of Coloured Peoples to Joseph Needham. Photograph by Joseph Needham, reproduced courtesy of the Needham Research Institute

the 'half Chinese' heritage was making this impossible. This was probably fortuitous because on March 29th 1951 my mother wrote to the Needhams saying, *"Now I come to the hardest part of the letter and I feel you may both be rather cross with me! I have after much thought decided to keep the baby myself. I have tried to think it all out logically and as unemotionally as possible from every angle."* Finally these points decided me in favour of keeping her:

1)The difficulties already in the way of adoption

2)Adoption anyway is no guarantee of perpetual security, love and happiness during childhood

3)Her sex which should make it easier to bring up single handed than if she had be a boy

4)A silly reason maybe, but I love her so much

The letter was written from Maternity Block 2, Edgware General Hospital, Edgware, Middlesex and explained that the confinement had been ghastly but she hoped to be getting up for the first time that day. I had been born 6lb 6oz and 20 inches long and very strong and healthy. My mother goes on to say that she has called the baby Zoë Kim. The Kim was after Kuang-Chün as it was the name she and their friends always knew him as. She said baby was very like him and a bit like her and *"actually she is most attractive and the nurses are continually telling me how sweet she is"*. The story she told me was that her confinement was extremely long, difficult and painful. When I was finally born she would not look at me however the doctor who had delivered me kept talking to me saying how pretty I was and that he felt sure my mother would want me soon—and so eventually she was persuaded to take me in her arms and then of course changed her mind and wanted to keep me! The confinement clearly had some major problems because she ended up being kept in hospital nearly a month due to major hemorrhaging when she first got out of bed.

The letter to Dr. Needham goes on to explore the difficulties she envisages in finding a job that would enable her to keep me with her and her thoughts that it would be unlikely she could get back into a County Council home, though perhaps some privately run homes or schools might employ her. She finishes the letter thanking the Needhams very much for everything that they had done and saying *"I shall write to Kuang-Chün and am hoping that over the years he will take an interest in his daughter; write to her and maybe send her small things. She shall know the truth about her birth from the first moment she asks any questions about it. And I still hope that one day she will visit Shandan."*

On May 7th 1951 my mother wrote to the Needhams giving her new address as the Middlesex County Council Mother and Baby Home, 167 Willesden Lane, London NW6 where she has been placed since end of April—having been in hospital for nearly a month following my birth. She describes the conditions at the hostel, as an improvement on the ones at the previous hostel, and that I am thriving, very like Kuang-

Maternity Block 2,
Edgware General Hospital,
Edgware,
Middlesex.
March 29th, 1951.

Dear Dr. & Mrs. Needham,

My baby was born on March 21st & was a girl. She was 6 lb. 6 & 20 ins. long at birth & is very strong & healthy. The confinement was ghastly — doesn't bear thinking about even now! — but I feel quite fit again & expect to get up to-day for the first time.

Now I come to the hardest part of this letter & I feel you may both be rather cross with me!

I have after much thought decided to keep the baby myself. I have tried to think it all out as logically

Letter dated March 29th, March 1951 to Joseph Needham from Susan Eunice. Photograph by Joseph Needham, reproduced courtesy of the Needham Research Institute

Chün and even have his smile. She notes that she was still awaiting a reply from him. She finishes the letter by asking the Needhams if she may give their name as referees when applying for jobs and that it was looking increasingly difficult to find a position where she could have me with her.

On May 30th 1951 she writes again from that address thanking them so much for the letter and frock that they had sent for me—commenting that white was the best colour for me—as the traditional 'pink for a girl' was not flattering to my skin colour which was too dark. She said that the night before she had gone to the Britain-China Friendship Association meeting at the Holborn Hall but had had to leave before Dr. Joseph was called to speak [the hostel required them in by 9:30 p.m.]. She was pleased to report that she had found a job in a residential nursery where she could keep me and would be starting work there the following Saturday. She said that I had just been christened, not something she had a strong desire to do but it pleased the Church Army Sister, who was her Moral Welfare Worker, to have the ceremony. She thought it would amuse the Needhams to hear that I had been christened Zoë Kim Anne, the latter name being at the good Sister's insistence because she said, "Zoë Kim sounds so ungodly!" She finished the letter by thanking the Needhams once more for all their help and encouragement during the last trying months and saying she would not forget.

Chapter VII
Following the Employment Possibilities (1951–1957)

In June 1951 my mother started work as a Nursery Nurse in a residential nursery Brook House near Crowborough, Sussex. After two months the proprietress had to ask my mother along with other members of staff to leave as she could not make the nursery pay sufficiently well to continue to employ them. Eunice says in a letter to the Needhams that she was not sorry to leave, as it was a very bad nursery from many angles.

She went on to secure employment as a Senior Nursery Nurse in a small family-type nursery near Andover, Hants. She approved of the proprietress in this nursery and the plans to keep it small and thus not institutionalized—contrasting it with the poor practice and large size of the previous nursery.

Eunice wrote a letter to the Needhams dated October 19th 1951 from this new nursery saying that although it was further than she would wish from her friends she felt she would settle there whilst Zoë Kim was tiny. She went on to say that, in answer to the question in their last letter, she certainly had not changed her mind so far as keeping Zoë Kim was concerned. She was emphatic in the letter that she would never change her mind now and would not part with Zoë Kim under any circumstances. She thanked the

Needhams however for writing to tell her about contact from some prospective adopters. She then went on to outline how well I was developing and how good tempered and easy to manage I was "*very lively, intelligent and full of fun*". Eunice said she was weaning me onto vegetarian food, as she was a vegetarian, and enclosed some photos as the Needhams had requested. She said she was not very good at taking photos and it would be good if Dr. Joseph could take some of Zoë Kim just as he had done of her father.

Towards the end of letter she says that she had still not heard from Sun Kuang-Chün and that she planned to write one more time [the third letter] and ask him to reply c/o the Needhams address in Cambridge. She went on to say that if this third letter did not bring a reply then she would write no more. She said she was only writing for his and the baby's sake and if he chose to take no interest in his daughter then she could do no more. Nevertheless Eunice felt that it would be good for the baby to know that she had a father who cared for her, even if he was on the other side of the world.

The "prospective adopters" that the Needhams had contacted Eunice about had written to Dr. Needham on October 3rd 1951 from a Barnes, London SW13 address. They had heard about the possibility of a baby for adoption and wanted to explore further. There was another prospective adopter's letter dated December 9th 1951 from a London SW16 address, who had heard via the League of Coloured

My mother and me 1952

Peoples that there might be a half-Chinese baby for adoption and they were interested in taking it. It was interesting to read these letters in the Needham "Adoption Case" file and think of the different turns my life might have taken.

It was at the nursery in Andover that my mother met and became friends with Sylvia. In January 1952 Sylvia took temporary work at that nursery for a month prior to getting married. She remembers one day in February that year she had just settled the children down for a nap and was busy washing the babies' nappies when the door burst open and "*Susan appears—Oh dear Sylvia the King has died*". Sylvia said that my mother's reaction was that this was very important news—never mind that they had work to do! Sylvia and my mother kept in contact after Sylvia had left and one day Sylvia received a letter from her. She wrote to ask if Sylvia would look after Zoë Kim as she had a neck problem and was going into hospital for a few days.

The "neck problem" turned out to be TB Glands of neck

and Eunice was moved into a convalescent home Rosamira Balcony, St. Peter's Covent, Maybury Hill, Woking, Surrey. She remained in the convalescent home for 3 months and during that time Sylvia and her family took care of me.

By this time my mother knew both Dr. Joseph Needham and his wife Dr. Dophi Needham equally well and would write to either or both of them as seemed appropriate. On July 14th 1952, Eunice wrote to Dr. Dophi Needham from the convalescent home address, thanking her for the pleasant weekend that she and Zoë Kim had spent with her. She asked if there was any news from Dr. Joseph who was in China, and particularly if there was any news of Sun Kuang-Chün. She included in the letter to Dr. Dophi a letter she had written to Kuang-Chün, which enclosed a photograph of Zoë Kim. She asked Dr. Dophi if she would mind sending it in one of her letters to Dr. Joseph with the hope that he might be able to get it to Kuang-Chün.

The letter continues with Eunice commenting on the political events of the day and shows her left wing sympathies *"Dr. Hewlett Johnson has landed himself in a storm has he not! As was to be expected from the press apart from the 'Worker' has given such a distorted view of his message. I feel that he must be a very brave and sincere man."*

She went on to say that taken as a whole there could be a lot worse places to spend 3 months of enforced idleness. She notes it was an Anglican Convent for the training of novices of the Order for the care of the aged and invalid nuns of the Order. Taking in TB convalescent patients was a way for the Order to earn some money. She said the nuns were very sweet and her bed was on the balcony for TB patients. It felt just like sleeping outdoors as the windows ran the length of the outside wall and were kept wide open day and night. She had to stay in bed until after lunch and was then allowed to get dressed and go in the grounds until 7 o'clock supper. Visitors were only allowed for a short period in the afternoon in the grounds, not in the ward. She said she was missing Zoë Kim a lot but that Sylvia would be bringing her to visit from Salisbury.

During these early years the Needhams were a great support and help to my mother, sending presents of little frocks for me and inviting us both to Cambridge to stay with them. There is a letter from my mother to Dophi in the file dated December 8th 1952 in which she thanks her for lending her books to read whilst she was in St Peter's Convent and apologizes for not yet returning them. She said that one of the reasons for the delay in returning them was that several of her friends had borrowed, and enjoyed, her Chinese Science one. She goes on to say that she has read with great sympathy and interest Joseph's reports in the newspapers on biological warfare in China. She said that she felt from his writings that he was *"obviously honest and sincere and I am sure that all right minded people recognized that"*. She goes on to say that

Joseph must have had a very exciting time while in China and she looked forward to hearing the stories when next she visited them.

This letter, dated December 1952, was from another address Great Hollanden Nursery, Underriver, near Sevenoaks, Kent. And it explains that she had gone to work at this nursery having left the convalescent home a month ago. The previous nursery in Weyhill, Andover had had to close due to falling numbers and it looked like this new nursery in Underriver, Sevenoaks was similarly going to have to close at the end of the month. Eunice explained that with so many private nurseries closing she wasn't sure it was a very secure sector to be working in and felt that *"all these changes are so bad for Zoë Kim; it would be a blessing to a find a permanent post"*.

A point of difference that has emerged from doing the research to write this book is whether or not my father knew that he had fathered a child before he returned to China in 1950. I had always believed that he did not know she was pregnant and this was also the view of others. For example H.T. Huang [of whom more later] states in his published life story *"My Life Across Three Continents: A Memoir"* that *"During our trip to the Northwest in 1943 Rewi Alley and two of his students at the Bailie school Shuangshipu came with us all the way to Dunhuang ... .later the two young men were sent to England to receive training in textile technology.*

One of the two, Sun Kuang-Chün [孙光俊] had an affair with an English nurse named Susan. After he left, she gave birth to a girl, but K.C. never knew that he had an English daughter ..."

However Susan's letter to Joseph Needham in January 1951 seems to state clearly that he did know. It is only the desire for accuracy in this book, which is encouraging me to read the source material carefully and strive for clarity! My sister Sun Kun and my niece Juanjuan think that if K.C. had known Susan was pregnant he would certainly have felt very ashamed because in Chinese culture if a woman is pregnant before marriage then people think the boyfriend has behaved very badly. He would have been torn though, about what to do about it because BUAC and Joseph Needham were making it very clear that both the 'Boys' must return to China and contribute to building the new society. His sister Sun Lanfen remembers that K.C. did talk to her on his return to China about his girlfriend in UK and that they had slept together, and he was worried that she might be pregnant. In 1996 when K.C. was first asked if he remembered Susan he said of course he did and when he was told that they had a child he never doubted it. He then told FY and Sun Kun that he had a child in UK and said that Susan wouldn't lie to him and he took comfort from that. So we will never know the truth of it—and it probably doesn't matter!

Another point of interest and contention is that, given

the difficult circumstances that Eunice found herself in, why didn't she turn to her family for help? My mother was firmly of the conviction that they had all rejected her and told me the story of how it happened. Her mother and father had come to visit her in hospital and they saw me for the first time. They apparently told her to get me adopted, and me being half Chinese was at least part of why they were so insistent that she should do so. When Eunice refused, apparently her mother turned to her father and said "come Ernest we must go—this is no daughter of ours!" My Aunt Isabel tells another part to the story, which centres on a conversation she had with their mother and father before the visit to Eunice, as they were staying with her. Isabel asked them to tell Eunice that she was welcome to visit her [Isabel]. Apparently when their parents returned to Isabel having visited Eunice they said she had replied in relation to that invitation "*if it will satisfy her curiosity then tell her she can visit me*". Isabel said she did not go and visit her and that Eunice had always kept herself separate "hidden herself away". Her brother Ernest noted *"Early Adulthood 1944–1957: I did not see anything of Eunice during this time when I was in the Royal and Merchant Navy at sea. As I was away at sea I was not involved in all that went on then and only heard about things 'third hand' as it were"*.

Whatever the truth of it—the fact was that my mother had no contact with her family until I was eleven years old—

of which more later.

One member of the family that that did try to track her down was Auntie Maisie, Miss Elizabeth Griffiths, who lived at 1 Cambridge Street Pimlico. Margaret Dunn, my mother's cousin, recalls that Auntie Maisie asked her to knock at the door of a friend of my mother's who lived not five minutes away in St Georges Drive, London. Auntie Maisie felt that Eunice and her daughter might be living there as she thought she had seen Eunice in the street. Margaret Dunn says that Auntie Maisie was anxious to find and support Eunice and baby Zoë however no one answered the door. Auntie Maisie was another relative that I did not meet until I was 11 years old.

I do remember staying at St Georges Drive with Marjory and her younger partner [as we would term it these days] David. Marjory was the mother of Frank who had been at School with Eunice. Lanny described Marjory as one of Eunice's communist friends. Another of her radical friends who was introduced to her by Marjory was Ray. She said she remembered Eunice as a highly intelligent woman with very wide interests and that her love of her daughter Zoë Kim made her decide to qualify as a nurse. She said my mother was always very ambitious and driven and was determined to open her own nursing home or nursery and run it properly [unlike the examples she had been working in over the previous years]. Whether I can actually remember time with these radical, interesting, adults who fully engaged with me as a child, or simply remember the photos is a mute point. However David was a great photographer and there are photos of me at my birthday party in their flat, playing with my dolls' pram and walking in Kew Gardens which feel like memories to me! These were happy times with a close friendship group for her and me to be part of—a sense of being taken care of, David and Marjory treating us as their own family.

From 1953 to

Zoë Kim third birthday party

In Kew Gardens 1953 in coat made by Susan Eunice

Playing with dolls in a pram 1953   Susan Eunice and Marjory

1957 Eunice achieved the relative stability of employment and accommodation that she was seeking. Still in the private nursery/children's home sector, she worked first at The Grange, Hindhead, Surrey 1953 to 1955 and then at Ruthven House, Shores Road, Woking, Surrey 1955 to 1957. From memory the same proprietor owned both these homes. He made accommodation available for staff that had children and was generous in looking after them. For example I believe he paid for the children to attend a small, local private school— The Grove School, Hindhead, which I attended from Autumn term 1953 to May 1955; I was just over two years when I started and according to the first school report for Autumn 1953, *"Zoë captured all hearts at her first appearance and is a dear little girl with a quite amazing vocabulary for her age."*

Zoë front row at school 1953

I can remember some incidents when we children were leading wild, unsupervised lives in the house and grounds of these homes. The children that were placed there to be cared for had physical and mental disabilities and I can recall us looking at the children in their cots with no understanding of them and making unkind remarks for example about one of them who had a very large head (hydrocephalus). We ran around the grounds and I can remember running through a thunderstorm and enjoying the pounding rain. Once we were playing chase across the safety bars that were placed across the windows and one of the bars broke away from the window frame as I pulled on it and I fell to the floor—I still have the scar on my chin to this day.

I have happy memories of life with my mother in these institutional settings—I would spend a lot of time on my own in our room although she would be able frequently to come up and see me and check all was well. I was a great reader and could entertain myself with my games. I spent a lot of time off school with tonsillitis [until my tonsils were taken out] and again the institutional setting was a fine place to be off school and still looked after. I have many of the books my Mother and others gave me, which bring back happy memories of a solitary but enjoyable early childhood. The Alison Uttley series of storybooks including Little Grey Rabbit and her other animal friends and their gentle adventures; the Flower Fairies series and others by Cicely Mary Barker—the first one of which was given me by David [partner of Marjory] and is inscribed from him for my second birthday March 1953 and a later one which is inscribed from my mother, *"Zoë Kim, for being a good girl! From Mummy May 2nd–5th, 1957"* I have wondered what that was about? the Beatrix Potter series of little books—all these little books were wonderful to own and read and to enter the world they presented. On my 6th birthday my mother gave me a full sized book—Heidi by Johanna Spyri and to this day I have such strong memories of enjoying entering that world.

She met and made friends with two other unmarried mothers who worked and lived in the children's homes with her, because they too had children with them—Mary and her son David and Fitz and her son Peter—both of whom were to feature later in her life. She also became friends with the parents of one of the children she had looked after—Fred and Gladys, and with one of the cooks Freda—and they too were to feature in our later lives. My mother and I also visited other friends during this time and went on trips to London together. I have strong memories of attending the Trooping of the Colour celebration of the birthday of Her Majesty the Queen on June 13th, 1957.

Susan Eunice and Zoë Kim

Chapter VIII
At Last Training to be a Qualified Nurse (1957–1962)

Just as K.C. had an ambition to be an Engineer so too Eunice had an ambition to be academically qualified and recognized in her profession. By chance being an unmarried mother had taken her into the caring sector—looking after children as the only employment that provided living-in accommodation where you could also look after your own child. She now wanted to become a qualified nurse. She worked within the maxim, which she discussed with me at the time, "give me the child until he is seven and I will give you the man." In other words she had given me the stability of close parenting until I was 7 and now it was okay for her to pursue her career aspirations, which would inevitably mean we would need to be apart. I recall her discussing with me whether I wanted to go to boarding school or to stay with friends and I chose the latter.

Eunice always wanted to push herself academically and others have testified that she was bright but unfulfilled. She found out about the Four-Year Scheme of Integrated Training giving qualifications in both psychiatric and general nurse training [I have amongst her papers the article she read about it from the Nursing Mirror 11th May 1956 which describes the experimental course arranged between Holloway Sanatorium, Virginia Water and St. Mary's Hospital, Paddington] and decided this was what she wanted to do.

A letter from the South West Metropolitan Regional Hospital Board dated 21st June 1956 sets out, in response to her enquiry, the process for applying to join the integrated training course. A letter dated 14th November 1957 from the Holloway Sanatorium Hospital, Virginia Water, Surrey confirms that her application for the post of student nurse had been successful and set out the terms and conditions. Her salary was to be in the scale £362–£420 per annum less £124 for board and lodging, and she would be required to work a 48-hour week. She would be supplied with uniform but was required to provide herself with black stockings and plain, rubber-heeled, black shoes. Her training commenced on 30th December 1957.

From that post she then applied for and was successful in obtaining a place on the Four-Year Combined Scheme of Psychiatric and General Training arranged between Holloway Sanatorium Hospital and St Mary's Hospital, Paddington. This was confirmed in a letter dated 25th March 1958. On 30th June 1959 she transferred to St. Mary's Hospital, Paddington, London W2 to undertake her Two-Year General Nurse training.

During this period my mother kept up with the friends she had met in her The Grange and Ruthven House days including Fitz whom I recall visiting. She worked for one of the big hotels on Richmond Hill Surrey called then the Hotel Stuart and I can remember visiting her in the staff quarters at the top of the hotel. It has remained in my memory because I burnt my arm quite badly on the paraffin stove, which she used to warm the attic room that she lived in! We also went to visit Sylvia and family in West Runton, Norfolk, Freda and family in Sheerwater, Woking Surrey, and Fred and Gladys and their daughter Julia in Coombe Gardens, New Malden Surrey. I have strong memories of staying with Lanny's parents in their bungalow in Wonersh, Guildford, Surrey who treated me like a grandchild—saving special treats for me like picking the first tiny strawberries and tomatoes in the greenhouse. Peter, Lanny's husband, would play with me with small, metal traction engines.

In 1957 once Eunice's job at Holloway Sanatorium had started, I could no longer live with my mother as all nursing posts were residential. My first placement, as it were, was with Sylvia and her family in West Runton, Norfolk. Sylvia's husband, Terry was a butcher's shop manager and so this abruptly ended my vegetarian upbringing! They had 2 children and the eldest one Tina was a couple of years younger than me. We both went to the local school at East Runton and, according to Sylvia, both hated it! It was difficult for my mother to visit me very often given the distance and I never settled at the school according to Sylvia, so I was moved to live closer to my mother in London.

During her training Eunice always used Marjory and David's apartment in St Georges Drive as her home address and we were frequent visitors there and also with Ray and Harry and family in Kenton, Harrow.

Susan Eunice and Zoë Kim; Sylvia, her children; her mother and other children 1961

In 1959 I went to live with Frank, Marjory's son, and his wife Debbie in a Council block of flats in East London. I can remember life in a rather crowded maisonette, with them, their children, Debbie's mother and me. Nan, as we called Debbie's mother, joined in games with us children—we would eat our boiled eggs and then turn them upside down in the egg cup and offer them to her, and of course when she cracked the shell they would be empty! Much laughter and fun on a daily basis! I attended Olga Primary Junior Mixed School in Bow, East London and still have the book awarded to me by the Headmaster Mr. Bennett in 1959 for Progress—the book was called Zoë's Zoo by

Ralph Anno.

Ray describes this as a warm and loving home for me whilst Eunice studied hard. My mother was able to visit me much more frequently than when I lived in Norfolk. Frank had been at school with Eunice where they were great friends. My staying with Frank and his family rekindled that friendship and it developed, as I understand it, into rather more than a friendship. I was not privy to the details but understand that for the good of their marriage it was decided that I should no longer live with them so that the opportunity for Eunice to see Frank was removed. I have since found the hand written letter, dated 13th July 1960, from Mr. Bennett the Headmaster, to my mother expressing his extreme sorrow on hearing that I would not be returning to the school, particularly as I

Zoë Kim living in london

would have gone into the scholarship class the next term, which would have enabled me to obtain a Grammar School place.

So after the school holidays in 1960 I was moved from Frank and family in London and found myself living with Lanny and her husband Peter in East Grinstead,

Sussex, in a small house which they shared with some friends Christine and Lesley. I moved to Baldwins Hill School, East Grinstead and have few memories of that school apart from playing shinty, a sort of Scottish form of hockey, which convinced me that PE was not for me! For a brief time I went to live close by with Wilf, Paula, their young daughters and boxer dog but that didn't work out, so soon I was back with Lanny and Peter. I think adults thought I would prefer to live in households with other children, whereas of course given my early childhood with my mother, I was much more comfortable in adult-only settings. It is also undoubtedly true that the children in these households where none too keen on a peer interloper! By the time I returned to living with Lanny and Peter and their small dog, they had moved to another

Zoë and Lanny in later years

part of East Grinstead into a small flat, where I remember clearly listening to Ella Fitzgerald and other jazz singers and enjoying my new life. Lanny reflected *"Perhaps my lasting debt of gratitude to Eunice is the legacy of Zoë who has given me, and Peter, such pleasure. I have known Zoë since she was a few days old and we were her guardians until her majority. It would be far too sentimental of me to share details but I am so happy to still regard her as an honorary daughter."* I remained close to them visiting regularly until Lanny died in 2011, several years after Peter had passed away.

During this period 1958–1962 my mother was undertaking the hard work involved in her nurse-training course and as Lanny recalled, Eunice had an enviable ability to pass her nursing exams at very high grades—although often her studying was done on Green Line coaches travelling to visit Zoë Kim! She was second with 79% [the person placed first had 80%] in the St Mary's Junior Hospital exams, for example, and was awarded a prize for first place in the Holloway Sanatorium Hospital Junior Examinations in 1959. On 3rd November 1961 she attended a prize giving ceremony and was awarded a special Psychiatry Prize. On 5th November 1962 she was presented with a prize by Her Majesty Queen Elizabeth the Queen Mother and congratulated by the Matron at the successful completion of her Four-Year Combined Training Course.

Meanwhile, unbeknown to us, Eunice's sisters Isabel

and Lavena had decided that they would try and track us down. Lavena contacted the Salvation Army who it appears were able to put us in-touch because Isabel recalls seeing me for the first time on the steps of Boots in Cambridge where my mother and Lavena had agreed to meet. I then discovered I had a whole Reed family and over a short period met Lavena and her husband Harry and their 3 children Susan, Christopher and Martin; Isabel and her husband Philip; Ernest and his wife Kathleen and their children Michael, Sally and Helen. I remember one of the first people I met was my cousin Sue at Isabel's flat in St Christopher's School, Letchworth, Hertfordshire where she ran one of the boarding houses. A number of famous people's children were boarders at the School including Peter Lessing, son of Doris Lessing, and Isabel enjoyed looking after them. Later Isabel was to move from this job and take over the needlework and craft programme for the school.

Chapter *IX*
Running and Owning Nursing Homes (1962–1973)

In 1962, after completing her nurse training course, Eunice moved to Hull, Yorkshire to work for her friend Mary [who by this time had married] at a nursing home for older people that she had bought, Rossmore Nursing Home, 66 Sunny Bank, Hull E. Yorkshire. I think her motivation in moving to Hull was in-part because I had failed my Eleven Plus examination, which meant that my post-eleven years old school education would be in the secondary modern school system not at a grammar school. This would mean that I would be unlikely to get to university. My mother was aware of the vital contribution that a good education provides to a good life and found out that Hull offered a 'second chance' examination to children in their secondary modern schools enabling those that pass to move into the grammar school system.

So I went back to live with my mother at the age of 11 years and went to Welton High School, Hull—the local secondary modern school. We lived in a flat in Sunny Bank close to No.100 where Mary and Albert, her husband, and the 4 boys—David, Michael, Patrick and Andrew – lived. We all got on well and my mother became lifelong friends particularly with Patrick who trained and practised as a GP. Patrick's brother David, who was one of the children with me running around The Grange and Ruthven House in the early 1950s, was much older than Patrick and took over running the nursing home business. David told Patrick that Susan worked with their mother at Rossmore Nursing Home and that she was the real driving force that helped develop the business with a particular focus on the highest standards of care.

In 1963 I took and passed the "second chance" exams and transferred into Kingston High School, the local grammar school, in the September. I can remember clearly the smell of the fish docks wafting across the school playing fields when the wind was in the wrong direction! For reasons that I don't know, in 1964 I was on the move again! This time it was to live with Freda and Arthur and their son Christopher in Sheerwater, Byfleet, Woking. Freda was another friend my mother had met whilst working at The Grange and Ruthven House in the mid 1950s. They had a very nice house that backed onto the canal. Freda by this time was a cook at a small private girls school and so for one term I attended Oakfield School in Woking.

In March 1965 I went to live with my aunt Lavena and her husband and children at 51 Westbury Road, New Malden. I attended Wimbledon County School for Girls and mostly have memories of domestic science lessons—learning how to brush your teeth and making fairly disgusting meat and vegetable stew [which we found years later in the back of the pantry still sealed in its Kilner Jar!] My aunt's family home was a large, rambling house with a big garden mostly inhabited by their bull terrier dogs. My most vivid memories are of us children all sitting at the long table in their

Susan Eunice in backyard of Rossmore Nursing Home in nurses uniform

breakfast room attached to the kitchen [with pantry beyond] and talking about our days at school and plans and ideas. There was a stove in the room to keep it warm and I can remember sitting in there late at night, watching the silverfish attracted to the warmth of the stove, after others had gone to bed, as I wanted to finish the jumper I was knitting! My cousin Chris was closest in age to me and he and his friends were great jokers so it was always fun to be around him. Chris was to die in a microlight accident in the 1980s but I went on to have good family friendships with Martin and Sue.

As it turned out I had been moved south because my mother's plans were not to remain in Hull. She applied for the post of deputy matron at Benslow Nursing Home, Benslow

Benslow Nursing Home 1964

Rise, Hitchin, Herts, and, by letter dated 17th October 1964, was offered the post. Her commencing salary was £ 16 per week. Her duties were to be the complete care of the patients and management of the nursing staff, and to take complete charge in the absence of the owner. She was expected to work 44 hours per week and if the night staff needed advice to be on call.

She met Nan there and as Lucy, Nan's daughter reflected:

"Susan took over running the Benslow Nursing Home in the 1960's. As senior sister my mother [Nan] was to be her deputy. It very soon became clear that the pair of them were to get along famously and soon became firm friends. Susan was a caring and generous boss—my mother was very fond of her. "

Quite soon after her arrival at this new job, the owner of the nursing home announced that she wanted to sell up and retire. She asked my mother if she would like to buy it. It had been Eunice's ambition for many years to own and run a nursing home so she seized the chance. She invited Fitz, another friend from the early 1950s days, to join her as a business partner and together they managed to raise enough money to buy the nursing home. My mother's approach to running the business was rather different to Fitz's and they soon parted—Fitz having a stronger view of the need for tight financial control than my mother, went on to be a successful rest home owner in the area. Fitz required the capital back that she had put into buying the goodwill and lease of Benslow, and this had to be arranged.

Shortly after my mother took over ownership of Benslow Nursing Home, she rented a flat in the town and in 1966 I came to live with her at Flat 4, Park House. My mother had given me the option of going to St Christopher's School, where Isabel and Philip worked, which was in the adjoining town of Letchworth, or going to Hitchin College of Further Education. I chose the latter and studied both my O and A levels there. I was then 15 years old and met some fellow students who have remained my good friends to this day. One of these was Theo, who, because his parents were in the Forces, came and stayed with us, so that he could continue his education at Hitchin College, and this meant he also got involved in the business. He vividly recalls the excitement and fun of those days as Susan determinedly set about running her nursing home with quality and enjoyment for the patients, staff and those around her as the absolute priority and with the finances left rather to manage themselves:

"Susan really cared for the old folk in the Benslow, having no time whatever for anything less than total care—even for those who had completely lost it; absolutely unacceptable for the doctor not to try his damnedest for a frail, bonkers old lady.

"Susan passed her driving test after many trials and tribulations—a huge triumph!

"Blithe confidence that two lads [Tony and I] could repair practically anything; I owe my current DIY skills in no small part to the mistakes which Susan allowed me to make."

In 1967 we moved into The Bungalow, Station Gates, Hitchin. This was nearer the Nursing Home and, incidentally, to Hitchin College, and was also part of the Benslow Nursing Home estate, and thus didn't require additional rental to be paid. Theo's reflections here too capture the spirit:

"Living in the coal cellar of The Bungalow on a put-you-up bed; Susan at her "make it up as you go along" best! Tio Pepe nightcaps—still my favourite."

As I mentioned earlier, attention to finances wasn't my mother's forte and those from whom she had borrowed money to buy the Nursing Home were not best pleased about this. Others with no financial interest in the place but a more censorious view on life would tut at her extravagances—however for her, life had been hard and finally to get to the place of freedom, doing what she was passionate about delivering high quality care for her patients, and with access to funds meant she wasn't going to be stopped. It wasn't that she was deliberately spendthrift, just simply that she felt the money would work itself out somehow and there was no need to account for every penny. Theo again captures this beautifully:

"Trying to make the Benslow petty cash balance at year-end; hundreds of bills, slips and box of money that wouldn't add up. Eventually Susan tore up a few slips, put some money from her purse into the box and voila it all balanced! Off for a good dinner to celebrate!"

Patrick also captured those days, when as a child he spent time with us in Hitchin:

"The Cinema Restaurant—I can't recall the name but Susan suggested I try the Crepe Suzette, a most amazing dish that involves flames and the chef coming to the table. Susan knew how to make a memorable occasion into something

really special—a meal into a banquet. Memories like this reflect her warm heart and generous nature.

"Susan knew

Patrick and Susan Eunice in Post Office Tower restaurant

how to 'do London'

in style but one particular memory sticks out was a meal in the rotating restaurant at the top of the Post Office Tower. We sat by the window at night watching London spinning around below us. An evening I will never forget –eat your heart out London Eye!"

Eunice was still reconnecting with family members having made contact again only a few years previously and Brian another family member remarked:

"Most people of my generation can remember where they were when they heard that JFK had been shot—I certainly can! I can also remember the exact day I first met Eunice—it was Sunday 18th March 1968, the day after I had taken part in the now famous Anti-Vietnam War demonstration in front of the American Embassy in Grosvenor Square. I went to visit Eunice at her home in Hitchin with Auntie Maisie and was given a delicious cream tea. I can remember Eunice gently rebuking me for attending the demonstration as there had been photographs on the TV News of police horses injured by the demonstrators [not by me!]"

Lanny also remarked on her hospitality:

"Over the years we saw a little less of each other but when visiting her in Hull, Hitchin and London her generous hospitality was appreciated—she pulled out all the stops. Her taste in the colour schemes and furnishings of her flats and the Bungalow was attractive to me."

During this time I managed to do sufficient study at

Hitchin College to pass O and A Levels that enabled me to go to university—this had been my mother's academic goal for me and she was very pleased and relieved that I made it. I was at Chelsea College [now incorporated into Kings College London] and made a great friend Annette. Annette is from Trinidad, returned there after University and recalled:

"My memories are dim but sweet. I liked the way Susan looked. She always seemed to stride with confidence. I liked her welcoming ways—it seemed as if the moment she met me, I was not just a part of Zoë's life but of hers as well. I regret that I did not write to her while she was in Barrow. She will never know that I thought of her and treasured those happy memories in Hitchin."

In 1972 Eunice decided that she wanted to return to life as a professional nurse in London. She was finding the business side of Benslow Nursing Home harder and harder and no longer liked the small town feel of life as a nursing home owner in Hitchin. She had always struggled with conventional constraints wanting to be a free spirit and now, having taken up with one of my College friends a man about 25 years her junior, no longer wanted to be seen as middle aged and responsible. She wanted to be rid of all that, recapture some youth she felt she had lost, and become a carefree nurse once again. I can remember trying hard to persuade her to put a manager into Benslow so that she could return to the business in later years—but all this was to no avail. As she had always done in the past—she wanted a clean break, end the past and have a new beginning in a new setting and with a new career.

Going through her effects after she died—I found a large cardboard box of papers relating to her time at Benslow Nursing Home. The papers were largely related to the business and represented the difficulties of running a small but complicated business with many debtors and creditors. I also found the invitation for my mother to attend the centenary celebration event of Girton College Cambridge 1969 first established in Benslow House—because a ladies college needed to be far away from the men in Cambridge! Amongst the guests was Shirley Williams MP.

It was clear from the documentation that despite the bills and correspondence from accountants, solicitors and bank managers, Eunice was not getting the support she needed to run what was a quite complex business and the finances were running out of control. The profit assessment, presumably used as the basis on which she and Fitz had bought the business, was based on the previous 5 years of running the home. It was a handwritten document in pencil without any evidence to back up the figures and this calls into question whether it was ever possible to run the business at a profit. There seemed to have been a constant chase to get the money in and then delaying payments to creditors until the last moment. This must have been truly concerning and what started out as a great adventure with high hopes of doing the right thing and providing the best possible care, was rapidly becoming a worrying nightmare. No wonder selling the business and returning to life as an employed nurse seemed such an attractive option.

The business goodwill and lease were sold by early 1973. The papers included assessments of capital gains and tax owing from sale of business dated February 1973; agreement to overdraft October 1973; letters chasing for unpaid capital gains tax dated March 1974 and it is clear that selling the business did not clear the debts which probably explains Susan's decisions some 10 years later on in life.

Chapter *X*
Final Years (1973–2005)

On 1st April 1972 Eunice started back at work at St. Mary's Hospital, Praed Street, Paddington, London where she had completed her training in 1958–1962. She enjoyed her time on De Hirsch Ward and stayed until 31st March 1973. During this time she moved from the Bungalow in Hitchin to Essendine Road, Maida Vale, London–a rented flat–with her partner my college friend staying with her for much of the time.

Responding to a call for help from her friend Mary, Susan returned to stay with her for a while in Hull. As Patrick remembers, his father was becoming increasingly unwell, drinking heavily and gambling. He had manic depression and Susan was able to persuade him to be admitted to hospital for treatment. Patrick thinks that this almost certainly saved his father's life.

On 7th May 1973 Eunice started work as a Staff Nurse at the National Hospital, Queen Square, London. The salary was £ 1,191 p.a. with an additional £ 126 London Weighting allowance. The hospital was a specialist hospital for people with Neurological Diseases and she absolutely loved it! The high tech work with very unwell patients and all the drama and quick decision-making that was required really played to her intelligence and inclinations.

In 1974 she switched back to St Mary's Hospital, living in the nurses home in Guildford Street, London WC1 and working at the Lindo Wing. At this time she also lived briefly in Highbury, London N5. The Lindo Wing is the private wing of the hospital and is where, for example, members of the Royal Family have their babies. Isabel recalls that Eunice told her that in fact she preferred working with more disadvantaged people such as those she had encountered in her mental health training.

In 1974 the opportunity arose to rent another flat in Essendine Road, in a different property in the street than she had lived at a couple of years previously. Through the landlord she then had the opportunity to buy the flat and took up residence again in Essendine Road in 1975 whilst continuing her work at the Lindo Wing. At this time she was also doing extra shifts in other hospitals as a bank nurse as well as evening and night work, sometimes for famous people, to try and increase her income [mindful no doubt of the debts such as Capital Gains tax from Benslow Nursing Home still requiring payment]. Eunice was also studying for an Open University degree and continued studying modules throughout the rest of her life. During her nursing career she also undertook sewing jobs as yet another way to make money. As everyone says she was very talented—and she certainly worked very hard!

In June 1977 she started work as Relief Assistant Matron for the London Borough of Hammersmith and left the post in August the next year. Her employers, Hammersmith Social Services Department, said that they very much appreciated her willingness to change and move about with little notice in what was a very difficult role. She had left Hammersmith having obtained a role as Assistant Officer-in-Charge for Hounslow Social Services starting work at a home in Heston, Middlesex, starting salary £ 3,621 per annum. In 1979 she left to become the manager of Age Concern Day Centre, Eligin Avenue, Westminister—she was called the "Lady in Charge" by the older people who frequented the day centre and was much appreciated by them all.

1980 was the year that Richard and I got married and Richard's mother remarked that Susan Eunice seemed a very private lady, very proud of her own family and particularly of her daughter. Richard's mother and father were pleased that she had agreed to our wedding taking place in Walsall, where they lived. My friend Diane remarked that Susan was an independent spirit, wearing long skirts and tops "hippy" style and not a traditional "mum" which meant that that she always enjoyed discussing "issues" with her more as if she were a contemporary. This attractive but unconventional dress sense was more of an issue in those days when there were clearer definitions of what conventionally middle-aged women should wear.

Richard and Zoë wedding day 1980

On August 3rd 1981 she took up post as Relief Assistant Head for London Borough of Camden Social Services Department, and on 1st February 1982 became the Head of Home at Ingestre Road with a salary of about £ 10,000 per annum. This was to be her last employment in the public sector and she retired in November 1985. This was triggered by continuing ill-health and in 1986 she had a number of operations connected with her back and knee. These were partly in the NHS and partly private which contributed to her financial problems. Also during this period her partner left her, she was devastated of course but in true Eunice style knew that she had to find her own way through it all.

Eunice had been to a sales and marketing event in

London where the small chalet style "mobile" homes were for sale in various locations across the country. Mindful of her many debts to be paid off and without a job or partner to anchor her in a particular place, suddenly the idea of selling up her Maida Vale flat, paying off some of her debts and taking off to a fresh start seemed attractive. As before, I questioned the wisdom of such a radical step—but Eunice was always someone who once she had made up her mind, jumped into the action with no looking back.

So in August 1988 Eunice moved to Walney Island, Barrow in Furness, Cumbria. My husband Richard's brother Andy helped her pack up the flat and drove the van with her possessions in it to Cumbria. He says he especially remembers her being very patient as he had never driven a van before, and had to navigate west London traffic on a Bank Holiday weekend too! He said it was very reassuring to be told that he was doing a good job, and can remember clearly Eunice's calming influence. 235 West Shore Park, Walney Island was an idyllic setting in the summer with views across the sea and wild life to watch on the dunes. Ernest her brother remembered spending holidays in her lovely chalet home on the beach and touring with her in the adjacent Lake District. My family and I also enjoyed Christmas and summer visits there.

However in the winter there were months of horizontal rain and strong winds all of which caused the mobile homes to deteriorate rapidly and made venturing outside difficult. By chance one day someone knocked on Eunice's front door and enquired whether she would be interested in a house swap as he owned a house in Barrow town and wanted to move to Walney Island. Eunice had the house surveyed and the report came back that said a swap must be considered 'somewhat

Susan Eunice, Kate and Simon on Walney Island sand dunes

of a bargain' and so the swap was legally transacted and she moved in to 39 Church Street, Barrow in Furness, Cumbria. She was pleased to be in solid bricks and mortar in a terraced house near the town centre. This gave her access to amenities not available on Walney Island and to a small network of neighbours to pass the time of day.

Then on May 2nd 1992 her life was to undergo a massive change again—this time also triggered by me. On that day I was attending the Memorial Service in honour of Lu Gwei Djen, Joseph Needham's second wife. At the tea reception afterwards Joseph, who by now was a frail 92 year old, introduced me to H.T. Huang who had worked with Joseph for many years, accompanying him to Dunhuang in 1943 when my father was also on the same journey. After the tea reception I went with Joseph back to his office at the Needham Research Institute and got involved in a conversation he was having about his care needs. From the conversation it was clear that it was being proposed that a Chinese student might look after him and equally clear that this was not what Joseph wanted. I stepped forward and asked if he would like me to see if Susan, as he always knew her, could look after him? She was expert in the care of the elderly, was retired so free to start work and had always said she would repay her 'debt of honour'. As she had put in her letter to Joseph on May 31st 1951, she would not forget the help and encouragement the Needhams had given her during those trying months around my birth—this she had always referred to when talking to me as her "debt of honour". Joseph was most grateful for this suggestion and so there and then I made the call. I rang my mother in Barrow in Furness and explained the situation and that Joseph needed her. She accepted without question and arrangements were made for her to come to Cambridge and take up post.

In June 1992 Susan moved into 2 Sylvester Road, Cambridge. This was in the grounds of the Needham Research Centre [NRI] and was a large ground floor flat, which Joseph lived in and with a separate room for a carer. Upstairs there was a flat used by long term visitors to the NRI, one of whom was H.T.Huang who recalls his first meeting with my mother:

"The first time I met Susan was when she came to Cambridge in June 1992 to be Joseph Needham's carer. Joseph had told me a good deal about her, so I felt I was meeting an old friend that I had not seen for a long time. She was an attractive, warm and energetic lady. I have pleasant memories of the teas I had with her and Joseph on Sundays whilst I was in residence at the Needham Research Institute. A couple of times I took them for a Chinese dinner at the Jade Fountain Restaurant, which we all thoroughly enjoyed."

Susan tried hard to ensure all Joseph's wants and needs were met, including for example burning his toast and crumpets because that was the way he liked them! When it became clear that Joseph needed 24 hour care, she ensured that other staff were employed to provide appropriate cover. As long as he was well enough, Joseph would go over to his office in the NRI, which would require someone to push him in his wheelchair. He would visit friends and would also entertain others—some of them quite famous people.

Isabel would visit my mother as Cambridge was very near where she lived. She remembers the time that Terry Waite came to visit Joseph. Terry Waite was the Assistant for Anglican Communion Affairs to the Archbishop of Canterbury in the 1980s. As an envoy he travelled to Lebanon to try to secure the release of four hostages. He was himself kidnapped and held captive from 1987 to 1991. At one point

Joseph sent Eunice to fetch Joseph's mother's bike out of the garage to show Terry, who then bought it for £ 5. Later, when Terry returned to show Joseph how he had repaired & cleaned it, Joseph said it was worth more than £ 5 and asked him for another £ 5! Eunice jokingly rebuked Joseph saying "I hope you think it was worth losing Terry Waite's friendship for the sake of £ 5!"

H.T.Huang recalls an encounter with another famous person:

"It was through Susan's kindness that I had the pleasure of having tea with Stephen Hawking. In the Fall of 1992 Joseph was invited to afternoon tea with Stephen who lived less than a mile away from the Needham Research Institute. Susan thoughtfully asked Mrs. Hawking if Joseph could bring a friend. And so I found myself sipping tea and eating scones with Stephen Hawking!"

Joseph, who was a tall, big built man, became more frail with Parkinson's disease at the same time as Susan's knees and back deteriorated and she needed another operation. He would increasingly fall down and the fire brigade would have to be called, to help him up because Susan did not have the strength. There was also a lack of clarity about who was actually in charge of Joseph's affairs and disagreements about how much and what his money should be spent on in terms of his care. All this led to Susan leaving Joseph's service in 1994 and returning to her home in Barrow in Furness.

Eunice's final years were spent in increasing isolation. The operations–spinal fusion and knee replacement–were not overly successful so she was never pain-free and she also developed breast cancer, which entailed a lengthy treatment regime. All this conspired to keep her at home in Barrow. She also became very uncomfortable staying with other people and said she had spent a lifetime living in other people's homes and now she wanted to be in her own place doing exactly as she pleased. She was a 'late riser, late to bed' person and was very fearful that if she ever had to move into residential care then such sleep patterns would not be tolerated. She continued to study modules of her Open University Degree–with increasing difficulty but never giving up, and developed a passion for sending for Readers Digest Books on the assumption that sending for the books increased her chances of winning the big prize draws. She never gave up hope—planning what she would do with her winnings to the end.

Richard, my husband's descriptions of my mother capture her final years:

"My first encounter with Susan Eunice was in the summer of 1977 at a folk/rock concert–a rather unlikely setting, which I soon realised, was somehow fitting. Then she was Susan—hospitable, generous, intelligent, never predictable and often prickly. She was working in care for older people, where she was passionate about

*their entitlements but often frustrated by what she saw as
"management's" inability to provide the means to deliver: we
used to "discuss" such issues!*

*"Then at home in Maida Vale I saw how she would
escape into the Age of Enlightenment and other parts of her
Open University Degree course.*

*"The move to Barrow in 1988 signalled what I saw as
her "retirement" —by then Susan had become Eunice, at least
to us. She retreated to an amazing location on Walney Island,
literally next to the sea and a glorious wild unspoilt beach; and
after a few years to the greater convenience of Barrow town
centre. She retreated too in other ways and certainly my links
with her became almost entirely through Zoë. I think Barrow
is a sort of metaphor for Eunice: it's a weird mix of the (very)
down to earth and a rugged beauty; it was once in Lancashire
and now is in Cumbria; and it really is (as the locals tell you)
at the end of the longest cul-de-sac in the country. But who
are we to judge?"*

In her increasing isolation and mental and physical frailty
Eunice had a few good local neighbours and friends who
looked out for her. It was her choice to move so far away and
I think done with the recognition that if she had lived closer
she would lose her independence and therefore her dignity.
She was passionately determined to die in her own home and
on no account to receive any social care or to move into any
form of institutional care setting. She achieved that and I am

Photo of Joseph, Dophi and Gwei Djin inscribed on the back "For Susan David-Reed, all love from Joseph Needham Cambridge 1993"

Susan Eunice caring for Joseph in his home

Susan Eunice and Kenneth Robinson outside Joseph's flat in the grounds of the Needham Research Institute

Susan Eunice, Joseph Needham and H.T. Huang

eternally grateful for the contact and support the local friends and neighbours provided for her in her declining months and years—something I was not able to do living so far away. She spoke to me about these people often and I thought I'd end this section with some of their thoughts.

Edgars wrote:

"About Susan—we met in 1990 when I retired and started to live in West Shore Park. After some time when she moved to Barrow and she had to go and stay in Cambridge she asked me to look after 39 Church Street—she was scared about burglars. Afterwards when she returned to Barrow I visited her—usually on her birthday 6th June and just before Christmas."

Dave wrote:

"Susan told me how she looked after Dr. Joseph Needham for some time and was very interested in his work. She said that marriage was mentioned but it didn't happen. I thought it was a pity that things didn't work out for them, although it would have meant Susan leaving Barrow to live with Joseph.

"Susan was a good talker but she was also a good listener. I would often find myself telling her about any problems I had, something you can't do with just anyone. She would always give me sound advice and was a friend I could always confide in.

"I think Susan had an ideal temperament and outlook

on life. *She had problems with her house etc like everyone else, but she didn't let things upset her. She dealt with them and forgot them. Also she hardly ever complained about anything—she had health problems, but rarely mentioned them unless asked. She set an example of how best to deal with life's problems."*

Noreen wrote:

"When we first met she use to walk around the park, we would say hello and all that jazz. Soon after I started cleaning for Sue, over the years we had some good laughs—we would talk about everything under the sun. She would tell me about the nursing homes she owned and had worked in. She was into reading a lot, watching television, and gardening. I was always there two hours; after I finished doing my cleaning we would have a cup of tea and biscuits. I found her a lovely person never had a bad word to say about anybody. She would talk about her family and friends—she went through a lot of pain over the years but she would have a smile on her face. I'm glad I knew Sue she was a kind of person that will be remembered for everything she did. She was my friend."

The last word in this section needs to go to Joe—he was the local newsagent who delivered her newspapers and came every Friday to collect his money. I suspect he was the last person to see her alive. He sent in several recollections of her:

First meeting—Susan repeated many times "I'm not from these parts you know" of course I did not know—but soon got used to it! Susan continued to give me a brief history of her life and predicaments of late. She reminded me many times of being on a par with me in business as she had run a home for the elderly sick.

"My calls were on Friday nights and she was very mischievous! She would say things like 'you again!' 'should I let you in?' 'I have no money' 'so can't pay you and lost pen and cheque book' and then she would present me with the cheque all filled in!

"Susan scolded me for interfering in her welfare when calling the fire brigade to repair her fire alarms; mentioning to Council to provide support if required; but later apologized as all was done in good faith as she reminded me often."

Part three

Zoë's Story
Anglo–Chinese Understanding

Chapter *I*
The Needham Connection

For most of my early years I thought that my father was dead. I fabricated a story, which I came to believe, that he had died of smallpox when I was a baby. My mother wore a wedding ring and so the assumption was that she was a widow. Despite her plans before I was born to tell me about the circumstances of my birth as soon as I was interested, she did not give me any information. Various of the 'aunts' that I stayed with did try I think to fill the information gap, for example I can remember a conversation with my Auntie Freda and also have a book given me by Auntie Gladys and Uncle Fred on my birthday in March 1961 called Child of China by Maria Gleit. As I got into my teens I became increasingly irritated by the questions about my Chinese heritage—I found people are incredibly gullible and when the inevitable "where are you from?" question would occur—I took to saying "Sweden" and that seemed to prevent further questioning.

This was despite our continuing relationship with the Needhams and their kind attempts to connect me to my heritage. They sent my mother and I many books as birthday or Christmas gifts over the years—usually with a fond inscription inside with the date and the occasion.

The first dated book I have is on Christmas 1956 when they gave us Monkey by Wu Cheng-en translated by Arthur Waley. A series of other books followed every Christmas, including for Christmas 1958—I Stayed in China by William G. Sewell and for Christmas 1961—Young Traveller in China today by James Bertram. Christmas 1962 saw Folk Tales from China published in PRC for me and Yo Banfa! By Rewi Alley for Susan.

For Christmas 1965, Dophi and Joseph sent us two books Sanliwan Village by Chao Shu-Li translated by Gladys Yang and The Builders by Liu Ching translated by Sidney Shapiro. They included a small letter and said they hoped we would enjoy the books as they were interesting stories founded on what has been going on in the countryside [so important in China, the letter emphasised] and the letter went on to explain the Chinese characters which Joseph had written on the books. Joseph had given me a Chinese name Li Jo Chin [include Chinese characters] "precious as gold" and Dophi, who had written the letter, explained that Joseph had given me the same family name as them, Li, since the Chinese hardly distinguish between N, L and R sounds, so Reed and Needham could both be called Li. Joseph had also included a small piece of paper [written on the back of a reused scrap cut up from a larger piece—Joseph never wasted anything!] where he had written my Chinese name in characters and aligned each character to my English name, so Zoë = Jo. Beside Reed he had initially written the character for Sun [my father's name of course] but crossed that out and written the character for Li. We didn't notice this at the time only recently studying the papers and thinking about the significance. Dophi's letter goes on to say that the other characters written on the book cover include her and Joseph's names in Chinese and the fact that they are giving me the books as a gift. The letter finished with the information that they hoped to buy a new car and then would hope to run over to Benslow Nursing Home and visit us so that they could explain the Chinese naming and characters in person.

Photo of these two books with Joseph Needham's Chinese writing

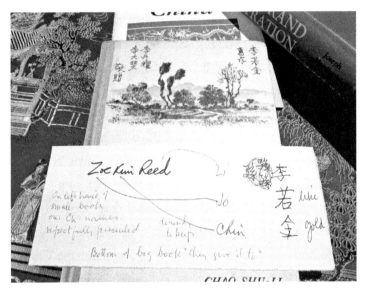

Photo of the piece of paper with my name written in characters by Joseph [showing Sun crossed out]

More books followed every Christmas including 1969 when they gave me *The Grand Titration–Science and Society in East and West* by Joseph Needham which was newly published that year and included the dedication*"to Lu Gwei-Djen the explainer, the antithesis, the manifestation, the assurance of a link no separation can break."* For my birthday on March 21st 1979 they gave me *Moulds of Understanding– A Pattern of Natural Philosophy* by Joseph Needham and *China and the West: Mankind Evolving* of which Joseph was one of the contributors.

It is with some regret that I now look at all these books on my shelves and realise the wealth of knowledge about

Photo of the books the Needhams gave me on the silk cloth the Needhams gave us for our wedding present

China that I could have been gleaning through the years of my childhood if I had read them all. The truth of the matter was though that without any personal relations with China I did not see it as legitimate to claim to have a Chinese connection and so developing an understanding would not be something I would pursue. Britain was a great deal more racist growing up in the 50's and 60's and the seemingly constant need to explain myself at every new encounter [and given the life my mother and I led, I had many of them during my childhood] "Where are you from?" was always the opening gambit. I felt a fraud to claim being half Chinese when I couldn't then point to any relations from China. So outwardly I refused to claim any Chinese heritage because I couldn't evidence any connection with it.

On 1st June 2004 when my husband Richard and I went to the Cambridge University Library and retrieved the file called "Reid (sic) Z.K." in Joseph Needham's Archives I learnt more of my past and understood perhaps some of what I was really thinking at the time and the roots of my ambivalence towards claiming a Chinese heritage during my childhood years. The first letter in the file is from me dated 11th November 1973 and it is quite a thing to confront yourself as you were 31 years earlier as I did that day, which was completely unexpected as we had no idea what would be in the file when we requested it, in that small library room in Cambridge! Writing this book has given me the opportunity to reflect more on what the file contains and says about my interest in my Chinese heritage during my University years.

The first letter in the Reid(sic) Z.K. file was dated 11th November 1973 and was a handwritten one from me and began *"Oh, Joseph and Dophi—so often these days I feel I'd like to communicate with you both, in the selfish hope that you will be able to clarify my thoughts ... ."* And the letter then goes on to explain that Some months ago Susan finally told me the story of my father. I say, finally, because I've always disbelieved this story of his death during my childhood: always thought he was alive and alive in China what is more. *"I know it is easy to say such things when you have the knowledge—but its true—and another thing I've felt for a long time is that one day I shall meet my father: or people who have known him in his later life; and that this will occur in China."*

It is a long letter and I go on to wonder what to do with the news? Should I send off a letter to my father in one of the envelopes, which Joseph had addressed for Susan to use when writing to him at the time of my birth, or perhaps write to Joseph and ask him to try and find him again? It also clearly triggers me to read some of the wealth of books we had— apparently when Susan told me the story of my father she lent me the copy of "Yo Banfa" which the Needhams had sent her. By the time of writing this letter to the Needhams I was part way through reading the book and talk about what an inspiring story it was and how appealing the idea of collective living was.

I was in my fourth year at University having undertaken a research placement in the third year. I was clearly disillusioned with the motivations and purpose of researchers and upset by my social science lecturers whom I said seemed to want to confuse students with lectures on *"Reality is Socially Constructed and Reality is Negotiable!"* I was clearly struggling with the move from 'hard' science to social science, which was reviewing the role of science in society including the thinking of Marx. One of the essays I had to write for the

Science and Society course was "Why did modern science not develop indigenously in China?" and The Grand Titration was on the reading list—so I was cheekily writing to the author for any handy hints. Our Population Studies course lecturer had indicated he wanted to discuss population control in China but seemed to think that what figures we did get in the west about Chinese population are biased—so I was asking Joseph for help with some unbiased figures.

Joseph always hand wrote his letters before they were typed and sent. So in the file I found both his typed reply to my letter and the carefully constructed handwritten version. His reply dated 24th November 1973 set out how pleased he and Dophi were to get my letter and to know that not only that I now knew about my father Sun Kuang-Chün, but that I had been inspired by it. Joseph said *"I can assure you that he was an absolute charmer when young, and I am sure must be a fine man (a textile engineer) now, if he is still living, as we all hope."* He goes on to express caution however about making contact saying that Kuang-Chun may not even know what happened to Susan, and he may well have married and brought up a family in China, if so, he may never have told his wife about his love in England. Joseph said in the letter that there was only one person who might be able to help in tracing him and that was obviously Rewi Alley and that the time may now soon be ripe for a discreet enquiry through him. He went on to say that all the other things I had talked about in my letter would be practically impossible to discuss without a personal talk. He understood I was feeling rather disoriented as between science and sociology, absolutism and relativism and invited me over to stay a weekend with them in Cambridge to discuss.

The next letter in the file is from me thanking them for the invitation and confirming I will be arriving on February 16th for the weekend. The following letter is dated 25th February 1974 and is from Joseph Needham to Rewi Alley. Again the file included Joseph's carefully handwritten draft of the letter as well as a copy of the typewritten version that was sent. After some initial pleasantries Joseph writes that the real purpose of the letter is to ask if Rewi could possibly find out what has happened to Sun Kuang-Chün; reminding Rewi that he was one of the two boys that had gone with them to Tunhuang [as it was spelt in English then] in 1943; remarking that Joseph was fond of both boys but that Kuang Chun was particularly attractive. He explained that after they came to England Kuang Chun had a love affair with a nurse named Susan Reid (sic) and after he returned to China a love-child was born. *"Since Susan is a courageous, tenacious and altogether sterling personality, she brought up this little girl, whom we have come to know well too ... Zoë was staying with us here a week or two back ... After he went back to China he never wrote, and though Susan tried for some years to write to him there was never a reply."* The letter goes on to say *"Now, both Susan (always very professional and competent, now a Matron) and Zoë (extremely intelligent, knowledgeable, progressive and leftist) are splendid people. Susan didn't tell Zoë about her background until a year or so ago, and I then provided some lovely photos of Kuang-Chün. Now she is very proud of her father, and her dearest wish is to visit China and see all that the revolution has done, and if possible to meet him and make herself known to him."*

Photo of K.C. in frame which Joseph Needham had by his bed and gave to me

Joseph goes on in his letter to say that that is the reason for approaching Rewi—as the one person in the world who could find out how the land lies. He asked Rewi whether K.C. had married, whether he had had children, whether it would be possible for me to meet him and for ideas about how I might get to China—stating that he had of course mentioned to me tours that were arranged by SACU and that perhaps they could help me financially. Joseph felt that the Chinese authorities are rather human-hearted, so that if one could press the right button, as it were, some arrangement from the Chinese side might be conceivable. He finishes the letter by saying that surely Kuang-Chün would like to know that

Joseph Needham's hand written letter to Rewi Alley.
Photograph by Joseph Needham, reproduced courtesy of the
Needham Research Institute

Susan has done a wonderful job, and that Zoë Kim is a young woman with really something to give to the world, however impeded by the unethical society of the West.

The next letter in the file dated 16th March 1974 is from Rewi Alley to Joseph Needham. After an update on his health and circumstances, he explained that he initially saw a great deal of Sun and Wang as they had come back to school before he had left. He said that K.C. had married a girl student from Shandan who's father and uncles had been with the school since Shuangshiphu. He did however have some concerns that there had been some difficulties for the family which was put down by some to their close relations with me and he went on to advise that *"On the whole I think it better if Sun is left alone with no more explanations to make and that his daughter just takes China as she finds it when she comes. He is a sensitive person, and I would not like to give him additional burdens."* Later in the letter he says he would be happy to meet me and do anything he could for me whilst I was in China and, in relation to another matter said *"Best sometimes to let sleeping dogs lie. Which is what I advise with Sun"*.

Dophi sent me a copy of Rewi Alley's letter as soon as they received it and a month later Joseph sent me some more photos of K.C. I replied on 17th April 1974 saying I was quite surprised at the level of my disappointment on receipt of Rewi Alley's advice but had concluded that on reflection his advice

is a nurse in a county hospital. On the whole I think it
better if Sun is left alone, with no more explanations to make
and that his daughter just takes China as she finds it when
she comes. He is a sensitive person, and I would not like to
give him additional burdens. It is not easy for his daughter
to understand, I know, but that is how it is.

As for Wong, I last saw him in 1966, when he
came to Peking with the Red Guards. He is a teacher in the
textile college in Hsienyang near Sian. He could not find
lodgings so I lent him a big blanket.

I would be very pleased to meet Zoe and do
anything I could for her while she is around.

Last year, when I was in Lanchow, many Bailie
boys did call, but I was too rushed to see them all. But the
NW is the NW, and one must understand local problems. Best
sometimes to let sleeping dogs lie. Which is what I advise
with Sun. I did go to the woolen mill last summer, but
no one mentioned him. There have been many changes these
years and probably he has been transferred elsewhere.

Yes, I do remember with much pleasure our
journey to Tunhuang, and the gay company those two kids
gave. And all the discussion with you. I keep in touch
with Hungying, who expects to be able to come this year
sometime, if it is possible for her to see her relations.

Hope the spring is treating you well, and
that your work goes steadily on despite all.

Love to all,

yours,

Extract from letter from Rewi Alley replying to Joseph Needham 1974.
Photograph by Joseph Needham, reproduced courtesy of the Needham
Research Institute

to let sleeping dogs lie was sound and that I would hope to
go to China some day, perhaps after the completion of my
year's teachers' training course that I was then undertaking.
The letter then goes on to tell the Needhams all about my
involvement in the Essex University sit in, demonstrations
and picket lines and arrest of the "Essex 90"—these were
all students, one of whom was my then boyfriend. It seems
that I'd been extremely caught up in delegations from my
University's Student's Union going to support the arrested
students—rather to the detriment of my studies!

The file contains a few more letters between us around

the time of my marriage and between Susan and Joseph through into the late 1980s when she continues to seek his advice and guidance on her life because she says she was not happy and not clear on the right next steps to take. Joseph's advice was always thoughtful and sympathetic.

Chapter II
Finally Making the Connection with My Father

During the two years that my mother looked after Joseph, 1992–1994, I saw more of Joseph because he was there when I visited her. He was always pleased to see me and we had some conversations however the Parkinson's was taking its toll on him making communication difficult. I did try to ask about how to connect with K.C. however, by this time Joseph had become very frail and was never quite able to get round to beginning the process of making links.This was slightly difficult to understand because we knew by then that K.C. and Joseph had been in communication.

K.C. wrote to Joseph in February 1993 expressing condolences at his loss, given the death of Lu Gwei-Djen and also once more thanking him for his help back in the 1940s. K.C. also wrote that he and Madam Wang (his old teacher so he always called her by this title) were considering ways to preserve the memory of those foreign friends who had supported the development of the Lanzhou Bailie School. He said that since 1992 he was having regular meetings with Wang Xian Lin (formerly of the Lanzhou Bailie School), who told him of Lu Gwei-Djen's death. Joseph Needham replied to this letter in April 1993, assisted in the process by Susan who by now of course knew K.C. 's home address. Joseph reflected in his reply letter on the fact that he had been happily married to his first wife Dophi for 64 years of which she suffered with Alzheimer's for the last five. By contrast he and Gwei-Djen were only married for two years *"after the long years of separation"* before she died *"lucid to the very end"* . He then related to K.C. that he was now being looked after by Susan Reed who *"is much the best person to do it since she is so nice"* .

During those visits to Cambridge I also got to meet and know HT Huang whom I'd first met in May 1992 at Lu Gwei Djen's memorial service. He was a lovely thoughtful man and very easy to talk with. I discussed with him my desire to meet my father and I also corresponded with him when he was not at NRI but back in Alexandria, Virginia USA where he lived. He had been the young secretary to Joseph Needham in 1943 when he accompanied Needham in his role as Head of the Sino-British Science Cooperation Office, in peregrinations across Northwest China. He met K.C. Sun as one of the two Bailie School Boys bought along to help Rewi Alley and Joseph Needham with their domestic needs on the journey. In February 1994 H.T. wrote to me saying he had written to K.C. Sun using the address which Susan had given him but had had no reply. He said he was thinking of visiting K.C. next time he was in China to appraise the situation in the meantime he would remind Joseph to give him K.C. 's address in Chinese.

Joseph Needham passed away in 1995 and I attended his

Memorial Service on 10th June. One of the many other people present was H.T. He had arrived from Washington, USA the day before and taken lunch with a number of people including my mother at the University Club before the Memorial Service. I was very pleased to meet H.T. again. We discussed what might be the next steps in contacting my father and H.T. decided the best route was for him to contact Madam Wang. He said he was happy to help on the understanding that if K.C. declined then the matter should be dropped. Susan was pleased to support my efforts but for her the relationship was consigned to the past. H.T. had maintained contact with Madam Wang and in January 1996 wrote to her explaining that I would like to contact my father. He explained that I did not wish to cause him any embarrassment and hoped that Madam Wang would be able to raise the matter with K.C. .

Madam Wang held two private meetings in 1996 with K.C., at the second of which she confirmed to him for the first time that he had an English daughter. K.C. then went home and told Fengyun and Sun Kun (his daughter) about me and how I had now got in touch with him. They both told him that he had responsibilities as a father and that he must make contact with me. K.C. had told both his wife and his sister about his relationship with Susan soon after his return to China; the rest of the family had become aware of the story but it was never discussed.

After he had obtained his wife and sister's approval

it was agreed that he should respond to me with a warm welcome from my Chinese family. So in February 1996 Susan and I received letters in English from K.C. expressing his delight and welcoming us into his family. He wrote to Susan that in nearly half a century this was the first time he had spoken her name, and signed the letter with the name by which she had known him, Kim. K.C. concluded his letter to me saying he would like to know me by the Chinese name of Sun Ru Yi (which translates as "everything one could wish for" and phonetically is close to Zoë). He also hoped that I would agree to being known as his daughter.

Letters continued to be exchanged during 1996: K.C. wrote often to Susan but it was clear that she was happy to leave it to me to pursue the relationship. They told each other about their family situations. K.C. was now retired and he and Fengyun were living in the apartment near to the mill in Lanzhou. K.C.'s sons had moved away, two of them with their families whilst the youngest one was soon to return home after a series of short-term jobs. His daughter Sun Kun lived nearby with her husband and young daughter: they were particularly close to Fengyun and K.C. , who was very interested in the future of their granddaughter.

I was able to tell my father that I was happily married and then working at a senior level in local government in London. He was also delighted that he had two English grandchildren, a girl and boy. We began to discuss how we should meet for the first time and we made some detailed plans.

My very supportive family, Richard my husband and our young children Kate and Simon, set off with me on a journey into the unknown. We had photos but I did wonder whether my father and his family would actually turn up at the appointed place and appointed hour. We arrived in Beijing and checked in to the Swiss hotel and then on my birthday in March 1997 under the National Flag in Tiananmen Square we met for the first time, over 47 years since K.C. had returned from England.

Between 1999 and 2007 I made five further visits to China to meet up with my father. My husband Richard and I visited him and his family in their home city of Lanzhou for the first time in 1999. He wanted us to see him and his family just as they were—so, for example he told me, although he had considered installing a western toilet in their flat before we arrived, he decided against it.

We stayed in the second flat he owned in the compound of the top mill: it was March so the heating had been turned off despite snow falling. He showed us the nearby health clinic (with both Chinese and Western medicine) and as he had a dental problem we went with him to see the dentist based at the local hospital. We also went to see the square, which had a statue of Rewi Alley on the site where the Bailie School had been. Whilst we were there we saw the wards where Fengyun had worked before retirement. He took us on a tour around the top mill which was by then in a sad state of decline with very few of the machines which K.C. loved so dearly operating. We also went to visit K.C. 's granddaughter Juanjuan in her school—we stood at the front of a class of 65 lively but well-behaved children. We spoke briefly to them in English and answered some questions, but drew the line at singing for them despite pressing requests!

By 2001 we felt we wanted to get to know other parts of China and so all four of us went as a family again. This time we met my father and my sister, her husband and niece in Jinan, the capital of Shandong Province (two hours by train south of Beijing). Here we met K.C. 's sister Sun Lan Fen and her extended family. We were greeted with great hospitality including the mandatory huge banquet in a private room in a restaurant owned by a friend of the family. Sun Lan Fen had four children who were all present with their families, most of them taking part in karaoke. Everything we said, every action and every mouthful of food that we ate was watched and we caused

K.C. at the dentist 1999

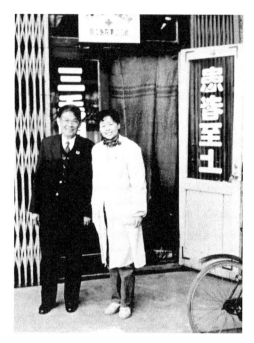

K.C. outside the Clinic with his doctor 1999

K.C. , Zoë and FY with Rewi Alley Statue in Lanzhou 1999

unintended offence by not eating the dumplings and not tasting everything!

I decided for my next visit, in 2003, to travel on my own. My father and his family thought this was very strange but I was trying to find a way of spending time with him to understand his story and to get to know him. I realised by then that during our visits he had to spend the whole time laboriously interpreting from English to Chinese and back again. As everything the English visitors said or did was analysed and discussed, so everything had to be translated! I asked that the two of us take a train ride together—just so we could sit and talk. We caught a train from Lanzhou to Xining three hours away further west—with a chilly walk at the end to view the Buddhist temples and I did indeed feel that I understood him a little better after our trip.

In 2005 Richard and I went to visit my niece Juanjuan who by this time was at university in Yibin in the south east of Sichuan Province. Yibin is a small city by Chinese standards and at that time was relatively unsophisticated: Juanjuan was very proud that she had managed to track down the one café in the whole town which served coffee so that I could have a much needed cup. She was very impressive the way she tried hard to understand and accommodate our wishes even though they were sometimes very strange to her. And increasingly as her English became fluent she was becoming more important in our getting to know Chinese ways. We travelled onwards to Lanzhou via

Chengdu, with an obligatory visit to the Panda Research Centre and then completed our journey to Lanzhou by overnight train.

The last time I saw my father was in 2007 when my son Simon and I went to spend a week in Lanzhou after taking in Chengdu and the pandas. We stayed with my sister and her husband who had moved into a lovely apartment, albeit on the 7th floor with no lift. Simon enjoyed getting to know my youngest brother Sun Long and Sun Kun's husband Xiao Hu—both of whom are great teasers; their encouraging him to have just "half" more of a beer was a constant meal time refrain. We had all gradually come to understand more about how we lived our different lives. Certainly my language studies helped me understand more about the Chinese culture and its expectations. I was impressed at the way our various cultural blunders were forgiven by my new Chinese family and they began to understand that no offence was meant. For example, K.C. found it hard to explain to his family why we would travel all that distance to stay for one week in Lanzhou when they clearly thought we should stay for several months. We in turn learnt not to take offence when cultural niceties that we anticipated were not reciprocated. Together we came a long way in building small understandings between East and West.

K.C. died in 2008 aged 82 from a short leukaemia related illness. He was buried on the outskirts of Lanzhou in a funeral plot with an appropriately auspicious view. I visited his grave two months after his death with my own family and my Chinese relatives. We were touched to see that as is tradition, my name and that of my husband and children were on the gravestone along with the names of my father's other children and their families.

K.C.'s graveside outside Lanzhou August 2008

A few photographs follow from our first visit to Beijing in 1997.

K.C. and Zoë meet for the first time on 21 March 1997

To Susan my dear, Love Kim.

Our family

A happy family

Simon on the Great wall

In Beijing 1997

Chapter III
Pursuit of Anglo-Chinese Understanding:
Personal and Political

So on 21st March 1997 I had finally achieved my personal connection with China—I acquired a father for the first time and brothers and a sister. K.C. brought his wife, daughter, son-in-law and granddaughter, and also a nephew and his wife and baby because they lived in Beijing, to our first meeting. So there I was suddenly with an extended family—but based in China! I had also arrived in a country were many, many more people were the same height as me and had looks similar to mine. It was a pretty extraordinary sensation!

It did indeed have the effect of legitimizing for me the pursuit of my 'other half'. Before travelling to China I had started Chinese lessons—and am very grateful that my first teacher taught me with all the precision that is used when teaching Chinese children—extensively practising how to write the characters in the right stroke order for example. Learning the language is something I continue to do as my grasp of it remains very poor—but it is still great being able to catch and understand the odd word spoken by a Chinese person on the London Underground for example—it has the effect on me of feeling a connection with China.

Since 2000 I have been a director in the NHS working for a large mental health trust providing services in southeast London. In my work too I have created opportunities to connect with China and have been involved in a number of visits from Chinese health professionals keen to find out about managerial systems and clinical practice in the NHS. By working closely with the British Embassy in Beijing, one of these visits turned into the building of a partnership with a mental health hospital in Shandong Province and a month long training and observational clinical placement for 6 Chinese doctors and nurses. Developing such partnerships takes a lot of persistence and determination and I am sure it is my commitment to building the understanding between China and UK that has driven me in this work.

In 2009 I became the Chair of SACU, the Society for Anglo-Chinese Understanding. My mother and I were both members of SACU, and when I attended an AGM talk in the early 2000s I volunteered to join the Council. I attended Council meetings as an ordinary member for a while and when the then Chair stood down, I was encouraged to apply for the post. Since then I have, I guess, been fulfilling my 'debt of honour' to Joseph Needham who, whit others, founded SACU, by working with colleagues in the SACU Council to fulfill our mission. In 2013 I led a SACU tour, the first one SACU had made for some considerable time, which followed the journey Needham had made in 1943 when my father had been one of the people accompanying him. We travelled from Chongqing to Dunhuang stopping at Lanzhou, Shandan and other places on the way. It was particularly exciting for me as we left Lanzhou, 70 years on, and followed their path to Shandan to visit the Bailie School and onto Dunhuang.

In 2015 SACU celebrated its 50th anniversary. At the anniversary event on 30th May 2015 His Excellency the Chinese Ambassador Liu Xiaoming officially opened the conference and his speech contained the following passage

"Confucius said 'At fifty, I knew the mandate of Heaven.' Today SACU turns fifty. On this very special day, I give SACU my best wishes from the bottom of my heart. I believe you not only know your mandate but are fully committed to it. It is the mandate to advance China-UK understanding and friendship. It is the mandate to carry forward, in this new age and with new ideas, the lofty cause of bridging gaps and strengthening bonds."

Dr. Joseph Needham and others established SACU in 1965, as a bridge between British and Chinese people. It had thousands of members in its early days and was the only route to China in the 1970's. Throughout the country's era of international isolation, SACU maintained strong links with China.

Today, SACU is a small voluntary organisation, working in partnership with other organizations that share its mission. SACU's basic aim is to spread knowledge of China in Britain, dispel misconceptions and counter misrepresentations. We have established the SACU 2065 Project—to fit our organisation to fulfil its mission for the next 50 years, bridging gaps and strengthening bonds—in a new age and with new ideas.

SACU's 50th Anniversary Event May 2015

In 2015 I was also invited to the Annual Award Ceremony of the Sino-British Fellowship Trust. This was another unexpected angle to our story in that my father and his colleague were apparently the very first students from China to receive a SBFT grant when they came to UK in 1947. The money to form the Fund had been gathered at the instigation of Sir Stafford Cripps, The Lord Privy Seal in the British Coalition Government, who persuaded his wife Lady Isobel Cripps to lead an appeal for funds and Dr. Elizabeth Frankland Moore (whose name at that time was Mrs. Miller) became the organizing secretary.

Zoë receiving award at the SBFT Annual Award Ceremony 2015

THE SINO-BRITISH FELLOWSHIP TRUST
中英學術基金會

BRITISH
ACADEMY

THE
ROYAL
SOCIETY

THE TRUSTEES OF
THE SINO-BRITISH FELLOWSHIP TRUST

Look forward to the pleasure of the company of

Zoe Reed

AT THE ANNUAL RECEPTION AND CERTIFICATE PRESENTATION 2015

*Jointly hosted by the British Academy, Royal Society
and the Sino-British Fellowship Trust*

to honour scholars supported by

THE ROYAL SOCIETY/SBFT INTERNATIONAL FELLOWSHIP
THE SINO-BRITISH FELLOWSHIP TRUST
AND THE KATHERINE WHITAKER BEQUEST

To be held at

THE BRITISH ACADEMY,
10 CARLTON HOUSE TERRACE, LONDON SW1Y 5AH
ON THURSDAY 25TH JUNE 2015
12.30PM – 2.30PM

Please Note: The Presentation Will Begin At 12.30pm prompt

POUR MEMOIRE
*If you are **unable** to attend please contact
Debbie Haine, Trust Secretary, Sino-British Fellowship Trust
23 Bede House, Manor Fields, London SW15 3LT
email a.ely@btinternet.com*

Invitation to the SBFT Award Ceremony 2015

247

The Bailie Boys arriving in UK and being greeted
by Mrs Moore BUAC/SBFT 1947

A national appeal with the title of British United Aid to
China (BUAC) was launched, and raised nearly three million
pounds. This was used to provide relief across the war-torn
land and a committee headed by the British Ambassador in
China, Sir Horace Seymour, was set up to distribute the funds
throughout the country.

So, the family connection has given me the purpose for
my journey of Anglo-Chinese Understanding. As a child my
mother had told me very little about my father but one story

I do recall was that he was a very good swimmer. In the way children do I embellished the story so that in my mind he had swum the Channel! She also spoke about what a good artist he was but it wasn't until she and I were much older that she showed me the self-portrait he had done in pastels. Apparently he had been sitting at the kitchen table with her and using a mirror had quickly produced the drawing. She kept it rolled up for years and years and then when I was in my 40s one day she gave it to me. It was on a rough piece of paper, with unequal sides, which made it quite a task to have framed.

But from 1997 my father moved from mythical figure to concrete reality. He and his family became real people and since then my family and I have made many visits to family in China. We have come to realise just how different out two cultures are—coming as they do from different civilizations. We have all learnt and adjusted over the years. Unfortunately my father passed away shortly before our arrival in August 2008—actually on my mother's birthday in June. When I was finally told— after the event as seems to

K.C. Sun self-portrait

be the Chinese way—I remember being physically shaken and upset at the loss. I had only had a father for 11 years—but as I told him he had given me so much more than if he had stayed in UK in 1950—he had given me a whole Chinese family, my "full Chinese" sister and her daughter, my niece, both of whom I feel a great warmth and connection with.

In between visits we keep in touch, mainly via Juanjuan, using email, WhatsApp and occasional Skype phone calls. My sister Sun Kun is learning English and making rather more progress than I am with my Chinese. In recent years we have continued to visit my sister Sun Kun, husband Geng Xiaohu and their daughter Juanjuan. Our son Simon got married to his wife Keri in 2012 and Sun Kun and Xiaohu

Simon and Keri's wedding 2014

came and stayed with us for a fortnight and joined the wedding celebrations. This gave them an opportunity to met up again with my Cousin Sue's daughter's Nina and Christa who had visited them in Lanzhou in 2002, and with my Aunt Isabel

In 2013 Juanjuan and Qu Deye got married and Kate our daughter spent 10 days with the family in Lanzhou and was their bridesmaid. In 2014 our wedding present to the happy couple was to have them come and stay with us here in England for over three weeks. In June this year [2016] Kate and I will be visiting Lanzhou to meet Juanjuan and Deye's baby daughter Yueyue. As Kate says—they feel like real family, they are our family.

Deye, Juanjuan and Kate outside her shop in St Margarets, Twickenham August 2014

Final Thoughts

My daughter Kate contributed the following thoughts after her grandmother's death:

My mum, Zoë has often said that I inherited my love of the decadent and luxurious things in life from Eunice. Well I don't know if that's true, but what I do know is that my lasting memories of Eunice are of fun times. Having afternoon teas in Selfridges, and once having a cab ride all the way home from central London! Indulging the childhood delights of Barbies and china dolls and discussing the merits of different TV programs. Eunice was also one of the few adults to discuss seriously, and co-create an effective day care program with a nine year old for her pet hamster!

But it was certainly not just a purely superficial connection; I'll also always recall how from when I was very small it always felt like I had a great deep friendship with Eunice. We would sit up late chatting, her telling me about the boarding school, and her upbringing. And talking about the wonders of her favourite Nelson Mandela, and K.C. with his "slow boat to China". I think some of my earliest discussions of life, and death, and morality were with Eunice, we would basically try and put the world to rights!

I think it was Eunice's ability to really talk to people

properly, regardless of the usual things, which hold people back, which make her truly special, a unique one off.

My cousin Sue who herself has since passed away, reflected:

"My Aunt Susan Eunice seemed mercurial and unpredictable, here today and gone tomorrow. Sharp, intelligent, discerning, stylish and strong yet also vulnerable, fiercely independent, bold and self-reliant, she would say what she believed without fear of the consequences. My aunt was never ordinary nor dull and unquestioning, a bright spirit is gone and the world will be duller without her."

My own final thoughts about my mother are complex. I had always felt a strong connection and responsibility for her and as she became more and more frail I struggled with what was the right thing to do. She was determined to die in her own home fiercely independent to the end—however I could see that she wasn't coping. She refused every avenue for help. In early September 2005 I had decided that notwithstanding her wants and needs, my levels of anxiety were such that I needed to insist that she receive some regular help in her home, or move to a safer setting. She was not answering the phone, something that had occurred before, and I decided the time had come to confront her. My dear friend Diane met me at Preston station and drove me to Barrow—along that longest cul-de-sac in the world. As we drove I rehearsed with Diane how to present a persuasive case to my mother that she must accept some help. I approached Barrow with dread in my heart because I knew she was either dead or it was the end of our relationship if I insisted she accept help. It turned out that it was in fact the former—and I was so grateful for the support from Diane who helped me through that difficult discovery. My mother had bolted the door inside so I was unable to gain entry using my key; I called the police and they broke in and advised that Diane and I should go to the hotel and await hearing from them about what to do next. I was grateful that my mother had bolted the door and the sensitivity of the police in handling the matter.

Reflecting now on my mother's life and background, which on many occasions had the trappings of being one thing but was actually another, I can understand how much of her fierce independence and outward aggression was a defense against fear of loss and hurt. She was a great contradiction being intelligent, lively and engaging with so many people with enormous strengths and energy and yet vulnerable too. She was always planning for a better future and yet would dwell on past injustices. She preferred that our relationship was that of friends rather than mother and daughter although was as proud and loving of me as a mother would be; she did not want to be seen as a conventional grandmother although loved her grandchildren dearly. Fundamentally she was very fearful of and affected by societal ageism, the conventional behaviours it requires and the injustices she felt it imposed; as a consequence she didn't accept the natural stages and phases of life.

It is interesting for me to also reflect that both my mother and my father were absent as parents—my father because he was the other side of the world and my mother because of the challenges and trials of her life. But both gave me so many strengths and gifts—for example I can remember being enormously proud when Joseph Needham on several occasions reflected that some action or remark I had made was "very Chinese". I'm sure I have many of my mother's strengths and characteristics too and am grateful that I am adaptable and flexible—a skill no doubt acquired because of my childhood moves. I have also learned from the life she led and my early years about what is important for me in my life. I have always been clear of the crucial importance of strong family life and love and the need for my children to grow up in one place; feeling part of work places, communities and organizations and maintaining connection with colleagues and friends has been vital; and now that I've reached my 65th birthday owning ages and stages of life are all essential lessons I've learnt. However like her, I too am independent minded, given to big ambitions and not accepting when things appear unachievable!

It is clear that the short time that my mother and father had together, left a powerful legacy which remained with them throughout their lives. When my mother passed away I found amongst her things the piece of woven material that

K.C. had made and given her when he was in the UK. She had bundled it up with a scarf she used to wear at the time and one of my first pair of shoes. After K.C. passed away, I went to visit his widow Fengyun and she gave me a few of his personal possessions. In accordance with tradition she had burnt most of them together with all his papers so that K.C. could have what was his with him on his journey. She had kept for me a few of his Chinese-English dictionaries, which he held so dear and used every day, including one that he had used in the UK. She also gave me the Fair Isle sleeveless sweater, which my mother had knitted and given him all those years ago. So both of them had preserved these mementos of their precious time together throughout their lives, and I now have them together as my mementos of them.

The Fair Isle sleeveless sweater my mother kitted for my father

致凯特、赛蒙和娟娟
继续英中两国之间的理解

引言

我第一次见到父亲，是在1997年3月21日。那一天，是我46岁的生日。我和丈夫带着两个孩子从伦敦飞往北京，而父亲则乘着火车从甘肃兰州缓缓而来。与他同行的，是他的妻子、女儿、女婿和外孙女。下午3点，我们在天安门广场的国旗下见了面。

在此之后，我又去看望过他5次。2008年，我还没来得及趁着北京奥运会再去看看他，父亲就过世了。就是这几次见面，让我拼拼凑凑地了解到父亲传奇的一生。每次见面，我们都会用英语聊上好一会儿，平时也常常通信，后来他还寄给我一组回忆录，里面记述着他不同阶段的人生经历。

在第一次见面之前，我根本不知道世上还有他的存在。那么多年以来，我一直以为父亲已经去世了。1947年，他跟着20世纪中国历史上两位重要的西方人——新西兰人路易·艾黎和剑桥大学研究中国科学文明史的著名专家李约瑟——来到英国，结识了我的母亲。通过父亲的叙述以及对艾黎和李约瑟的研究，我了解了父亲在英国的经历，以及1943年他与两位先生一同前往偏远的甘肃西北部，考察敦煌莫高窟的故事。母亲则帮助回忆了他们在一起的短暂时光；而她也于2005年去世了。

以下是我父亲自述的故事。这个男人克服了一度难以想象的苦难，凭借着自己的坚毅和智慧，在人生的道路上勇往直前。他结识了两位对中国有着重要影响的西方人，对西方世界，尤其是英国产生了诚挚的感情与崇敬，并始终热爱和忠诚于自己的祖国。他在中西方之间架起了一座桥梁，为我们这些有幸与他相识的人留下了丰富的回忆。

孙如意

2012年8月

2016年5月附笔

经北京大学孙华教授的介绍，北京出版集团找到我，说要用中英文两种语言来出版我父亲的故事，我非常高兴。能用双语的形式出版这本书是我一直以来的心愿。但他们希望书里的素材能再丰富一些。原书只是蜻蜓点水般地提到过我的母亲。但出版方认为，读者也同样有兴趣了解我母亲在同时期的生活。因此，书里应该包括当时（包括1939—1945年二战时期）在中国和英国发生的故事。此外，出版方也很好奇，我为什么会愿意以英中了解协会①主席的身份，自发自愿地推动中英两国之间的关系。而事实上，我就是在协会的工作中才认识了孙华。

于是，新书在2012年的基础上增加了一些素材，加强了有关父亲的记述，并将有关母亲和我的内容从父亲的这部分中独立出来，挪到了别处。

现在，在这本新书里也可以看见我母亲的故事了。过去的她

---

① 全文中的协会均指英中了解协会，即Society for Anglo-Chinese Understanding，简称SACU。——编者注

一直带着几分神秘。家里人都说，她总是"起床就不见人影"。她"很自我，而且容易动怒，动辄生气""我们都数不清她究竟跳过几次槽"，而且"我们各走各的路"……因此，他们之间不可避免地存在误解和不同的看法。我很感谢大家与我分享这些看法，尤其是伊莎贝尔小姨。她是母亲这一代人中唯一还在世的。她制作了一本相册，像家史一样地记述了大家的生活，还帮我回忆了很多往事，拼凑出过去的轮廓。她还给我看了外祖母80多岁时写的日记，帮我穿越到他们在非洲的时光。

关于自己的生活以及生命中出现过的人，母亲曾经和我有过几次深谈。这些都对本书的形成起了重要的作用。此外，母亲还一直保留着家人、朋友寄给她的所有信件和卡片。母亲过世后，我去整理她的一箱箱遗物，心里不禁感慨：现在用书信往来的人已经很少了，以后的人也不会再需要整理如此多的文件了，但同样地，也不会有这么丰富的资料留存下来！

为了追悼母亲，我将这些素材归入了若干个文档。我看到了各种各样的文件，包括她的护理考试证书、奖项和奖励；工作录取通知书；离职纪念卡；加入工党和工会的证明；滚石乐队演唱会门票；给伦敦交通行政部的投诉信，抱怨"售票员看我要开车窗，态度很差"；身份证；等等。这些文件帮助我更好地了解了母亲，也帮助我区分清楚了它们所发生的时间和地点。

同样也是为了追悼她，我做了一张时间表，并给认识母亲的人都寄了一些报事贴，请他们写下记忆中的苏珊，帮我填满这张时间表。通过这样的方式，我从更多的角度和更详细的细节了解了我的母亲。

我很感谢李约瑟博士将所有的信件都保存了下来。正是因为如此，我才得以在剑桥大学的图书馆里找到"李约瑟档案"，并拜读这些信件。

北京出版集团的编辑告诉我，这本书将被列入"国际名人看中国"丛书。这套丛书旨在介绍外国友人对中国的援助和情谊。虽然本书也会谈到一些外国名人的生活，包括李约瑟、路易·艾黎、斯塔福德·克里普斯爵士和伊莎贝尔·克里普斯夫人、乔治·何克等，但书里的主角却是另外两个人——他们有过不同于常人的生活经历；从两个不同的大陆出发，经历一系列事件后，在另一个大陆相遇；凭借智慧和决心，为自己创造了多姿多彩的生活。他们给了我生命，以及非常有趣的生活经历。我很感激他们。

我也很感谢北京出版集团给我这个机会，让我认真思考自己不平凡的父亲和母亲，解开他们谜一样的过去，并且第一次完整地记叙我的童年。

最后，无论对于只写到父亲的原书，还是这本新书，我都要感谢在中国和英国的家人，感谢他们的帮助和回忆。我也要感谢我的丈夫理查德以及凯特的丈夫亚当给我的建议，以及在技术上对我的支持和帮助。

孙如意

2016年5月

目　录

第二部分　　　苏珊·尤妮斯的经历
　　　　　　　　母亲的故事

第三部分　　　孙如意的成长
　　　　　　　我与英中了解的故事

第一部分

孙光俊的自述
父亲的故事

18岁左右的孙光俊[1]

[1] 除非另有说明，否则所有照片均为私人收藏。

第一章　幸福的童年
（1926—1938年）

我叫孙光俊，生于1926年3月17日，农历二月初四。我的父母共生了12个孩子，但只有6个活了下来，我是其中最小的一个。我有三个哥哥，两个姐姐。除了最小的一个姐姐外，其他的都比我年长许多。当我还是个孩子的时候，他们就已经结婚生子了。作为家里最小的一个，我总是得宠些，甚至难免有一些被溺爱。

我的家在河南，一个叫作"岭岗"的小村庄，靠近今天的开封市尉氏县张市镇。河南位于中国中东部，其悠久的历史多与横贯北部的黄河有关。2007年，尽管全省人口已达到9900万，但河南仍是全国城市化程度最低的省份之一。在20世纪20年代，这里完全是一派农村的景象。那时，孙家和其他许多人家一样，就靠着种田和小买卖来养活自己。

小时候，家里人管我叫"四淘"（淘气的老四）或者"云彩客"（来自云的礼物）。长大以后，取名为"光俊（Kuang Chün）"，我的英文名字"K.C."就取之于中文名的首字母。仗着自己是家里最小的孩子，我总是好管闲事，也常常淘气。我胆大而好奇心强，想到什么就说什么。虽然小姐姐比我大两岁，但我常会拼命地戏弄她，为此没少惹来母亲的一顿好骂。母亲有时还会拿根棍子追着我打，想要惩戒我。可我很快就学会了用快跑来躲避责骂。每次都要一直跑到听不见母亲的声音了，我才会停下来，然后去找别的小朋友玩。

小时候，父亲与我并没有那么亲密。他是个严肃的人，话不多，但却对我的成长产生了很深的影响。除非我特别淘气，否则父亲不会管我。而且即便他很生气，也不会打我。他志向远大，一心想通过努力工作来让家人过上好日子。我不知道他从爷爷那儿继承了多少家底，总之，他很快就做起了各种小生意。根据我们当地的习俗，他还在世的时候就把家产分给了几个儿子：做父亲的，要为儿子安排婚事，分配家产，确保儿子们衣食无虞。女儿在婚事上也要听从父母之命，但分不到家产。

我比几个哥哥要小得多，生来也不具备父亲的商业头脑。我只记得每天等着父亲西装革履的下班回家（他总是穿得很讲究），看着他掸去身上和鞋上的尘土，洗干净脸，然后坐下来吃饭。

虽然基本都是农民出身，但孙家在当地一直还算是比较富裕的。父亲把家产分给几个成年儿子时，他一共有1.5亩地，一家老式的菜油坊（使用人力和马力）和几间小屋。我的大哥（孙光尧）接管了油坊生意。二哥（孙光庭）当了小学教师。三哥（孙光震）只读了几年中学，结婚后便和父亲还有大哥一起工作。

农忙时，父亲会带着所有人下地干活。农闲时，年长一些的就会去油坊，用花生、芝麻和棉花籽榨油。

父亲的生意做得很红火。20世纪30年代初，父亲又买了80多亩地和4间院子，分给几个年长的儿子。那时几个哥哥还有大姐都已经结婚了。大姐雇了一个叫王铎的工人，负责喂驴子、马和牛，管理马车。我们都叫他王哥。家里人都很喜欢他，他和我们在一起生活了很多年。

当时，我们和大多数乡亲一样，也在田里种了些鸦片。但在我们家里，只有父亲可以把收下的鸦片留下来，自己在房间里抽。根据当地的习俗，人们谈生意的时候，最开始是边喝茶边谈，接着是在密室里边抽鸦片边谈，不让其他人进入。如果生意一直谈不完，他们就可能抽上一整天。等客人走了，父亲会清理干净所有的用具，然后，包括他在内的所有人都不得碰这些用具，直到再招待下一位客人为止。他是孙家唯一碰过鸦片的人。虽然他这一生都常常要陪客人抽鸦片，他却一直控制自己，不致上瘾。父亲55岁时去世了，而那会儿，我还是个很小的孩子。在我的记忆中，父亲是一个好人，他一生辛劳勤勉，以保家族兴旺。

岭岗村一共有四五十户人家，住的都是简单的房屋。村子四周围绕着高墙和深沟，东西两头各有一扇门，中间连着一条路。我家就在村子东北角上。孙家大多数子孙都住在村东头，比其他村民要富裕，并且更"进取"或者说"眼光更长远"一些。

我们一起出钱开办了一所"新式学校"，还请了一位先生来教书。这类学校又称"洋学堂"，意指"仿效西方"。仅从学校招收女生（这对一个村子来说，是非常先进的做法）这一点就能看出来。姐姐孙兰芬读书的时候，我还只有四五岁，但我也跟着她一起去上课。从那时起，我俩的命运就愈发紧密地联系在了一起。

由于我从小就被捧在手心，再加上我天性好玩，在学校惹了不少麻烦。像我们这样的小学一般只有一个老师，要负责教所有学生。老师名叫白宇杰。他总是善于鼓励学生仔细观察周围发生的事情——天、地和人。而在村里的其他地方，教书内容就要传统多了，无非就是孔孟之道。

白老师并不是我们村的。他在学校里支了一张床，然后按照各家送来上学的人数，轮流去学生家吃饭。一个夏日的午后，我在返校路上，听见远处一位伯伯唤我的名字。这位伯伯很和蔼，很有学问，过去还曾参加过科举考试。他看见一个瓜农，就给我买了一片西瓜。我兴高采烈地接过，一边吃，一边往学校走去，也顾不得会迟到了。

孙兰芬见我没来上课，就开始担心起来。她总是想要保护我，还常常替我受白老师的惩罚。白老师可是说打就打的。可姐姐也有绝技——每当老师的小棍落在背上的时候，她都会用自己的长辫子当作垫子。虽然听起来打得很重，但她总说自己什么感觉也没有。我一直不知道她是不是真的不疼，但她就是这样永不止息地爱护着我。

等我回到教室，手里的西瓜还没吃完，根本没注意到白老师。谁知他一巴掌拍在我的后脑勺上，将我打倒在地。西瓜弄了我一脸一身。我当时的模样肯定一团糟，尴尬极了。同学们开始嘲笑我，我忍不住大哭起来。白老师也跟着笑起来。见我躺在地上不停地哭，白老师让姐姐先带我回家，拾掇干净。姐姐照办了，然后再自己回学校上课。那个下午，我就待在家里，觉得无比尴尬和难堪。

凑巧那天该轮到我们家请白老师吃饭。所以当姐姐放学到家的时候，我知道白老师肯定就在后面不远了。我爬上门外一棵高大的柿子树，等着老师来。二哥当时也是老师，所以他和白老师走在一起。我大声喊道，家里馒头没有白老师的份，还说了他很多难听的坏话。

二哥孙光庭抬头看见我，让我下来。白老师也抬起了头，他羞得脖子和脸都红了，这倒叫我很开心。那天的晚饭吃得很快。可白老师走后，二哥却狠狠地揍了我一顿。我以前只是很忌惮父亲，可从那以后，我也不再相信二哥了，还总想尽办法躲开他：我可忘不了这顿打。

但总的来说，我的孩提时代还是非常幸福的。我整日无忧无虑。和大多数同龄的孩子一样，可以毫无顾忌、自由自在地嬉闹玩耍。男孩女孩们在满是灰尘的院子里一起玩——躲猫猫，或模仿婚礼甚至葬礼等当地习俗。夏天，男孩儿光着身子满村乱跑，下塘游泳、入河摸鱼。他们可以爬树、掏鸟窝，也可以去池塘里捉青蛙，到田里捉蚱蜢和蟋蟀。夏秋季节，大多数人家都会有鸟笼，里面全是鸟儿，尤其是麻雀。还有蚱蜢。幼鸟被从窝里抓出来，塞进笼子里，等着鸟儿的父母们衔来虫子和其他食物，伸入笼网中喂食。每天从早到晚，都能听见各种鸟儿的歌声。

村里的孩子大多姓孙。我有一个好朋友就叫孙光群。他与我同岁，小名也一样。村里的孙姓人中，有些是近亲（比如同一个祖父），有些则远些。其他不姓孙的孩子也大多比我年长些，但这并不妨碍我们打成一片。

童年的平静和幸福因父亲的去世而被打破。而几年后的1937年（我11岁），由于发生了一连串不断升级的"事件"，中国爆发了抗日战争。从此，我的生活被彻底改变了。

迁 徙

仅仅几个月后，日本就发动了全面侵华战争。随着日军占领湖北省的战略要塞武汉，河南也被推向了战争的前线。

邻村的村民和日军发生了不少冲突。此外，也有少数村民变节投敌。听说邻村发生了多起日军强奸妇女的恶行，我们村里的人已经非常愤怒和紧张了。所以，当我们听说有一小股敌军和他们的狗腿子在村子附近集结时，村民把所有能找到的武器都集中起来，所有男丁纷纷出动，准备防御。虽然缺少武器，但人数上远远超过了对方。对我来说，在那么小的年纪，保家卫国是一件让人无比激动和充满同乡情谊的事情。我们热情高涨，仿佛一群人等着捉打过街老鼠一般。但这种兴奋感并没持续多久。当天下午，我们就听说，日军会分批进村，杀光村民，烧尽房屋。

不过，我们家人和其他村民根本就没时间担心日军会不会报复。就在当晚，为阻止日军西进，蒋介石政府在花园口炸开了黄河大堤。我家也被淹了。黄河被人为地从东西流向改为了南北流向，只见天与水相接，混成一片。所有的田地都被淹了，浑浊的河水冲垮了村里的房屋。尽管我们无从知道这次改道究竟直接或间接造成了多少人的死亡，但数量无疑是巨大的。此外，还有更多的人因此流离失所。

我们家不得不面对这个事实。大哥现在是一家之主，他相信一句老话：坐吃山空。于是几天后，他决定举家迁移。我们倒不怕日本人，但没有粮食、没有生意、没有买卖，我们活不下去了。于是，又过了几天，包括我和姐姐孙兰芬在内的第一批人马就乘坐木船先行离开，往河南南部方向开去。和我们一起的还有我的母亲、二哥孙光庭、二嫂，还有他们的3个孩子。这几个孩子中最大的不过10岁，最小的还在襁褓之中。

我们历经千难万险，最后到达了河南省中部的许昌市，被当地政府接收为难民，分得了一些食物并安排了临时住所。当然，与我们有同样遭遇的人还有很多，为的是躲避洪灾，躲避日本人。我们一家和其他共100多人被分配到了300公里外河南东南方向的信阳地区。根据安排，在我们到达信阳之后会再被分别安排到小村、镇，甚至是地主家。我们一家人被安排在地主家住。

从许昌到信阳，我们在路上花了很多时间。当时根本没有任何交通工具，难民们只能带着锅碗瓢盆和衣服步行过去。东西较多的人用手推车推着或拉着往前走；而东西较少的则直接扛着走。我们当中有携家带口的，也有独身一人的；男、女、老、少，还有各种残疾人；有些孩子太小了，根本走不了，甚至还有嗷嗷待哺的婴儿。更让我吃惊的是那么多裹了小脚的女人。对她们来说，哪怕很短的一段路程，走起来也是很痛苦的。

我们几乎用了20天才走到信阳。即使在那样的情况下，一路上的安排也还是很妥当的：难民们可以去指定的歇脚点领取食物。如果天气不好，我们就住在寺庙或教室里。不然，我们就睡在露天环境，有时会是树下，一个挨着一个以得到些支撑和安慰。

我们8口人算是比较大的一家，行李也比其他人多。二哥不是很强壮，所以我们推了一辆独轮车，载着二哥家的行李和两个比较小的孩子。我在车前拴了根绳子拉着走，二哥在后面推。可我们都没经验，总是把小车弄翻。于是，我们听取了同行其他人的建议，很快掌握了技巧：我在前面，要确保路上没有障碍物磕磕绊绊，二哥在后面推的时候也要灵活一些，以保持小车平衡。因为我要不停地踢走石头、牲畜的干粪等，所以鞋子很快就磨破了。

我们白天赶路，晚上休息。难民们还为此编了首歌。说来奇怪，我们竟都很享受这20天一起说、一起笑、一起哭的日子。一路上，我过得很开心。大家互相帮助，日子很快就过去了。

等我们到了指定的地主家，却发现早已人去楼空，因为不堪日本人在信阳周边的滋扰，房主一家早就跑了。走了20天，我们都筋疲力尽，决定先住一阵子再说。废弃的农田里长着麦子和豆子，刚好可以收割。虽然只是些最简单的食物，但也够吃了。然而没过多久，佃户们也开始来收粮食，看来是支撑不了几天了。于是，二哥决定去城里找些零工，并给全家人都分配了任务：姐姐负责照看较小的两个孩子；他的大儿子和我负责找柴火、水和鱼；母亲和二嫂负责出去讨吃的，这对她们来说并非易事。毕竟过去我们是地主家，不是普通的农民，不习惯于别人的施舍。

全家人都很沮丧。这样的生活对我们来说太艰难了。于是，我们决定搬去附近一个叫"元台"的小镇，再做筹谋。可计划赶不上变化。几天后，我们听说从陕西省（河南以西）来了一位姓李的交流教师。他来自那儿的一所孤儿院，此行是为了收留日军占领区的孩子。家里人决定让我和姐姐孙兰芬，还有最大的侄子孝忠一起去孤儿院。几天后，李老师找到了二十几个孩子，于是我们准备离开河南。

在和家人道别之后，我们步行到了洛阳火车站，乘火车前往北临黄河的陕西潼关。由于这条线路接近日军驻地（在黄河南岸），所以火车只能夜间运行，不亮灯，也很少喷蒸汽。在通往潼关的路上，火车要经过一处山口：我们称这趟火车为"空中快车"。不过，除了真正不怕死的人，大多数人还是认为这条线路太危险了。

于是，李老师决定让孩子们下车，步行过山口。年长的孩子负责照顾年幼的孩子。大家基本上都没有什么行李，因此走路也不成问题。我、侄子和姐姐各带了一套换洗衣裳。姐姐还带了一个小木盒，里面装着镜子、木梳和头绳。夜里，我们利用树丛做掩护，沿着火车的线路，穿过山口。我们刚从其中一个山口钻出，重新呼吸到新鲜空气，警报就突然拉响了。我们赶紧躲入附近的防空洞。才刚进到洞里，炮弹就炸开了。防空洞里哭声、叫喊声乱作一片。有人开始祈祷。但我却很平静，一点儿也不觉得害怕。

等走出防空洞，我四下望了望，发现一个男人被炸死了，他的腿被炸飞了挂在树上。我们继续前行，终于抵达目的地——位于陕西西安以西的凤翔县王家堡孤儿院。

第二章　在孤儿院的日子

（1938—1942年）

这时，我已经12岁了。从1938年起，我将要在孤儿院度过3年多的时间。这是一间很大的孤儿院，可以容纳近1000个孩子。我姐姐也住在这里，直到1941年，她去了当时新开办的宝鸡女子职业学院，离孤儿院不远。但侄子没多久就被二哥（他父亲）接走了，带回去和家里其他人一起生活。我偶尔会和他们联系，包括我母亲，但从没回到他们当中。孤儿院虽然条件艰苦，却让我觉得安全。我只能靠自己了。

孤儿院效仿军队编制。每10个孩子为一个班，设一个班长；5个班为一个连，设一个连长。吃饭的时候，每个班可以分到一碗蔬菜，每个连的50个孩子共可分得两桶粥。班长负责将粥稳稳当当地盛到每个人的碗里。而连长在确定所有碗都盛好粥之后，就会吹一下口哨，示意大家动筷子。于是，只听见一片饿狼吃食般的声音，因为大家知道，谁吃得快，谁就能再多吃点儿。

饭菜毫无质量可言：肉食只偶尔才能吃到，大多数时候就是些馒头、玉米或小麦粥、煮豆子或炒豆芽。所以孩子们都营养不良，很难抵御各种疾病和传染病。有些人得了疥疮，很可能会威胁到生命。我在孤儿院的时候也生过病，但总归还是挺过去了。

孩子们也大多衣衫褴褛。孤儿院就靠着政府的一点儿救济来采买物料，但救济还总是推迟发放。往往天都已经下雪了，过冬的棉衣才刚刚准备好。然后我们要一直穿着棉衣入夏，直到单衣做好。所有的衣服都是难民们自己做的，五年级及以上的孩子都要自己动手。

孤儿院的教育

孤儿院的一个重要部分就是学校。在孤儿院，我下定决心一定要继续上学，为了能够过上更好的日子。我很好学，在村里的学校被大水淹没之前，我的成绩也一直很棒。到了孤儿院后，通过和其他学生的交流，我觉得自己应该能升入三年级或者四年级。因为分到几年级是按能力，而不是按年纪来定的。

到了分班的时候，所有新来的人都得到通知该去哪个年级，唯有我被漏掉了。于是，我就去了四年级的教室报到。老师在黑板上给我出了道算术题，想看看我水平如何。但我根本看不懂老师写的加减乘除这些符号，所以她把我送去了三年级。可是，同样的事发生了：我已经习惯了打算盘，否则根本不会算数。我一言不发，这惹火了那位姓高的老师，直接把我拖去了二年级。我一下子慌了，大哭起来。我为自己的无知感到十分羞愧。

幸运的是，负责二年级的李老师是和我们一起从河南逃难来的。他是一个和蔼、正直的人，很受大家尊敬。从河南来的这一路上，他给孩子们讲了很多传统故事，比如《大闹天宫》《包公案》《薛仁贵征东》，还有我最爱听的《唐明皇梦游广寒宫》，等等。高老师说，我完全不懂算术，所以只能把我交给李老师。说完，高老师便离开了。

李老师看着我，让我止住眼泪。他给我找了个位置坐下，然后对我说，他知道我只学过算盘，不会算术。但他可以教我，不必难过。但我仍觉得难为情——我在这么多人面前丢脸了。姐姐虽然比我大，但也一样在二年级。所有人都看着我，只有她低着头，沉默着。她知道，要不是考算术，凭我的语文能力早就够得上三四年级的水平了。

孤儿院不设一年级，因此所有水平差一点儿的学生都归入二年级。教室直接设在大堂里，没有桌椅板凳。孩子们只能坐在捆好的高粱秆上。每个学生有一本笔记本、一支铅笔和一块木板（上面放着笔记本）。教室前面有一块黑板。由于只有老师有课本，因此上课的所有内容都必须写在黑板上。我们再一字一句地抄在自己的笔记本上，就好像小百科全书。

到了寒冷的冬天，要抄写这么多内容就更困难了。外面飘着皑皑大雪，气温降到零下十几度，教室或卧室里连个火炉都没有，更别提暖气了。和大多穷人家里一样，孤儿院用的是最简单的砖砌地台，也就是炕。它的作用是在夜里通过炕内的火道取暖；但在孤儿院，炕始终是冷冰冰的。到了冬天，我的手脚经常会生冻疮。手指肿得像小胡萝卜，根本握不住笔。但我一心要学习，求知若渴。

在二年级待了半年后，我在老师和同学的帮助下升入了三年级。我很认真地学了一年。根据孤儿院学校的规定，每年夏天，学生可以根据自己的学习情况决定考入哪个年级。因此，读完三年级后，我就参加了五年级的升学考试，并且顺利通过了。接下来的两年，我读完了五年级和六年级，并于1941年从小学毕业。再下来，我就可以读中学了。

生活条件

在这段日子里，生活条件每况愈下。政府督促难民迁移时所做的承诺根本没有兑现。我们缺衣少食，就连最基本的玉米粥都喝不上，每个人都面黄肌瘦。我也经常饿得肚子咕咕叫——白天吃不饱，晚上睡不好。

夏天是跳蚤横行的季节。每间宿舍有两张大炕，可以睡15个左右的孩子。谁要起夜的话（通常是为了使用屋子中间的尿桶），腿上就会叮满跳蚤。所以我一般会坐在炕沿上，迅速把跳蚤掸去，然后再回到被子里。但屋内还有更多跳蚤、虱子，有时候甚至还有蝎子、蜈蚣、大蜘蛛和蜥蜴，让我根本无法入睡。有一天夜里，终于轮到我被蝎子蜇了——真的很疼，我哭了一夜。有个小伙伴对我说，我可以哭，但不能叫妈，否则情况会更糟。传说中母蝎子生子后很快就会死去，所以蝎子都是没妈的。

我的被子破破烂烂，重量不足3斤。上面沾着血迹，脏得发亮，而且气味难闻。我盖了它那么久，从来没有洗过。被子原先大概有四五斤重，可后来被虱子蛀了。于是我就用砖头猛砸，想除掉虱子，结果把被子弄烂了。我的身下没有褥垫，冬天就用一层草席，下面铺满麦秆，而到了夏天就只用草席。至于枕头，冬天用棉衣，夏天用石头。那时，被子和衣服是我仅有的家当。

在这样艰苦的环境里，根本谈不上营养，卫生条件也只是最基本的而已。虽然孤儿院里有一间诊室和一位医生，但却只有极少的一点儿药物和治疗手段。如果疥疮太厉害了，医生可能会开点儿硫黄药膏。可若得了再严重一点儿的病，一般就没治了。有时候，煮点儿猪肝汤就能当药了。随着时间的推移，越来越多的孩子死于疾病。

起初，葬礼比较像样。村长会给死者穿上最好的衣服，打一口木棺材，而校长也会声泪俱下地说几句慰藉的话。但随着死者越来越多，仪式变得越来越简单。死去的孩子就穿着自己的衣服（如果他们还有衣服的话），然后被裹在草垫里，再用绳子扎紧，再由两个男孩将尸体抬到墓地，挖个坑埋掉。有时候埋好的尸体会被狗吃掉，空出的坑就留给下一个死了的孩子用。当地大多数人家都会养几只大狗来驱狼，而我听说，这些狗有时也会吃婴儿。狗会出现在葬礼上，然后争抢猎物。一开始，没人愿意参加葬礼，可后来有规定，凡是协助葬礼的人都可以获得两个馒头，于是一切都变了。我们极度渴望得到食物，而馒头就是生命，它也因此成了一种重要的货币。我参加过几个小伙伴的葬礼，每次都能得到两个馒头。

取　水

孤儿院位于高海拔的农村地区，满目荒凉。在这里，取水成了一个很大的问题：全村只有一口井，且水位于地下五六十米处。井口直径约两米——从上往下看，就好像一个饭碗。我和朋友经常向井里丢石头，听着它在井壁上撞来撞去，发出不同的声音，直至掉入水中。这口井距离孤儿院大约一公里。井口上有一个架子，上面安装了一台绞车。绞车上连着一根长长的麻绳，两端各拴一只木桶。两人转动绞车的手柄，一边将空桶放入井中，一边将装满水的桶往上拉。等到将这只桶拉出井口，再将里面的水倒入事先带来的另一只空桶里，让两个孩子挑回孤儿院的厨房。一年四季，不论什么天气，四年级以上的学生都要轮流来取井水。

水是限量供应的，以确保人人都有水用。每天早晨，我们10个人共用半盆水进行洗漱。我连手和脸都没法洗干净，更不用说洗被子了。我在孤儿院这些年，连一个澡也没洗过。好在孤儿院附近有个小坑，到了夏天被雨水填满的时候，我和小伙伴就会溜过去游个泳，洗个澡。到了冬天，手、脚和脸都暴露于风霜雨雪之中，常常会冻坏。但不论路有多难走，我们都要轮流去井里取水。如果鞋坏了，我就得光脚走在雪地里。这时，脚会冻得肿起来，于是我就赶紧回到房间，把脚放进被子里，直到消肿为止。脚本来冻得都麻木了，可肿消下去之后，疼痛感就会袭来，连路都走不了。

人生课

在孤儿院的这些年，我不仅接受了最基本的教育，也建立了让我坚守一生的道德原则。尽管生活艰苦，但我仍感激孤儿院教给我的一切，虽然我当时并不这么认为。

一个晚春的清晨，我和一个朋友打了一满桶水回学校，路上遇见了几个收苜蓿的村民。这些农民通常会把苜蓿收集起来，用开水焯过后在太阳下晒干，这样就能存到冬天当蔬菜吃。当时一大清早，我还没吃早饭，于是立刻放下水桶，抓了一把半干的苜蓿就狼吞虎咽地吃起来，好像是饿狼见到了肉一样。然后，我又抓了一把，边嚼边往学校走去。在校门口，我撞见了刘老师，他问我在吃什么，得知是苜蓿后，他扇了我好几个耳光，非常痛。他显然很生气：

"我怎么教你的？不管日子有多难，都不许偷东西！宁可饿死，也不能偷别人的食物！你必须要做一个诚实、正直的人！我希望你从此记住，永远只能做对的事情。你自己说，我今天是不是该揍你！"

我很羞愧地回答说："当然该。"我觉得自己确实应该受到惩罚。这件事我一辈子都记得。它提醒我要做出正确的决定，避免走错路。我决定要好好体会遵循正确的原则和价值观到底有多重要。

继续向前

1941年，我15岁，准备去上中学或技校，以求谋生。我想离开孤儿院，但首先得找到一个合适的理由，还有一个能收留我的地方。如果我偷偷溜走，一旦被抓回来，就会被关进小黑屋待3天，还很有可能挨一顿打。所以，我必须先想清楚怎么做才能走。

我有一个同学叫李明学，我们的姐姐就读于同一所学校。这所学校坐落在宝鸡以西不远处，是由新西兰人路易·艾黎为响应中国工业合作社①（C.I.C）运动而创建的，意在培养技术和管理人才。学校也得到了共产党的支持。无论是从教育水平，还是住宿条件来说，这所女子学校都比孤儿院要好得多。于是，我和李明学计划，要溜到姐姐的学校去。

1941年初夏一个周日的早晨，微风拂面。我们引开了孤儿院看门小男孩的注意，跑上向西的大路。姐姐的学校距离我们大约25公里。走出孤儿院，我们环视了一下四周，没有看见任何同学。于是快步走起来，还时不时地跑几步。所以，只花了半天多的时间，我

---

① 简称工合。——编者注

们就和姐姐们碰头了。

我们和姐姐们一起待了3天，讨论着未来——我们要做什么？要去哪里？可还没等我们讨论出结果，孤儿院派来的人就追到了，把我们带了回去。来追我们的人是孤儿院以前的一个学生，很和善。我姐姐求他替我们跟孤儿院的领导说几句好话——不要打我们或关小黑屋。他让姐姐别担心，说会跟他们解释，我们只是想姐姐了，并不是真的要逃走。等我们回到孤儿院，他果然信守了承诺。我们非但没受罚，还得了些面粉，可以做一顿好吃的饺子。

我第一次出逃的计划就这么失败了。但我并不安于现状，我坚信"失败乃成功之母"。如果我继续留在孤儿院，那我的未来只能是一片黯淡。政府给我什么，我才能有什么。成功就好比大海捞针。于是我又开始计划第二次出逃。

这次我找了另一个朋友，名叫高文姜。他比我年长些，认识一家小型棉织厂的老板。我们计划到这家工厂去当学徒。决定了之后，其他男孩就开始帮着我们一起攒馒头，准备留到路上吃。几个月后，馒头终于存够了。按计划，我们最多走10天，如果能搭上火车，时间就更短些。

1941的春节，我们离开了孤儿院。至此，我已经在这里学习生活了近4年的时间。我们步行至附近的虢镇火车站，准备搭火车去咸阳。可我们没钱，买不起火车票，只能寄希望于碰见好心的列车员，能免费捎我们一程。棉织厂所在的北潼关是一片煤矿区，所以我们可以搭乘运煤的火车，这样也比较不容易被抓。等我们到了厂里，只有一个看门的人在。他告诉我们，老板休假了，不知道何时回来。这可是个大问题，尤其是馒头已经吃得差不多了。

高文姜想了个办法：他有个婶婶住在咸阳，家里还有个12岁左右的儿子。她家离火车站并不远，一间小小的茅舍，只勉强够他们两人避一避风雨。高文姜向他婶婶介绍了我，说我是他的好朋友，如同弟弟一样。他解释说，我们是去棉织厂找工作的，他马上还会回去接着找。如果找到了工作，就回来接我。他让我把他婶婶当作自己的婶婶，听她的话，和她儿子一起干活。说完，他就离开了。

婶婶家的生活确实非常贫困和艰苦，比乞丐也好不了多少。他们的收入主要来自于婶婶为别人洗衣和缝缝补补。她儿子会去附近的火车站，捡些煤回来做饭用。

好在他们家附近有一个军营，婶婶就安排我睡在那儿。我每天只在午饭时间和婶婶一起吃顿面条，其他大多数时候都在火车站转悠，看看能不能等到高文姜。我很担心她没有钱再多照看我一个人，所以也坚持去捡煤。但她总不许我去，让我想待多久就待多久。她说她看得出来，我是个"好学的人"。婶婶对我很好，事实上也救了我的命，所以我一直很感激她。我等了高文姜好几个星期，却再也没有见到他，也没有听人说起过他。

姐弟团聚

在和婶婶一起生活了一个月后的某天，我和往常一样早早起来，去火车站捡煤。人群从车站进进出出，沿街摊位上的小贩叫卖着食物和饮料，一派生气勃勃的喧嚣场景。我却又饿又渴，想着能拿什么换一碗油茶、细豆沙，或是一块芝麻烧饼、几根炸得香脆的油条？可摸摸身上，我一分钱也没有，只能听听看看了。

天色将晚，车站内的人渐渐少了起来，我差不多是最后一个离开车站的人。车站外，一个贵妇人从我面前走过。她身着蓝色衬衫，怀里还抱着一个小男孩儿。孩子似乎睡着了，但手里还抓着一张钞票。突然，钞票从他手中掉下来，落在我面前。妇人并没有留意到，还在继续往前走。我四下望了望，没有人。于是，我用脚踩在钞票上，心怦怦直跳，仿佛怀里揣了只兔子。终于，妇人消失在了视线中。四下依旧无人。现在可以放心地把钱捡起来了。当务之急是联系上姐姐，所以我用这一小笔意外之财买了信纸、信封和一枚邮票。我给姐姐写了封信，告诉她我在咸阳的窘境。剩下的零钱刚好够买一块烧饼，那烧饼简直美味极了。我心想，我比那位妇人需要钱，她可能也根本不会发现孩子丢了钞票。

在那段日子里，我是咸阳火车站候车室的常客，基本上每天都要去一两次。春节刚过，很多工人和学生放完假回来，火车站熙来攘往。我并不讨厌人多；相反，我很高兴置身于人群之中。大家你推我撞，反而让我觉得暖和。突然，我在人群中瞥见一个认识的女孩，顿时大喜过望。她叫李梓怀，过去曾和我一起在孤儿院待过，现在和我姐姐在同一所学校念书。我大声喊她。她见到我先是一惊，然后就问我为什么会在火车站。我告诉她自己是怎么从孤儿院逃出来，又是怎么到了高文姜的婶婶家，接下来真的不知道该怎么办。我问她能不能帮我和姐姐见一面，她毫不犹豫地答应了。她说她今晚会去一个校友家，然后第二天就回宝鸡。她让我和她一起走，这样一定能见到姐姐。她还让我去和婶婶告个别，收拾东西准备出发。

于是，我几乎一路跑着回到军营，打包好行李，向收留我的哨兵致了谢，然后回到了婶婶家，告诉她我终于可以去宝鸡和姐姐团聚了。我向她深深地鞠了一躬，她含泪看着我离开。

梓怀还在我们分开的候车室等我。她吃惊地看着我："这就是你全部的行李？"我把行李放在她坐的长凳旁，然后坐下。我们聊了一会儿。我身上的疥疮好了一些，但还没有完全掉痂，和梓怀聊天的时候，我还会时不时地偷偷挠挠。梓怀拖着大大小小几个包，有些里面装着吃的。我推测，她的父亲是位军医，所以她的生活要比大多数人好一些。我们聊着天，时间很快就过去了。天色渐渐暗了下来，她从包里拿出一块又小又薄的糕点。我看着它，心想我一口气就能吃掉四五个。但我只接过她掰下来的半块糕，告诉她足够了。

终于，火车来了。我们向梓怀朋友所在的茂陵驶去，仅仅一站的距离。我们穿过村子，向她朋友家走去。所有行李都在我手上。这是一个美丽的月夜，天上星光点点。此时，不远处一声嚎叫划破了寂静。我让梓怀别怕，只是狗叫。突然，梓怀停住脚步，说她忘记朋友家该怎么走了，得找个村民问路。于是我们回到村里，找到一户亮着灯的人家。梓怀推门进去，只见四五个男人正在赌博。时值春节，赌博在农村很常见，因为农民都要休息一段时间，才会再下地干活。由于这是只在节庆才有的活动，所以政府通常睁一只眼闭一只眼。这几个男人赌性正酣，根本听不见问路。梓怀刚出房间，嚎叫声就停了。奇妙的是，她也立刻就找到了去朋友家的路。她咚咚地敲门，直到进门后才舒了一口气。

梓怀解释说，我们之所以会迟到，是因为她知道在不远处嚎叫的是一匹狼。她很害怕，所以装作迷路了，这样才能折回村子里。然后，她又鼓了鼓气，一路跑到朋友家，仿佛狼就在后面追着。梓怀上气不接下气地说着，把她朋友的家人都逗笑了，我却很镇定。过了一会儿，她终于平静下来，向朋友家人介绍我是孙兰芬的弟弟。对方邀请我们坐下来吃饭，还没等到梓怀婉言谢绝，我就一口应了。他们给我端上一个黑色的大碗，里面是满满的挂面和两个煎鸡蛋。我头都不抬地吃完了。朋友的妈妈看着我吃面的样子，眼里涌出了泪。看得出，我已经很久没有吃饱过了。

吃完饭，我踏踏实实地睡了一觉。第二天一早，我们赶往火车站，坐上了前往宝鸡的列车。我爬上行李架，藏在包后面，躲过了列车员的检票。不一会儿，我又睡着了。等我醒来，刚好到了站。因为没票，我从列车员面前走过时，故意拎上了梓怀的所有包裹，假装自己是她雇来的脚夫。终于，我们平安地抵达了女校。我和姐姐团聚了，姐弟相见，激动万分，我们都热泪盈眶。姐姐说她一直都很担心我，直到收到我从咸阳寄来的信，才确定我还活着。

第三章　在培黎学校的日子

（1942—1946年）

和姐姐在学校

　　我知道不可能一直和姐姐住在一起。说到底，她只是个学生，既没有收入，也没有自己的住处。但她很快就帮我在十里铺找到一份在织布厂的工作。而这个小镇距离她的学校也仅5公里之遥。

　　工厂有4台手动织布机，用来生产棉布。每台织布机由一名织工操作，另有两名学徒负责将纬纱递给织工。我就是其中一名学徒。这份工作很辛苦，也不付工钱，只不过每天管两顿饭。老板觉得我机敏肯干，答应送我一双

孙光俊与姐姐孙兰芬，
摄于1942年或1943年

新鞋。在工厂做工虽然没有工钱，但总好过在街上闲逛，而且总算能吃上正经饭了。晚上，我就睡在一个很窄很高的架子上：只要睡觉不翻身就没问题。一天晚上，我梦见自己睡在一张大大的双人床上……结果当然就是摔在了地上。

厂里的工人看起来都很喜欢我，可能就是因为我总是埋头干活的缘故——往地上洒水、扛纱线、取水、扫地、买食物。我很快就掌握了基本的纺织技术，可以给织工帮帮忙。我会将机轮转得飞快，让织工安心织布，累得膀子都酸了。但就是因为我干劲十足，所以不太会像其他学徒一样犯错误而受到责备或更严重的惩罚。一位织工还答应我，只要我的个头足够开织布机了，就教我如何织布，这样我就能赚些钱了。

一天早上，我正在做工，老板突然把我叫到院子里。我姐姐正在那里：她告诉老板，有人要接我回家了。她谢过老板这段时间对我的照顾，让我即刻出发。我被搞糊涂了。我在工厂干得很开心，而且我一直以为再也回不了家，怎么突然又要接我回家。等我们离开工厂，我问姐姐究竟是怎么一回事，她笑着说，她只是需要找个理由把我从工厂接走。事实上，有人主动推荐我去另一所学校——双石铺（今凤县）培黎学校。我激动极了，而且我在孤儿院时的老朋友李明学也被推荐去了。

推荐我们的这个人是我姐姐孙兰芬和李明学姐姐共同的朋友。他算是当地的一个诗人，与李明学的姐姐在恋爱。但当我们如约去取推荐信时，却出了问题。看起来，他对我的推荐有点儿不冷不热。如果只有一个机会，他建议学校录取李明学。如此明显的裙带关系，让我和姐姐都非常生气，毕竟我连工厂的工作都辞掉了。我们想了想，不能靠这样一份推荐信去新学校，于是姐姐和她的朋友去找了自己的校长寻求帮助。校长的回复倒是很令人意外：他同意破例录取我进女校，算是给我的特殊优待。

就这样，我进了女校。按照规定，我每天必须最后一个进寝室睡觉，早上第一个起床。直到此时，我的人生才真正开始有了转机。那一年是1942年。这间学校的特别之处就在于它的培训室，里面的木织机可以靠脚踏板和手摇柄来操作。通常情况下，培训室里同时会有四五个学生。我就一直忙着往木织机里送纬纱。如果哪台木织机出问题了，学校就会从当地的"工合"社请来维修技师。我对机械技术产生了浓厚的兴趣，并且很快学会了日常修理。于是，我得了个绰号叫"小技师"。在此之前，我的志向都只是成为一名技工，但现在，我更感兴趣于机器的工作原理，我要设计出更高效的新机器。从我第一次听人提到"工程师"这个词，就把它当作了我的志向。

这间学校非常适合我。它不仅提供理论学习，还安排了实践技能培训。当时新西兰人路易·艾黎在中国创办了多所培黎学校，并且担任了名誉校长。后来，我与路易·艾黎成了非常熟识的朋友，但因为他比我年长近30岁，所以我对他非常恭敬。我一直称他为艾黎先生，从不叫路易。

艾黎先生于1897年出生在新西兰，1927年来到中国。他原本在上海公共租界消防处任防火督察，后来担任工业督察长。他亲眼看到上海在日军的摧毁下变成一片废墟，见识了战争对工业的打击。

艾黎先生一直都支持不断壮大的中国共产党。他和多方合作，发起了工合运动。他和其他知名的外国人士一起，支持中国人民抵抗日本帝国主义的侵略。1940年，他创办了第一所培黎学校，目的是通过教育和培训，让中国的年轻人成为国家未来工业发展的领袖。教学内容结合了技术培训和文化知识。1942年，艾黎先生已经成为颇具影响力的人物，并与共产党建立了密切的联系：他得到过毛泽东的亲自接见，后来还与周恩来、邓小平等高层领导人保持了友好的关系。

见到艾黎先生

我到培黎学校后没多久，姐姐就介绍我认识了艾黎先生。此次会面是我人生中一个非常重要的时刻。我们聊了起来，很显然，我的知识和热忱打动了他，他决定收我为培黎学校的正式学生。他说我一定可以转去双石铺的学校，很快就会有新校长来接收我。

姐姐和我都万分高兴，因为我知道自己不可能一直待在女子学校。当时我已经16岁了，接近成年。在这以前，我一直都在流浪，活着是我唯一的目的。现在我终于有机会证明自己，为自己设定一条人生的道路。为此，我永远感激艾黎先生。此后的45年里，我一直与艾黎先生保持着联系，直到1987年他在北京去世。

学校以艾黎先生的一位美国传教士朋友"约瑟夫·培黎"的名字命名。一方面是为了吸引有同情心的外国友人给予资金支持，另一方面是因为艾黎先生不希望为自己和"工合"运动引来不必要的关注。日本侵略者害得我和家人背井离乡，然而即使在这偏远的陕西西部地区，日军也仍是不小的威胁。"培黎"也玩了一个文字游戏，取"培训"和"黎明"的意思。艾黎先生对我说，虽然旧中国还处于黎明前的黑暗，但我们要培养新中国的技术人才。

从双石铺到兰州

就在我与艾黎先生见面后没几天，我就被新校长乔治·何克接走了。这个年轻的英国人于1938年初次来到中国，不久后就认识了艾黎先生。两人致力通过工合运动来支持中国的发展。何克先生到达宝鸡时，身边还跟着他在当地其他"工合"学校收下的几个学徒。

我们经过长途跋涉，终于到达了位于双石铺的新学校。尽管何克先生和其他员工面临的工作条件非常艰苦，但学校还是在何克先生的领导下，成为这一带最成功的工合学校。和我一样，这里大多数的学生都是河南来的难民。到了1942年我们去的时候，学校的人数已经从12人左右增加至60人。何克先生把自己在学校的宿舍腾出来给学生住（他自己住在窑洞里），并且一直坚持改善学生的生活条件。

那时，艾黎先生和何克先生对国民党反动势力主导下的中国工合运动的创始组织有些失去信心。他们都希望有更个性化的教育体系，以造福当地群众。他们看中了偏远的中国西北地区，并开始制订计划。

我之前就听说，在相邻的甘肃省兰州市以西地区，还有另一所学校。在双石铺待了约一个月后，我和何克先生谈起有没有可能转到那所学校去。虽然我很喜欢双石铺，但还是想尽可能地远离日军还有战乱地区。

几天后（接近1942年年底），我们5个男孩儿乘坐学校的卡车到达兰州，进入了新学校。在这里，我一心苦读。我已经16岁了，从一个爱捣乱的孩子变成了一个谦恭直率的人。同学和老师都很喜欢我。艾黎先生仍然关心着我的学习情况，并且每次来兰州学校都要找我。从1942年年底开始，我在学校度过了4年左右的时间，并将兰州当作了我的家。我很快就在学校安顿了下来，成了众人皆知的好学生。

和李约瑟博士一同前往敦煌莫高窟

1943年9月，我有幸被选中，陪同著名的英国学者李约瑟（Joseph Needham）博士从兰州前往甘肃西北部考察。

李博士受剑桥大学调派，前往重庆任中英科学合作馆馆长。当时，随着日军步步逼近，国民政府想要寻找一块更安全的驻地，因而将重庆定为首都。

他的任务就是考察英国应该在哪些地区开展对华援助，以推动中国工业和技术的发展，从而改善中英两国之间的关系。李博士早年是生物化学专家，但他被中国文化所吸引，并成为20世纪研究中国科学与文明的著名西方学者。

李博士从重庆出发，准备前往甘肃西北部的玉门油田考察。可他乘坐的雪佛兰卡车却在双石铺抛锚了，等待维修。当时，艾黎先生正在为学校寻

1943年，前往敦煌的路上——李约瑟摄

找新址，因而对西北考察颇感兴趣。他欣然接受了李博士的邀请，加入了他的小考察团。

途经兰州时，李约瑟有几处地方需要拜访。兰州是甘肃省的省会，黄河穿城而过。考察团队提出需要两个学生做随行助手。艾黎先生在培黎学校的所有学生中选了我和我的朋友王万盛。9月18日，我们从兰州出发。对我而言，旅行不过是了解另一个陌生的地方，但这次不同，我和团队还肩负了特定的任务。一路上，我们遇到了很多艰难险阻，事实上，我们刚上路就碰到了麻烦。我们所乘的卡车一路上坏了好几次，机修工恐怕是团队中最忙的人了。

对我来说，这是一段全新的经历，无论对我的知识还是阅历都影响颇深。我根本没有想到，遇见李博士和艾黎先生会对我之后的人生产生怎样的影响。当时在路上，我看到一队队士兵沿路行进，他们当中有很多人年纪并不比我大多少。听李博士说，甘肃本是资源丰富之地，尤其是羊毛，但当地人却没有足够的能力把原材料制成商品。在距离兰州450公里处，我们经过一个叫山丹的县城。和我们之前见过的村镇相比，这里就是一片绿洲。这座四面城墙环绕的古城被李博士称为"最可爱的开阔之地，美丽的古建筑"。而艾黎先生也选中这里作为双石铺培黎学校的新址。

终于，我们在9月30日抵达了敦煌，接着又奔向24公里外的千佛洞。我们本打算在千佛洞逗留一天左右，到处看看，照照相，然后就回敦煌。千佛洞的洞顶和四壁上全是壁画及地仗，被李博士称作中国最伟大的艺术博物馆。可不料卡车又抛锚了，我们不得不等零件运来，于是在那里待了3周左右。李博士在本子上做了详细的记述，还配了些略图，而我和王万盛则忙着买菜做饭。此

外，我们还欣赏到了英国传统的莫里斯舞，而这只是李博士的众多
爱好之一。

我和王万盛骑着驴子去附近的小镇买过几次东西，还和李博
士、艾黎先生一起去参观千佛洞。我们的食物很简单，但足够吃
饱：一大块穆斯林面包卷，加少许羊肉。其他主要是水果，尤其是
瓜、梨、楹椁，还有土豆和蔬菜。我们经常按李博士说的方法做爱
尔兰炖肉。

有一天，我和王万盛未能按约定时间从敦煌回来，李博士和艾
黎先生开始担心起来。这段日子，两位先生始终放不下心，因为一
直有传言说哈萨克族人的武装就在附近并且四处寻衅。他俩跑到沙
漠里去迎我们，还在地上用粗盐生火，以驱赶野兽。太阳落山时，
他们才远远地望见了我们。只见我们每人手中拿着一根长棍，以
吓退狼和其他动物。看见两位先生在等我们，我们立刻举起棍

NW4_28

去敦煌的路上。照片由李约瑟提供，转自李约瑟研究中心

子，并抽打着驴子快些赶路。然而，当太阳从身后照射过来，拉出我们长长的影子，看上去竟像两个不怀好意的骑马人。两位先生转身就向营地跑去，直到听见我们的声音才发现自己看错了，于是大笑着转过身来，热情地迎接我们。其实，我们在回来的路上的确看到了哈萨克族人和狼群，但我们晚归的原因却是在银行排队。

在秋日的阳光下，千佛洞（雕有1000多尊石佛）构成了一幅绝妙的景色。树叶刚刚泛黄，美得如油画一般。在沙漠的环绕下，千佛洞仿佛一片溪水潺潺、树木葱葱的绿洲。蘑菇从木头中钻出来，因无人采摘而长得又高又大，仿佛一只鸡腿顶着个大大的圆脑袋。蘑菇白嫩，如果洗干净且炒得好的话会非常好吃。李博士给出了食谱，我和王万盛就负责在营地做菜和打理一些其他的事情。

有一天，我们从敦煌买菜回来（需要在敦煌过一夜），发现李博士和艾黎先生都有些不适。原来，他们自己做了一顿蘑菇，吃完以后感觉不舒服。我们告诉这两位著名的旅伴，做菜前必须先洗掉蘑菇上的沙子。他们竟然疏忽了这么个小常识，引来我们好一通嘲笑。

之后，我们愉快地返回了兰州，在黄河桥上告别。王万盛和我跟着艾黎先生回培黎学校，而李博士则要去城里其他地方会朋友。虽然告别，但我们和这位著名英国学者的友谊还会继续。

回到兰州

由于交通不便，我和李博士一开始不能经常见面。当时兰州还没有小车或巴士，只有马车和驴。整个城市只有一座桥能渡过黄

CFT4_23

李约瑟（左一），画家吴作人和王万盛（右一），摄于敦煌
月牙湖附近的沙漠。照片由李约瑟提供，转自李约瑟研究中心

孙光俊和卡车，摄于去敦煌的路上。照片由李约瑟提供，转自李约瑟研究中心

1943年，通往敦煌的路。照片由李约瑟提供，转自李约瑟研究中心

1943年，孙光俊（右）和王万盛，摄于敦煌。
照片由李约瑟提供，转自李约瑟研究中心

河，要不就只能乘羊皮筏。所以李博士决定从市中心搬到培黎学校来。在这里，艾黎先生自己拥有一间传统风格的小屋。

学校位于黄河北岸，距离市中心大约10公里。由于建在山坡上，学校呈前高后低的格局。所有的教室和培训室（纺织、机械、化学等）以及操场都在前半部。后半部靠近河边，比前半部大约低3米左右，是学生宿舍区和其他公共区域。

艾黎先生的小屋通常是锁起来的。但他要来住的时候，就会提前打开并打扫干净。小屋附近有很多花坛。客人要走到门口就必须穿过一条类似隧道的鲜花通道，通道两侧种着牡丹、菊花、豌豆花、牵牛花等各种花，春、夏、秋季，争奇斗艳。我很喜欢看到不同的时节有不同的花开，并呈现出不同的色彩：红、蓝、黄、白、绿……我常觉得，走近艾黎先生的小屋，仿佛走在一条鲜花做成的彩龙身下……我会帮忙打理花园，也会在适当的时节自己种些葡萄，结出来的果子很受艾黎先生和客人的喜欢。

1943年年底的一个下午，学校举行了一个小型仪式，庆祝李博士圆满完成敦煌之行。我们将桌椅搬到篮球场上，桌上摆放着为老师和客人准备的茶水点心：茶壶、杯子、西瓜子、葵花籽、蚕豆、冬果梨和其他水果。我、王万盛和大伙儿一起坐在地上，观看几个同学表演传统戏剧片段、介绍工合运动的历史、讲故事和说笑话。李博士带了两名翻译，一位是他当时的秘书黄博士（H.T. Huang），另一位是化学老师廖弘景。那天的气氛非常好；对我而言，这就好像家人团聚一般。

艾黎先生跳了一段新西兰毛利舞来助兴，还展示了毛利人传统的碰鼻礼。李博士也不甘示弱，跳起了英国的传统民间舞蹈。虽然已入11月，李博士还是跳出了一身汗，大家回报以热烈的掌声。而我则说了一堆不着调的"假英语"（只是发出几个单词的音），然后由同学"翻译"成中文。大家都很喜欢，尤其是李博士和艾黎先生觉得非常好笑。这次表演倒真的让我萌生了一个念头，或许我真该好好学英语，将来当个翻译。

我返校后没几个星期，好消息就来了。有一天，我刚在操场打完篮球，一位姓王的女士找到我，问我刚才打得开不开心。我说开心，但我其实篮球打得并不好，只是来凑数的。王女士让我去她的办公室。我跟在她后面走，心里一直在想她找我有什么事，我最近可没犯错啊。等到了办公室，我看见艾黎先生也在。王女士让我坐下，可我仍然担心不是什么好事，所以坚持说："不了，我还是站着吧。"艾黎先生对我笑了笑，让我坐下。

王女士开了口。她说，他们一致决定让我跟着李博士和艾黎先生去西方。显然，他们都很欣赏我在学校和敦煌所表现出来的态度和干劲。他们本想立即送我去英国一个月。但考虑到等我完成学业再去，对学校和我个人都会更好一些，因而推迟了行程，决定等到4年后，我年龄大一些，英语说得更好一些时再去。届时，李博士会安排我到英国继续深造。和我同去敦煌的王万盛也将一起去英国。

我既兴奋又不知所措，竟然说不出话来。我甚至怀疑自己是不是在做梦。我向王女士和艾黎先生深深地鞠了一躬，表示感谢。艾黎先生摸了摸我的头，鼓励我要更加用功地学习，有一个健康的体魄，将来为国争光。王女士表示赞同，她说会在下周一的晨会上把这个消息告诉全校师生。消息一宣布，我和王万盛就理所当然地成了大家谈论的话题。这个消息甚至还传到了其他几所培黎学校。有些人为我们感到高兴，有些则不然。

在兰州的生活

能够通过姐姐在宝鸡的学校进入到培黎，实在是我人生之大幸。现在，我已经是高年级学生了。对比童年的穷苦潦倒以及逃离战争时的险象环生，兰州的这所学校简直就是天堂。更何况我现在还可以憧憬英国之行。

我吃得饱，穿得暖，还有一张床可以睡觉；再不需要东躲西藏或是提心吊胆地生活。我还和大家一起，将兰州市郊的一座老旧的小皮革厂改造成了与西方接轨的新式技工学校。

学校里，所有房间都刷成了白色，打扫得干干净净；厨房、餐厅、宿舍、教室、机械室、化学实验室和缝纫室等一应俱全。学校周围也收拾得非常干净，看起来很漂亮。小路上铺着鹅卵石，花园里长着五彩缤纷的花朵，种着一些苹果树——这是美国前副总统亨利·阿加德·华莱士赠送的。我们还在学校里种了各种蔬菜，包括卷心菜、西红柿和辣椒等。我一生都很感激培黎学校的制度和它所传递出的价值。

学校奉行新的教育政策，强调手脑并用、理论与实践相结合；同时还鼓励培养学生严谨和独立的思维能力。学生人数迅速增加。同我当年一样，新生们大多来自被日军占领的地区，来自"工合"社，来自穷人家。

学校一开始只有一个混合班，不分专业。但很快发展为高、中、低3个班。所授的内容涉及各种理论和实践：数学、物理、化学、语文、英语、地理、历史和自然科学，以及纺织、机器、测绘、机械制图、会计、合作等等。教学设施也在不断升级，逐步配

1945年，孙光俊19岁时的照片——他
在前往英国前寄给母亲的照片（他
们已有10年未见）

备了纺织车间、染色和织毯区、机械车间（含车床、台钳、刨子、
锻铸机）和化工车间。通常，学校上午开设理论课，下午为实操
课，技术支持老师会帮助学生掌握技能并尝试创新。

接下来的4年，我一直在兰州培黎学校读书，直至1947年毕业。
一开始，我选择的技术专业课为土木工程测绘，一年后改为机械工
程，并学习了3年。

1943年年底，学校来了一位姓李的男老师。李老师是华侨，从
中国东南地区来到兰州。虽然他普通话说得不太好，但他高超的技
术制图能力立刻就给我留下了深刻的印象。他是一个很直接又很严
厉的老师，那些不太好学的孩子都不怎么喜欢他。他教会了我如何
利用最简单的测量仪器来精准制图，包括学校的示意图。我抵住了

同学的压力，和李老师相处得十分融洽；大家都批评他的教学手段过于严厉，我却不这么认为。

我决定把握住眼前的学习机会。我好不容易才摆脱了艰苦的生活，那种害怕回到过去的感觉依旧十分强烈。同学们秘密地开了个小会，计划要袭击李老师。我虽然拒绝参加行动，但也不会向校领导揭发他们。我谁也不想得罪。开会时，我一直低着头，没有说话。第二天一早，课刚上了几分钟，一个年纪较大的同学就站了起来，号召全班一起打李老师。老师迅速跑出了教室。整个过程中，我就坐在自己的座位上，一动也没有动。最后，几名涉事的学生被开除了，李老师也离开了学校。我这才不得已把自己的专业从土木工程测绘改成了机械工程。

在机械工程课上，我接触到了柴油机。整个学校只有一台样机，要供所有人学习使用。这台机器刚从上海运来，学校还没想好怎么才能最大程度地利用好它。所以到了该上课的时候，机器还没有配好底座，仍旧放在地上，就连外框都没有拆掉。常老师仔细地向同学们解释该如何发动柴油机器，然后我们轮流上去发动它。

午休时，我回到教室准备试一试（我太想发动它了），在此之前还没有人能发动成功。我决定先点燃发动机给汽缸加热，让柴油达到一个合适的温度。随着温度升高，我开始转动手柄。才转了几圈，就听见一声巨响，柴油机的排气管里开始冒出黑烟。这是之前都没有遇到过的。我赶紧跳到发动机车架上，往柴油机里加油：机器发动了，一开始很慢，不一会儿就在地上乱蹦了。虽然还是午休时间，但好多学生和老师都拥过来，想一睹究竟。只见我蹲在发动机上，努力想要控制住它，不让它上下乱蹦。这时候，常老师来了，大声地叫我使发动机熄火，说我实践课已经满分了。当时发动机已经转得飞快，我正慌乱得不知所措，听到老师说我可以直接关掉机器不管它了，顿时感觉安心许多。这是我上过的最重要的一节将理论与实践相结合的课。之后，学校把煤气灯和发电机都交给我来负责了。

随着学校规模的不断扩大，学生被分成了3个班。我进入了高级班，同班的有10个或12个同学。可是很快，有几个同学就因为各种各样的原因离开了，最后全班只剩下7个人。我们自称"七侠"，就相当于中国版的"罗宾汉和他的朋友"或"三个火枪手"。和我一样，同学们都很好学，并且都学以致用，将其所学充分运用到了日后的人生中。

我越来越热爱并专注于理论和实践学习，竟没有任何体育（或音乐）方面的特长或爱好。我做过的运动就是游泳、钓鱼和打乒乓球（真正开始玩乒乓球还是到了英国之后）。我从小长在黄河边，这才有了一点儿三脚猫的游泳技术。来了兰州之后也是去黄河里游。其实，我下河的目的一半是为了把游泳学好，一半是为了洗澡。长大以后，我改去游泳池，这才学会了自由泳和仰泳。钓鱼一直是我的一大消遣（当然，也是食物的来源），这个爱好伴随了我一辈子。

学校都很重视体育，所以我免不了要被拉去参加一些"大球运动"。但我通常都只是去凑数，尤其是在比赛时。好在这样的情况并不多。我唯一的优势就是听得懂对方球员间的喊话，因为他们一般用的都是英语。由于跟李博士相处了一段时间，我现在对英语也很感兴趣。我唯一真正上场的就是与教师代表队的比赛。当时校篮球队临时缺了一名球员，于是抽调我去。我满场奔袭，只要一拿到球就飞快地传出去。后来缺席的那名队员来了，我就立刻被替换下场，之后再没打过篮球。

在兰州时，我经常和艾黎先生见面。刚开始和他接触的时候，我就决定要好好地跟着他学。艾黎先生有一句口头禅让我一直铭记在心："没裤子，没袜子，没钱，什么也没法干。"我懂得了只有好好工作才能赚钱，才能过上体面的生活。如果人人努力，那么受益的不仅是自己，还有他人。他还常说："人人为我，我为人人。"我一生以此为座右铭。其意在鼓励人们奋斗，不可向贫穷妥协，因为那时候的许多中国人都把贫穷看作是自己应有的命运。

1943—1944年的那个冬天，乔治·何克途经兰州，我们又匆匆见了一面。之前，艾黎先生曾在去敦煌的途中，选中了山丹作为双石铺培黎学校的新址。而这次，何克先生正是带着60名学生从双石铺迁往新学校。不幸的是，何克先生在与学生打篮球时碰伤了脚趾，竟染上破伤风，于1945年7月病逝了。自此之后，艾黎先生就将更多的时间和精力投入山丹，较少待在兰州了。但我一直很景仰他，一心期待着1946年完成学业后与他一起去英国。

艾黎先生在去往山丹前曾和我一起吃了顿饭。他提醒我，去英国后要时刻牢记作为一名培黎毕业生和一个年轻中国人所应当肩负的责任。他说李博士已经为我做好安排，第二年（1947年）就可以去英国学习了。

我兴奋极了，却又不免担心起来：眼下的中国仍相对闭塞，极少有人能有机会出国，更别提像我这样出身的人了。艾黎先生宽慰我说，一切都会顺利的。像我这么大的人完全可以应付国外的生活，一定要洁身自好，不得召妓以致染上性疾病。这是我第一次接受到性教育。在中国，学校是不会教授性知识的，都是由父亲告诉儿子，妈妈告诉女儿。可我的父亲已经不在了。于是，艾黎先生就成了少年时期的我心中最贴近父亲形象的人。道别时，我们深情地拥抱。

第四章 前往英国

（1946—1947年）

李博士回到英国后，有感于在敦煌的所见所闻，开始撰写系列巨著《中国科学文明史》。这本书极大地影响了西方对中国的看法。他没有忘记对艾黎先生的承诺，要帮助培黎的毕业生继续深造，使他们有更强的能力带领中国实现工业和技术的腾飞。而这也能证明培黎学校以及李博士和艾黎先生所支持的"工合"运动的成效。于是，李博士与位于伦敦的英国联合援华会合作，争取了必要的资金支持，并着手制订留学计划。

随着这次"冒险之旅"行程的临近，我感受到了时局的变化。当时是1946年夏天，国共两党内战的枪炮声才刚刚响起。艾黎先生一直坚决支持中国共产党，认为国民党因循守旧，腐败无能。而李博士之所以来中国，也是因为英国等西方国家想要了解如何与共产党合作。相比国民党，共产党才是更坚决的抗日力量。

在这样的局势下，走陆路要比以往慢得多。10月，我和王万盛前往上海等地办理护照和其他所需文件。一路上，我们卡车转火车，再坐船到南京，一共用了6个星期。在英国大使馆办完签证后，我们又在南京待了几天，然后赶往附近的上海。中国工业合作协会上海办事处的人员接待了我们，并为我们安排了英语课程。我虽然跟李博士和艾黎先生学过一点儿英文，但这样高强度的学习还是头一次。我花了好长时间才逐渐掌握这门与中文完全不同的语言。

"工合"的人员负责照料我和王万盛在上海的生活，也负责把我们送往英国。我们被安排住在招待所里，一日有三餐，还能使用游泳池。我这才学会了怎么跳水。"工合"派出英方宣传干事皮特·汤森（Peter Townsend）作为我们的主要联络人。他后来也成为相当有影响力的当代艺术作家和编辑。我们的一应事宜均由他负责，因此我根本不知道在上海的这段日子开销有多大。

一直等到1947年3月，我们才拿到护照。我们从上海坐船去香港。抵港后，艾黎先生的一位老朋友陈益民来接我们。他是一名会计师，在当地非常有名，家境富裕。我们在远行的第一站就受到了他的热情接待。他请我们去家里吃饭，让我见识到一种截然不同的生活：餐桌旁，彬彬有礼的服务生帮我夹菜，清理食物残渣。这在过去只能是梦想而已。

我们被安排在一家小旅馆的一楼住了几天。虽然是3月，香港的气候已经非常潮湿，我们只得早晚开着窗。一天早晨，我起床后发现，洗完晾在窗户旁的衣服全都不见了。我打电话给酒店经理，他让我别着急，说一会儿会将衣服送回来。没过多久，一个男人就提着一个大包袱来到我们房间。他把包袱放在地上，打开一看，里面是各种各样的衣服。我们终于在里面找到了自己丢失的所有衣服。我很吃惊，询问酒店经理发生了什么。他说，一个小偷用一根带钩的长竹竿伸进打开的窗户里，把衣服挑了出来。经理报了警，告诉警察我们是从内地来的，马上就要出国，酒店是要对我们负责的。他还说，警察和当地的窃贼熟悉得就像一家人，所以没过多久，贼就被抓到了，衣服也被送了回来。

几天后，我们从附近的海边度假回来，接到陈益民的电话，说下午6点来接我们去他家吃晚饭。在他家里，陈益民介绍我们认识了英国人鲍勃·波蒂厄斯（Bob Porteous）。波蒂厄斯先生即将启程回国，并答应会一路照看我们。

我们乘坐的"堪波林（SS Chompollion）"号法国客轮原为军舰，因此没有什么舒适可言。我们和其他乘客一样，只领到一个临时的吊床，然后自己找地方搭。这一路上，大部分时间我晕船都很厉害，即便只是很轻微的摇晃。只有躺在吊床上才能稍微好一些。好在船每过四五天就会在港口停一次，让我稍稍喘口气。风强浪急的时候，我根本无法进食，简直难受极了。

当船驶入孟买港时，我觉得自己实在受不了了，真的想过要放弃行程。抛锚泊船后，我下海游了会儿泳，然后去城里转了转，还买了点儿东西吃。我感觉好了一些，于是就决定继续跟着船走。事实上，后来除非遇到特别大的风浪，我都能坚持。在这一个月的航行中，我通过和鲍勃聊天来练习英语。虽然我不会说法语，却还是可以用简单的英语和法国士兵交流，也很快就学会了一些最基础的法语。我还学会了下棋，甚至还赢过当时教我下棋的那个士兵。

习惯了船的颠簸后，我常会在甲板上走动，感受大海的无边无垠。我欣赏了之前从未好好体会的美景，尤其是海平线上的日出日落。彤红的落日仿佛燃烧的火球，缓缓滑入水里，等待着第二天清晨再一次破水而出，就好像一个老朋友。当然，海上还有其他风景：飞鱼在浪尖跳跃；鲨鱼在船边游来游去，寻找着食物；鲸鱼向空中喷出一团水雾；海鸥跟着船一路飞行，不时地落在船上歇脚。一天早晨，我看完日出后准备去吃早饭，却看见一只麻雀摔在我面前，我蹲下身子，双手将它捧起来。小鸟的生命迹象已经很弱，不一会儿就死了。我想着它是怎么飞来的，从哪里来，又想飞到哪里去。

船终于通过了苏伊士运河。河道很窄，可以清楚看见周边的情况。船在塞得港耽搁了两天，让我有机会稍稍感受一下埃及人的生活。狭窄的街道两旁，建筑物多为矮房。或许是卫生条件较差的缘故，当地很多人看上去都不太健康。

离开塞得港后，船驶向了马赛。抵达马赛后，我和王万盛在一家小旅店里住了几天。鲍勃此时还未与我们分开，于是我们3个人决定一起去城里逛逛。这个城市有很多战争留下的印记，商店橱窗里也没什么陈设。我猜想英国会不会也是同样的疮痍和贫穷。这就是我对欧洲的第一印象。我们在港口转悠时，我发现有3个年轻女人跟着我们，不免心生疑惑。我问鲍勃知不知道她们的用意。鲍勃说，她们是妓女，正在招揽客人。我牢记着艾黎先生的嘱咐，赶紧离开了。

在马赛的第四天下午，我们搭飞机去了巴黎。鲍勃就此与我们道别。我们在巴黎逗留了一夜，准备第二天转机去伦敦。此时，我的所有热情又被重新点燃了，迫不及待地想要出发。第二天早饭后，酒店前台帮我们叫了一辆出租车，我们踏上了此行的最后一段路程。然而，车子经过埃菲尔铁塔的时候却突然熄火了，司机使了半天劲儿也没能将车重新发动起来。看着时间一分一秒流逝，我们懊丧极了。就在我们走过去欣赏铁塔时，我觉得再也不能等下去了。虽然不会说法语，我还是请求这位大汗淋漓的司机帮我们另外拦辆车。终于，我们抵达机场，赶上了去伦敦的飞机。

第五章 留英生活

（1947—1950年）

　　艾黎先生已致信位于伦敦的英国联合援华会，称"山丹培黎学校来的两个男孩儿"（在英国时，我们的名字总被叫错）已经在路上了。5月，英国联合援华会开会商讨对我们的迎接事宜：我们将在伦敦住上几天，然后前往诺丁汉郡的斯坦得工合学校，那里将为我们提供膳宿和一些基本课程。此外，英国联合援华会还为我们报了诺丁汉技术学院的纺织课程。当时，"工合"运动在中国和英国都开展得有声有色。

　　6月12日，我和王万盛飞抵伦敦。由于无法确定准确的抵达时间，英国联合援华会并未派人到新开的希斯罗机场来接我们。在我们此行的最后一段，一个好心的出租车司机将我们送到了伦敦市中心，见到了在梅费尔区办公室里等待我们的委员们。

　　委员会正式接待了我们。喝了点儿茶，我和王万盛就被带到位于荷兰公园附近的酒店，随后前往伦敦市中心的一家中餐馆用餐。英国联合援华会的委员们认为这一天的活动应该算是结束了。可我们初到伦敦还十分兴奋，想要多看看。于是，我们去了伦敦北部的温布利球场观看沙地摩托车比赛。我们乘地铁到达球场时，比赛已经开始了，场内坐着6万名观众。一位球场代表招待了我们。比赛结

照片来自1947年7月的
《英国联合援华会月评》

束后，我们返回酒店。就这样，我们在伦敦待了几日，努力融入英国的生活。

大家对我们都很热情。我们也始终牢记艾黎先生的指点，尽力给对方留下一个好的印象。在伦敦短暂停留数日后，我们就前往了北部的斯坦得学院，即刻开始新的学习。斯坦得位于诺丁汉郡的乡村地区，以前是一间豪华的古宅，现在成为英国合作社联盟下属的住宿制学院。学院坐落在一片茵茵绿草间，湖水环绕，同过去在兰州的景象形成了鲜明的对比。学院里有来自世界各地的学生，不过只有我和王万盛来自中国。

我们抵达学校时正值暑假，一直要等到10月份才会正式开课。于是，我们在诺丁汉"工合"社的运输机车间里度过了3个月的有趣时光，学到了不少知识。此外，我们还经常去学校的游泳池和花园里玩，同时努力提高英语水平。

1947年10月，学院课程正式开始。基本上，我们一周有4天需要前往诺丁汉技术学校（30分钟车程）学习各种纺织知识和技术（面料分析实验、原材料、纺织品检验、应用设计和纺织技巧），培训课程既包括去实验室和车间实践，也包括听课。在车间里，我们接触到了手动和机动式织布机。剩下的一个工作日和周六，我和王万盛就留在斯坦得上英语课，并了解"工合"运动（周日休息）。

我还去过其他一些地方，有时是为了参加培训（如诺丁汉的面包厂），有时是为了观光（如爱丁堡）。

我的主要障碍就是语言。虽然我在日常交流上已经进步很多，但在课上涉及技术问题时，还是觉得不够用。因此，我和王万盛都学得非常吃力。与此同时，远在中国的艾黎先生对整个安排也保留着意见，他在写给李博士的信中说：或许应该让我们留在兰州或前往山丹培黎学校继续学习的。

李博士也尝试着联系过我们，他在墨西哥执行联合国教科文组织的任务时，还给我们寄过两张明信片。但直到1947年12月，也就是我们抵达英国半年后，才与李博士联系上。之后，我们还去剑桥与他和他的夫人李大棐相聚了一段时间。此外，我们还去了谢菲尔德，实地考察合作社并协助英国联合援华会筹集资金来扶持中国的发展。

逐渐地，我也掌握了一些技术方面的英语。但很显然，原定的12个月学习结束后，我和王万盛都没能取得太大的进步。我们访英的主要目的就是为了了解英国纺织业的情况，并把知识带回国以带动中国的工业发展。为此，英国联合援华会办事处、远在中国的艾黎先生和剑桥的李博士帮助我们获得了追加资金，以确保我俩能够在英国继续学习一年，一直到1949年夏天。

于是到了1948年，我能够继续在斯坦得和诺丁汉技术学院学习，同时还在英格兰西部格洛斯特郡的一家纺织厂打工。在这里，我们实地接触到了梳棉、纺纱、编织、染色和修饰等棉纺工艺。我们就住在当地一户居民家中，他们对我们很照顾。此后，我们还保持了一段时间的联系。1949年春，我们第二次前往剑桥拜访李博士，学业上已经取得了不小的进步。

1949年4月，我们结束了在诺丁汉技术学院和斯坦得工合学校的学习。短暂的复活节假期过后，我们在李博士和莫凤麟博士的安排下，参观了几间工厂。我们在利兹附近的加尼特工厂待了几天，他们专门制造机器，用于纺织厂的废品回收。我们对此非常感兴趣，因为中国一直存在新原材料匮乏的问题，所有东西都必须物尽其用。我们还参观了位于萨里郡汉斯米尔的一间小工厂，学习了纺纱机的组装技术，想着以后可以带回山丹。此外，我们还匆匆参观了一下埃塞克斯郡的克劳得工厂，见识到许多有趣的真丝和人造丝生产工艺。

与此同时，我在另一个方面也有了进展。在斯坦得的时候，学院里只有为数不多的几个年轻女同学。而我就遇见并爱上了其中一个。她名叫尤妮斯·里德，大家都叫她苏珊。学院里当然也有其他女性，不过主要都是负责伙食、行政和校内事务。1949年年初，苏珊来到学院。她花了一先令，参加了由"工合"社组织的写作比赛，得了一等奖。作为奖励，她可以在斯坦得商科免费学习一年。

我们第一次见面可能是在一节国际"工合"课上。我们的关系发展得非常迅速。很快地，同学们就看出我们互相吸引，拿我们打起趣来。

在确信我们的语言能力后，李博士希望我们能充分利用在英国的这段时间。于是，他带我们参观了纺织厂，还向我们展示了他在进行中国纺织业研究时收集的一些资料。他希望我们能够延长在英国的学习计划，去拥用先进机器的纺织厂工作，以获得一些实践经验。于是，他开始为我们争取实习机会。我很感激他，至少这样也能延长我和苏珊在一起的时光。

英国的四季变换比中国要分明许多。我特别喜欢春天的到来，尤其是看着叶绿花开。这是人们在一年当中最享受的时节。因此，

1949年的复活节，我和苏珊去伦敦玩了几天，住在一个朋友的公寓里。为了得到允许，我还特别对英国联合援华会解释说，自己将独自去徒步旅行。

　　这是让我终生难忘的一周。我体验了在英国首都的生活，也品味了恋爱的甜蜜。我特别喜欢在公园漫步，可以一边观察着路人，一边和苏珊聊一聊生活。我还参观了伦敦动物园。当时，英国广播公司正发起倡议，鼓励大家去给生病的大熊猫"联合"送竹子。英国广播公司想知道解放后的中国会不会再给英国送一只熊猫。这就是熊猫外交的开始。后来，我还去了卡尔·马克思的墓地，瞻仰了这位共产主义创始人的半身像，这让我不禁回想起国内的生活。

　　苏珊还带我去了伦敦的很多地方。在邱园，我惊叹于各种各样的奇花异草，看见温室里种植的香蕉，欣赏向上生长的棕榈树。这绝对是世界上品种最齐全、最令人欣喜的植物园。

　　参观完植物园，我和苏珊在一片草地上躺下，聊着一天的见闻。我们正准备回家时，几个年轻人（男孩和女孩）过来邀请我们一起玩球。我们欣然答应了。我跑来跑去，很快浑身就湿透了。突然，我感觉到一阵尿意，苏珊指向旁边一间公共厕所。我拼命向厕所跑去，却一不留神冲进了女厕所

孙光俊，1949年摄于北威尔士的
霍利韦尔

里，引来一阵大笑。

苏珊还让我体验了更高的文化追求：我们去欣赏了歌剧、看了几场电影、听了两场保罗·罗伯逊的演讲。在伦敦的这几日与我在中国的生活简直是天壤之别，不仅拓宽了我对世界的认识，更丰富了我的人生。

一方面，李博士继续动用他的人脉，为我和王万盛争取更多的工作机会；另一方面，英国联合援华会正为我们在课业上的进步过于缓慢而担心；还有，经费也用得差不多了。一开始正是因为李博士的努力，英国联合援华会才会资助我们，否则他们的奖学金一般只会颁给经验更为丰富的高年级学生。于是，英国联合援华会开始计划送我们回国。

就在最后时刻，李博士联系上了一位在北威尔士霍利韦尔的工厂主托马斯·瓦特豪斯，他对我们很感兴趣。1949年5月12日，就在李博士听说英国联合援华会已经为我和王万盛订好回程票后的两天，瓦特豪斯先生给李博士去了信。李博士立刻接通电话，取消了回程票。瓦特豪斯先生听说我们会使用工厂里的动力织布机，于是答应带薪聘用我们做12个月的织工。

为了让我们继续上学，李博士不仅为我们提供了有力的个人支持，甚至还同意为我们做经济担保，以防止我们在霍利韦尔出什么岔子。我写信给李博士，表达我由衷的谢意。我还特别提到，当所有人都打算放弃的时候，是他为我们做了这一切（我也替苏珊转达了她的感谢）。1949年5月19日，我和王万盛乘火车前往霍利韦尔。

工厂原名瓦特豪斯毛条厂，建于1777年，当时正值工业革命时期。选址于霍利韦尔是考虑到格林菲尔德谷的供水问题。工厂规模在19世纪达到顶峰，共雇用了1000名工人，其中就有来自贫民院的孤儿。之后，工厂逐渐走向衰落，直到托马斯·瓦特豪斯接手并更名为霍利韦尔纺织厂后，才在20世纪四五十年代逐渐走向成功。工厂目前位于工业遗产保护区内。

在霍利韦尔的生活与斯坦得的田园风光和相对奢华大为不同。我和王万盛的住所离工厂很近，楼下就是小餐馆。我们的房间很小，几乎没有热水供应，食物也很差。但工作内容倒是非常有趣，我很快就拾起了动力织布机的操作方法。工厂机器的质量给我留下了深刻的影响，虽然已经好几年了，但用起来却仍跟新的一样。

我每周工作5天，此外还要抽出时间来学习和读书。我到霍利韦尔后没几周，苏珊便来看望我。我们在兰迪德诺海岸边的度假村里过了一夜。很快，她就在附近的一家孤儿院里找到了一份舍监的工作。我们一起去了切斯特、莱尔和其他想去的地方。有一次，我去格洛斯特郡参观一间纺织厂，被一家女性机构邀请去做演讲。苏珊帮了我大忙：她把我要说的话都打印出来，好让我直接读就可以了。

夏去秋来，吹进山谷的海风愈发的凉了。我想念起在培黎学校时穿着过冬的棉衣，但以我和王万盛的工资根本买不起。工厂主的儿子兼工厂经理斯图亚特·瓦特豪斯致信英国联合援华会，说明了我们的情况，并请他们借给我们一些钱。然而，回信的内容却像冬天般寒冷。英国联合援华会的秘书长说，在她丈夫的工厂里，工人必须要靠省吃俭用来买衣服。于是，李博士又一次伸出了援手。他很快就答应了我们的请求。这让斯图亚特非常吃惊，于是立刻从公司的钱里预支了这部分给我们。

斯图亚特告诉李博士，大家对我们的进步都很满意，认为我们

与王万盛在霍利韦尔，1949年8月

两个既聪明，又招人喜欢。他建议我们在明年5月离开英国之前，再延长一段实习时间。此时，我和王万盛已经搬到了更好的住处，日子也过得舒服多了。李博士来看了我们一次，觉得很满意。他向英国联合援华会表示，对于夏天回国一事，我们并没有任何不悦，英国联合援华会听到的说法是错误的。当时的许多中国学生在接受资助完成学业后，都一心想着要改善自己的生活。但我们和他们不同。我一直觉得自己有责任将所学的新技能带回国，让别人也跟着受益。况且艾黎先生也已经致信李博士，明确表示希望我们俩学成后回国，去山丹培黎学校（原先的双石铺培黎学校）任教。

到了1950年的夏天，我在英格兰和威尔士已经待满了3年，收获颇丰。我对机械动力设备的操作，以及对人生，都有了更加深入的理解。在这一点上，我必须要感谢我的老师和苏珊。我还和一些好朋友共度了短暂的假期，这其中就包括李博士以及莱斯特小姐，后者是当时已经过世了的乔治·何克校长的姨妈。我的英文水平有了明显提高，并且此后一生都说得很流利。

在我离家去往英国的时候，英国人还没怎么见过中国人，所以我觉得自己代表了一个处于关键时期的国家的形象。当时，国内对一些留洋的中国学生多有诟病，认为他们在国外花了大把的时间来学习社交，然后回国四处捞钱。我从不以赚钱为目的，对能够买得起大房子的人也往往怀有戒心。我虽然去过西方，却并不会跳舞。对于这一点，我是很骄傲的，因为这正说明我并没有浪费过时间。

虽然当时的英国正处于战后的紧缩状态，但毛纺行业仍保持在世界前沿水平。我在中国学习的主要是手动机械，几乎没有接触过自动设备。而英格兰和威尔士的纺织技术则令我大开眼界，我见识到了速度更快、质量更好的毛纺工艺。我接触到纺织行业的方方面面，包括织物的使用，但真正吸引我的还是机器。我努力将与机器相关的所有知识都牢记于心。不过，我偶尔也会觉得培训内容过于简单。于是有一次，我就买了一把锦纶毛刷来研究它的纤维构造。

我越发按捺不住了。我不仅想将所学运用于实践，更想尝试脑中不断出现的新想法。我在英国的毕业设计就是从原材料开始，制造出一条成品的羊毛围巾。我把围巾带回兰州，送给了一直都在帮助我的姐姐。我还将苏珊织给我的一件无袖费尔岛杂色图案的毛背心带回国，并将我的一件纺织作品回赠给了她。我一生都很感激那些给予过我帮助的人，并保持着对英国和西方的爱。

我在霍利韦尔的工作一直进行着，直到1950年11月我和王万盛乘船回上海。在此之前，我一直和苏珊在一起。但此时，我已归心似箭，也劝她放弃了陪我回国的念头。10月底，我和王万盛最后去了一次剑桥，看望李博士和他的妻子，并停留了数日。随后，我们就坐火车去了伦敦。没过多久，李博士就出任了英中友好协会的会长。11月7日，我和王万盛乘"春山（SS Chusan）"号离开伦敦。"春山"号是大英轮船公司新近投入使用的一艘班轮。该船在巴罗因弗内斯打造，专门服务于新开通的远东航线。

第六章　回到中国

（1951—1988年）

教书匠的生活

1951年年初，我和王万盛来到艾黎先生创办的山丹培黎学校任教。此时的中国与我1947年离开时相比，已经发生了翻天覆地的变化。1949年，毛泽东宣布中华人民共和国成立，并任中共中央主席，周恩来任政务院总理。这对艾黎先生和培黎学校而言无疑是一个积极的信号：艾黎先生认识这两位先生，尤其是和周恩来比较熟悉。这样一来，不仅能提高艾黎先生的个人影响力，更能让中国展现出更多活力。

可当我踏上回国路时，心里却不太踏实。从抵达上海的那刻起，我就发现自己在人群中是那样的突兀。码头上的其他人都积极响应毛主席的号召，穿着朴素的无产阶级列宁装，而我却仍然穿着从英国买来的洋服。1951年，朝鲜战争正酣，中国与西方各国的关系陷入紧张。我发现大家都在看着我，我不希望太过招眼，于是立刻找机会换掉了衣服。

虽然政府也尽力挽留，希望我能够在上海工作，但我还是执意要回兰州。我知道兰州的学校已经搬走了，现在主楼里住着之前的兼职校长常关廉和他的妻子王贤林一家。他们都很熟悉我，邀请我去家里同住。我在他们家住了大约两个星期后，艾黎先生就乘校车从山丹来接我了。他说已经在山丹为我备好了房间，我只要把梳棉机和精纺机装好就可以上课了。艾黎先生见我特意弄了些合乎国情的衣服，但眼看冬天将近，这衣服不足以御寒，于是递给我一双他自己的打了补丁的毡靴和破旧的驼绒长袜。这双鞋袜温暖了我好些年。

而我的朋友和旅伴王万盛则留在上海，后来又去了北京。他一心想进入大学工作，却屡屡碰壁，最后也只得回到兰州。后来，他去了西安附近的一所技校教书，再后来，我们就各奔东西了。无论在英国还是中国，我都坚持接受文化知识和技术培训，但王万盛则更偏向于文化学习：他知道机器怎么开，但对工作原理和效果并不像我那样感兴趣。

于是，我去了山丹，负责装配新机器并担任技术助手——我要报答学校对我的付出。我很乐于教书，但我更希望能在纺织厂里将我的技术亲手传授给其他人。1951年，中国政府提出要让国内的纱厂数量翻一番。事实上，从1947年开始，纱锭的数量就已经增加了近一倍。对于我这样一个有技术、有动力的年轻人而言，正是出力的时候。而我在学校最初的工作就是修理一台从加拿大买来的旧发动机，让我在英国的所学能够发挥用处。

1952年，学校在山丹已经站稳了脚跟，但在政府的坚持下，又整体搬迁回兰州，更名为培黎石油技工学校。自1953年起，艾黎先生已不太参与学校的具体事务，主要在北京工作。这期间，他一直住在宾馆里，直到1958年搬入政府提供的小楼里居住，之后他一直住在那儿。1954年，山丹发生地震，大部分地区被夷为平地。以前的一个学生回到山丹带领大家重建校园，而我却再没回去过。1956年，"石油技工学校"升级为"大学"，于是我结束了教学任务，开始从事中英翻译与口译。我是公认的优秀教师，也算得上是技术专家，但心里却生出挫败感。因为我真正想要成为的是工程师。

1953年年初，我27岁，娶了张凤云为妻。她的父亲也是培黎学校的老师，早年就认识我，对我印象很好，于是介绍了我和他的女儿认识。张凤云比我小9岁，还是学校的学生。我留给她的第一印象只是个小个子。但我非常勤奋，因而俘获了她的心。她觉得，一个留过洋、借鉴过国外经验的人一定是有本事的。她离开学校后做了一名护士，之后大部分时间都在兰州第一人民医院工作，任产科高级护士，直到1990年退休。

圆梦工程师

1956年，我向兰州市政委员会自荐，要求参与兰州第一毛纺织厂的建设。自从回国后，我就一直深信自己能对兰州纺织业的发展做出贡献。我用了两年时间，参与工厂投产前的规划和设计工作。在顶峰时期，工厂共有5000个纱锭和2000多名工人。我在那儿担任了10年的技术总监，借此走访了全国各地，遍寻最好的纺织设备。

1958年，我出差去北京，竟在路上碰见了艾黎先生。我们已经数年未见。于是，他邀请我去家里吃晚饭。这一次重聚，让我们再续情谊。之后，我们每隔一段时间就会在北京和兰州见见面，而我也总会给他带点儿他最爱吃的甘肃梨。很显然，我已经成了培黎教育理念的成功作品，充分证明了艾黎先生和李博士当时送我出国的正确性。我对艾黎先生一直非常尊敬。于我而言，他是充满慈爱、给我鼓励的良师，他会及时纠正我的错误，但态度从不粗暴。他和全世界的大人物交往，也包括新中国的领导人毛泽东、周恩来和邓小平。但在我和许多学生眼中，他始终那么的平易近人。他教会我要尊重自己的搭档，无论男女；要热爱自己的国家；要对全世界敞开胸怀。

多年来，他的很多学生和中国朋友都常常会问他，为何一直未娶妻。他只是报以淡淡一笑，不置一词，又或者透过粗框眼镜看看对方，摇摇头。我自己也问过一次艾黎先生："好多人，包括外国友人，都会问我您为什么一直不娶，我该怎么作答？"艾黎先生思索片刻，回答说："从现在开始，如果再有人问，你就告诉他们，一旦结了婚，就会有家；有了家，就会有私心。"后来我有了成功的婚姻和幸福的家庭，但仍常常深挚地怀念与艾黎先生的对话和共度的时光。

1966年，"文化大革命"爆发，对整个国家和我个人都造成了极大的影响。我知道，自己因在工厂年薪较高而招来了许多邻居和同事的妒忌，其中有些人还记得我曾在西方留过学。我为自己的处境感到担心，只得扔掉家里所有与英文有关的或能显出我学历较高的报纸和材料。

所以，当有关人士找到我，要求我调离第一毛纺织厂，前往兰州棉纺织印染厂时，我反倒舒了一口气。新厂位于西固，距离兰州市区约15公里。当时，工厂急需一名工程师来组建新的棉纺织印染部门。我用了两年的时间来配置合适的机器并调试到位。这一段日子，我尽可能地保持低调，不再想要获得成功和认可。好在他们确实需要我的技术和经验，所以尽管情势艰难，我还是坚持下来了。我努力适应着新环境，穿得和普通工人一样，尽量不显出自己的职位与工人有任何不同。虽然我干的是工程师的活，却不再保留工程师的头衔。我和厂里的基层工人相处都很融洽，还交了不少朋友。

这时候显然不能透露我曾经去过英国或者会说英语。我一直把英语牢牢记在脑子里，虽然很多年都没有再说过。但我过去的经历终于还是传到了新厂里：我以前在兰州的一些同事来了西固，张贴大字报，说我曾与西洋勾结，还将我画成由一只羊牵着的样子，取中文的谐音"西"和"羊"。我整日提心吊胆，甚至想过结束这一切，好让我的家庭免于任何可能的报复。

孙光俊与张凤云，摄于1976年

在这段时间里，家庭生活成了我最重要的部分。从1966—1984

年，我们一直住在医院的家属院里。后来，凤云还把房子买了下来。1984年，我们将家搬到了新的毛条厂内，紧挨着黄河边。

1956年，我们有了大儿子孙成，之后又分别在1959年和1964年生下另两个儿子孙瑜和孙龙。1962年，我们有了女儿孙坤。我努力做好一个慈父，与孩子们感情笃深。当然，家里的大多数事情还是由妻子操劳，尤其是我离家在外工作的时候。孩子们总是期待着我回家时能带他们参加一些特别的活动，比如去黄河划船、游泳和钓鱼，顺便吃一顿本地特产做成的可口野餐。邻居家的孩子也常常一起来玩。

后半生的职业生涯

我在棉纺织印染厂一直辛苦地干到1982年，这期间经常会去全国各地出差。由于我的技术出众，总有人想请我去其他地方工作，可厂长始终不放我走。

但1982年，我的妻子张凤云却突然病了。她一直待在兰州市区，而我却在郊区西固工作。只要不加班，我每晚都会回去看她。我突然觉得，我们不该再分开。可西固的污染比兰州还重，所以我只得找机会回兰州工作。当时，政府计划在几个重点城市建8家毛条厂，其中就有兰州。于是，我加入了兰州毛条厂，负责洗毛机和精炼机的配置。当时厂里有几台上海制造的新机需要安装。有些企业会直接让厂家来装，但我坚信自己就可以。于是，我在3个技师的协助下，用两个月的时间完成了任务，得到了好评。新工厂建在黄河边，离我妻子工作的医院很近。我们一家就住在工厂的家属楼里，直到1988年退休。那时我62岁。根据相关规定，我和凤云还可以继续住在房子里。后来，我买下了这套房子，又在隔壁楼里买了一套房给家人住。虽然因"文化大革命"这些年过得很难，但我的事业很成功，收入也高于一般人家（退休后的养老金也很高）。凤云是高级护士，也有一份稳定的收入，还买下了自己的房子，现在给了我们的小儿子孙龙住。

1985年，我前往新西兰羊毛研究组织考察，并在那里工作了6个月。毛条厂承担了我来回的路费，而其他部分费用则得到了艾黎先

1985年摄于新西兰

生的资助。此行期间，我拜访了艾黎先生的妹妹，当时她已经80岁高龄了。4月抵达基督城后，我便进入了林肯大学。这是我自1950年回国后的第一次出国，也是35年来第一次有机会练习英语。

刚开始我有些听不懂别人的话，为此还推迟了与研究组织领导的初次会面（也让我有时间缓解一下第一次长途飞行后的疲惫）。两天后，我感觉好了些，于是见到了研究组织的罗斯博士。罗斯博士将负责照料我在学校期间的生活，并为我安排一些参观访问的活动。我和他谈到了当前的研发工作，并决定花一些时间来了解原毛的处理方法，以帮助兰州工厂攻克一直未能解决的问题。

我参观了研究组织的多个部门，并经介绍认识了一个叫作伊恩的人。在罗斯博士眼中，伊恩很特别，因为他用空闲时间养了500头猪。当我得知这么多猪全是伊恩和他妻子两个人饲养时，我惊讶极了。伊恩看出我感兴趣，就在一天下班后带着我去他的农场参观。小农场位于城郊，约20分钟车程，包括一栋单层的3居室小楼、一个专门用来换衣服的独立棚子和一间看起来更像工具间的大车库。猪圈就在离房子约100米处。伊恩向我展示了如何将各种各样的机器组合起来，以存放麦子（猪食的基本原料）并分送至各月龄的猪舍。在此过程中，机器还会自动地将各种营养物质添加至猪饲料中。

之后，我几乎每个周末都会到伊恩家，参与农场的各种工作：开拖拉机、给猪称重、将猪运去集市等。这些小猪既干净又健康，让我印象深刻。它们每日需要喂食两次，猪舍每日要彻底清洁一次。伊恩和他的妻子分工明确。他的妻子前一分钟还穿着非常整齐干净的衣服，下一分钟就能迅速换好衣服，毫不犹豫地前去给小猪接生，照料它们。

6年后，我已经退休，住在兰州。有一天，我外出钓鱼，碰见一个熟人。他手里有些地，说有兴趣和我一起养猪。于是，我们签订了合作协议，明确了分工，我负责提供初期资金，配置好设备。我们一开始只养了4只猪仔，很快就掌握了饲养的方法，增加到60只猪和猪仔。我借鉴了伊恩的做法，每日喂食两次，猪舍彻底清洁一次。附近的其他农民都笑我们说，我们的猪舍比他们的房子还干净。

可渐渐地，我搭档的热情开始减弱，邻居对我们的成功也有些嫉恨。但由于我们的猪终究没有新西兰的猪吃得好，没那么健康，我们的利润也就低了一些。后来，妻子和我开始自己喂猪和猪仔，但最终，我还是觉得这活对于我这个年龄的人来说太过辛苦，因而在春季时卖掉了所有的猪。这个生意做得基本不盈不亏，但我想做个商人的梦最终还是破灭了。

在新西兰，走到哪儿都能让人联想到羊。这个国家主要就依靠羊来获取羊毛和食物。此外，乡村里还能看见各种各样的数不清的动物。我觉得从某种意义上来说，新西兰本身就有点儿像羊——温顺，固执。有一次，我和一个朋友开车外出，我开玩笑地说："有几分钟没见到羊了，你一定觉得很孤单吧。""没错，"他说，"是羊让我们富有，让我们健康，让我们有美味可尝。"

即将离开新西兰前，我与康特尼·阿切尔见了一面。阿切尔先生曾在山丹培黎学校工作过，与艾黎先生私交甚好。他的父亲去世后，出于孝道，阿切尔先生只得回国，接管家族的面粉厂。我用阿切尔家的招牌面粉做了些薄饼，似乎很受大家的欢迎。搭配着泡菜和极美味的羔羊肉，我在离开新西兰前吃到了美美的一餐，久久不能忘记。

我一直留心着各种新机器，努力弄清它的工作原理，考虑它能给兰州的工厂带来多大的效益。在新西兰时,我发现了一种特殊的无捻纱,它只经过碾压,却仍保持了一定的强度。我没法得到图纸,只是把看见的仔细地记在了心里。第二年,就利用同样的纱线生产出了一系列样品,既柔软,又耐用。我觉得,把这样的技术引进回国是我的责任,尽管这并不会给我个人带来任何金钱收益。这又一次证明,培黎学校所提倡的学习方法是极其有用的,我只要明白了基本原理,就能照葫芦画瓢地做出来。

在新西兰时,我终于可以放心地给李博士写信了,这在我1950年回国后还是第一次。考虑到国内的政治环境,尤其是在"文化大革命"期间,给国外去信的风险太大了。艾黎先生时常提醒我,不要试图和英国的任何人联系。李博士很快回了信,说他从未忘记我和王万盛,以及1943年我们一起去敦煌考察的事情。得知我把自己在毛纺工程方面的经验带到了新西兰并积极向新西兰同行学习后,李博士表示很高兴。他邀请我有空去英国,看看正在建设中的剑桥大学李约瑟研究所。

从新西兰回国时,我带回了很多新的想法,还有各种不同的羊毛样品,但结果却发现,根本难以说服兰州的同事采用我的想法,或看一眼我带回来的"新羊毛"。1987年,我开始研究如何运用我在新西兰学到的特殊纺纱方法。可我的合伙人一心只想着赚钱,因而研究没有取得任何进展。于是,我自己又成立了一家类似的公司,计划利用我的专利在西藏新建一家地毯厂,但最后也没能成功。

自1950年我回国后,会说英语就一直是我的一个痛处。但"文化大革命"结束后,它的用处却逐渐显现出来。在工厂,我可以翻译英文资料;在当地,随着英语逐渐取代俄语成为学生普遍学习的第二语言，我可以教大家说英语。这也成了我的第二职业，让我退休后还能继续有事可做。1985年从新西兰回国后，我终于买了第一台彩色电视机、电冰箱和照相机。我一直提醒自己不要为了赚钱而赚钱，也不相信国内越来越多的那些"大人物"。我希望自己活得干干净净，凭本事和知识吃饭，而不是其他人的帮助。

1987年，我被指定为官方的英文翻译，陪同兰州纺织代表团访问西德。1994年11月，甘肃省政府派出27人的代表团访问新西兰、澳大利亚、新加坡等地，我也在其中。这是我最后一次出国。我因此结交了许多外国朋友，我和家人也在兰州接待过他们几次。

1987年访问科隆

第七章　谈谈家庭：东方与西方

　　虽然我和凤云的4个孩子都接受过良好的基础教育，但无一上过大学。"文化大革命"期间，由于大家知道我曾去过英国并在工厂里当经理，所以孩子们的日子并不好过。由于我的成分不好，长子孙成在毕业后一直找不到工作。

　　我努力工作，希望能给孩子一些好的机会。我的薪水不薄，但我仍然经常加班，希望多赚些钱。我每次出差回来，都会给孩子们带礼物。虽然我的事业有了进步，也取得了一些成就，但我仍希望继续过简单而有原则的生活。所以在孩子面前，我始终是个正派的父亲，除此并无什么特别。这4个孩子里，有3个在适龄的时候结了婚，我有3个可爱的孙女，丰富了我和凤云的晚年生活。

　　我记得在新西兰时，李博士曾回信给我，邀请我去英国看他。当然，我想再次联系上英国的朋友还有另一个原因。虽然我的家庭生活很美满，但我仍常想起苏珊，想知道她过得怎么样。虽然在我回国前，我们一直很亲近，但到最后，我们的关系还是淡下来了。我并不知道在我离开英国时，苏珊已经怀有4个多月的身孕。"文化大革命"期间，曾有一位陌生人给我的妻子凤云送来一张小小的黑白照片，上面是一个小女孩儿。她的长相偏向中国人，并不太像欧洲人。但送照片的人并没有说明或暗示这个孩子是谁。所以我以为他只是想问我认不认识这个孩子而已。

出于一些原因，我一直小心翼翼地保管着这张照片，虽然我并不知道这个孩子是谁。多年后，当我突然又想起这张照片时，却怎么也找不到。我想一定是在"文化大革命"时被毁掉了。在那个年代，被"红卫兵"抄家、没收财产都是常有的事。

1990年在西藏

2016年5月，娟娟[①]写给他外祖父的信：

亲爱的姥爷：

又是一年清明到了，当再次手捧着菊花去看望你的时候，

_____

① 孙光俊与刘凤云的外孙女。

你已经离开我们8年了。8年很长也很短。这8年里，我读完了研究生，找到了一份自己喜欢的工作，遇到了一个如你一样热爱生活、热爱学习的男孩子，现在还有了一个小女儿。这8年里，你一直都在我心里，每当我遇到挫折、心情烦闷的时候，你总会出现在我的脑海里，用你平静温和的话语告诉我生活本就有苦有甜，不论它给予了你什么，都要热爱生活，保持勤奋，美好的生活就会到来。

有你在的日子，总是过得充实又有趣。你带着我在大自然中体会生活的趣味。春天，你带着我一起去公园踏青，陪着我观察新近长出的绿叶和五颜六色的花朵；夏天，你带着我去河边钓鱼，教会我耐心等待；秋天，你带着我去田野里感受丰收的喜悦；冬天，我们一起堆雪人、打雪仗，在寒风里玩的热火朝天。你曾对我说过，生活可以索然无味，也可以有滋有味，就看你自己要怎样选择。

每天早晨，当我还迷迷糊糊在睡梦中时，就会闻到厨房飘来的阵阵香味儿——那准是你在为我们准备丰盛的英式早餐——香肠、培根、茄汁黄豆、煎蛋、吐司、麦片、牛奶。到了下午4点左右，你又会拿出蛋糕和点心，搭配上牛奶或咖啡，让我们尽享下午茶。于是，原本平淡的一天，在你出其不意准备的美味中，变得充满期待和喜悦。在这样的家庭氛围中，我学会了发现生活中平淡又独特的美，学会了与家人一起分享生活中简单又暖心的快乐。也是在你精心准备的美食里，我懂得了下厨的乐趣所在——自己精心准备的家常菜，更能令人大快朵颐。

从小学到初中，几乎每个寒暑假我都在你身边度过，你督促我做功课，教我学英语。每每当我倦怠了，你总是耐心地告诉我要坚持。在学习上，你一直都是我的榜样。还记得你都80岁高龄了，依旧每天记单词、读英语。即便是生病住院时，还要坚持学习英语。那时候我不懂事，不明白你为什么要这样——学习是个苦差事，不是吗？你告诉我学无止境，我却戏谑你这是打算攻读博士。现如今我的书架上有一本被你翻破了的英文字典，我总会用它来提醒自己如你一样坚持不懈、刻苦学习，不论何时都要保持一颗勤奋的上进心。

自你去世后，我时常写信给你，那一封封无处投递的信笺，记载着我对你的思念。随着时间的推移，我的日常工作越来越繁忙，信也就写得少了。就是这篇短短的信笺，也是在女儿的小睡中断断续续完成的。这8年来，你一直都在我心里。每每当我的生活有了新变化，我都会在心里告诉你，与你分享喜悦；每每当我遇到困难，我也会想到你，设想若是你在，会怎样为我指点迷津。亲爱的姥爷，愿你在天堂一切安好。

想念你的外孙女：娟娟

第二部分

苏珊·尤妮斯的经历
母亲的故事

20岁出头的苏珊·尤妮斯·大卫·里德

第一章　幸福的童年

（1926—1935年）

我的母亲有着幸福的童年。1926年6月6日，她出生在马拉维湖畔的一个名叫科塔的小村庄，取名尤妮斯·伊丽莎白·大卫·里德。这片湖当时称作"尼亚萨兰湖"，是英国在东非中部的殖民地。她的母亲叫艾格尼丝，父亲叫厄内斯特，有一个姐姐，叫拉文娜，还有一对龙凤胎弟弟妹妹，妹妹叫伊莎贝尔，弟弟也叫厄内斯特。

我的外祖父是受过军功奖章的一等兵厄内斯特·里德，曾效力于英国皇家陆军工兵部队，在第一次世界大战中受了重伤（直到63岁去世时，体内还残留着30枚弹片）。战后，他申请前往尼亚萨兰工作，因为当地温暖的气候更加适合养伤。后来，他进入英国中非公司，做了一名会计。该公司此前收购了几家从事零售和批发业务的欧洲贸易企业。曼达拉是其中最大的一家，不仅在城里有几间零售店，在农村也开了大约50间连锁店。外祖父的工作就是到这些农村店铺查账收钱。在他前往非洲工作以前，就已经于1920年4月和艾格尼丝·简·大卫成婚了。

外祖母向我讲述了她和外祖父相遇的过程，以及外祖父在战争中受伤的情形：

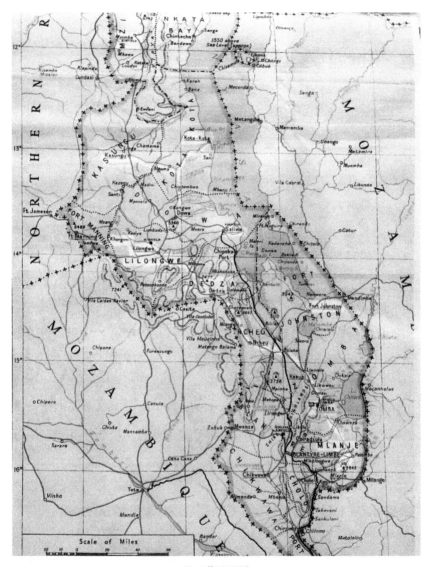

尼亚萨兰地图

344

1916年，我回到查塔姆，加入皇家工兵部队财务处，成为档案室的一名文员。1918年，我在考试中得了第一名，原本有望被调去白厅，坐上更高的职位，但人生偏偏就在这时出现了转折。那年我25岁，和朋友一起去附近的梅德斯通玩，那里毗邻川流不息的梅德韦河。我的故事应该就叫"茶馆偶遇记"。一天下午，我们在梅德斯通喝茶，店里还坐着两个受伤的士兵——穿着蓝色制服的兵哥哥。我的一生就此改变了。我爱上了其中那个高个儿（厄内斯特·里德），就此放弃了去白厅的机会。1917年，他在法国战役中受了重伤，当时才22岁。他抱着一挺德国机枪躺了好几天。一开始都以为他阵亡了，突然有一天，德国人发现了他，把他和德国伤员一起送进了德军营。当对方发现他是英国人后，便将他送回了英国阵地，然后又被送回英国，在几个医院辗转治疗了18个月。后来，他被授予军功奖章，以表彰他在战场上的英勇表现。1918年11月，他因身体原因无法继续服役而退伍了（他1914年9月入伍，当时只有19岁零4个月，被分配到皇家陆军工兵部队。1915年年初被派往法国战场，一直待到1917年4月受伤前）。

　　出院后（因为他拒绝截断整条腿，不想一辈子困在轮椅上），医生说他的健康状况很差，不适合待在英国，必须选择一个终日有阳光的国家。于是他选了非洲。不过在此之前，他必须要先回伦敦城市学院上学。按他的话说，是为了"充充电"。那么，我要等他吗？我当然是愿意的。所以，等他参加完入学考试，我们就在1920年4月结婚了。对我俩来说，那真是太美好了。

1920年，外祖母艾格尼丝与外祖父厄内斯特结婚时的照片

婚后没多久，外祖父就拿到了前往英属尼亚萨兰的通行证，也就是现在的马拉维。但在当时，通行证是不发给女性的，所以外祖父只能独自前往，让外祖母留守。好在公司承诺，只要开往南非的船上一有空位，就会把外祖母接过去和外祖父团聚。外祖母回忆说：

　　许多妻子都面临这样的状况。我只能盼啊盼……1920年12月4日，终于登上了开往德班的"博玛堡（SS Braemar Castle）"号海轮！简直喜出望外！但我从来没有一个人去过这么远的地方，心中不免忐忑。父母在蒂尔伯里港送我上船。我和另外两个姑娘住在同一间客舱里。船上载得满满当当。不一会儿，服务台叫我过去，说公司安排了一位高管和另外5名年轻的职员陪我同行。我真是太高兴了。从伦敦到布兰太尔，一切都已经安排妥当……于是，我焦虑全无，努力让自己适应这一切。

　　26岁前，我从未有过远行。可现在却要在茫茫大海上航行9000多英里[1]。经过英吉利海峡，驶入比斯开湾……每一天，我都感到自己离爱人越来越近。我们的船第一站停靠在马德拉群岛，短暂休息几小时后，又向特纳里夫岛驶去。有两次，我们都可以上岸待上几个小时，或坐小船四处转转，看看商店、教堂和其他景点。再之后是阿森松岛，但它是一个有线和无线设备的基站，所以不能登岛。岛上只有些工作人员和物资补给。最有意思的是，我们看到几头牛在岛上大摇大摆地晃悠，周围堆着一捆捆稻草。然后，我们又来到圣赫勒拿岛，这也是当年拿破仑的流放之地。这里风景如画，古色古香。你可以爬上长长的

---

① 1英里约合1.6千米。——编者注

坡道，或者像我们一样几个人同乘一部出租车——当然，如果你精力足够旺盛，也可以顺着365级陡峭的台阶（每级1英尺①高）拾级而上——到小岛的顶部看看，这里也是英国政府的驻地。

1920年12月31日，船抵达了开普敦。在这里，我们欣赏到了大山的壮丽。但因为只作短短两日停留，所以没法再细细品味更多的美景。然而，一想到已接近非洲海岸线，听着夜空里传来的教堂迎接新年的钟声以及轮船的汽笛声，我们就兴奋不已。在伊丽莎白港和东伦敦短暂停靠后，我们终于在1921年1月10日抵达了德班。我们登岸后住进了一家旅店，3周之后终于等来了前往东非海岸莫桑比克的船。在洛伦索马贵斯停留两晚后，我们如期抵达了贝拉市。

在贝拉市，我们又待了两周的时间才等到一艘渡轮，可以将我们接到赞比西河口流域，抵达英租界内的欣代港。贝拉是一座小城，当时还没有公路，只有沙石小道。当地有一种推车，由两个非洲人沿着煤车的轨道四平八稳地推着走。你可以坐着它四处转转。这里的店铺很少，旅店也只有两家。那会儿已经是1921年2月，我心急如焚地想要继续上路，因为我的丈夫一直在不停地给我发电报，问我究竟何时能到。

终于，我们登上了一艘小型渡轮，向欣代港驶去。但船上的客舱都位于甲板下方，随处可见黑色的大蟑螂。天哪，我绝对没法睡在那里！其他的40多名乘客也和我一样，不愿睡在甲板下面。似乎是因为船上运了糖，这才引来蟑螂。于是，大家全都搬到甲板上去睡了。

---

① 1英尺约合0.3米。——编者注

第二天一早，我们抵达了欣代港。结果麻烦来了！船不能靠岸，乘客必须站在所谓的"泊区"内，乘划艇上岸。可这时，新的麻烦又出现了！在距离木板铺成的栈桥还有10码①远时，划艇就不能再向前开了。所有人都只能被抬过去，我也只好照着做。两位身材魁梧的非洲大汉双手交叉，像抬轿子似的将我抬起。我紧张地伸出双臂抱紧他们的脖子，然后被送到了其中一块木板上。我就用这样奇怪的方式进入了东非。"英租界"里有几栋房子，但因为沙子太烫，必须沿着木板向上走才能到达。据说，那沙子烫得能把鸡蛋煮熟了！

我的神经一直绷得紧紧的。好在这几个非洲人都很友好，轻而易举地就把我抬上了岸，送到海边的小屋里。接着，我上了一艘小小的江轮。它和在美国密西西比河中行驶的明轮船非常相似——很小，两边还挂着小货艇。于是，最好笑的事情出现了：不知道为什么，其他20多名乘客在岸上随便找了个地方就休息了。只有我上了江轮，用了餐，并且累了一天下来，很早便睡着了。凌晨4点，我在一片明媚的阳光中，被乒乒乓乓的声音吵醒。那时才只是2月，非洲就已经热起来了。人们只能尽量早起，趁着大清早的凉爽工作——俗称"上工"，这样到了上午10点左右就可以下工了。

很快，其他乘客也开始登船。我们顺着赞比西河而上，开始了为期5天的航行。一路都很有趣，只可惜天气过于炎热，到处都是难缠的蚊蝇。黄昏时，船在"木头站"停了下来。这里可以买到点火的木材、水果、蔬菜等等。只要能在货艇上找到

---

① 1码约合0.9米。——编者注

地方落脚，非洲乘客就会上船，一直坐到下一个停靠点。其中有一个停靠点名为"修庞加"，这里立着大卫·李文斯顿妻子的墓碑。1870年，他的妻子被埋葬于此，在栅栏围起的一方小小的墓地中孤单长眠。由于她死于疟疾性发热，可怜的大卫只能将她"留下"，自己继续跋涉前行。

5天后，我们开始了最后一段的海上之旅，到达了布兰太尔的终点站——项迪奥。接着，我们又在火车上颠簸了两天一夜，于第二天黄昏抵达了布兰太尔。车站里，一群欧洲人和非洲人正在等待列车的到来。这趟列车每周抵达时总能引起不小的骚动。大家都想看看是谁来了，盼着能见到久别重逢的老朋友。我一眼就在人群中看到了我的丈夫，他正在焦急地等待着我。

这里可不会有戴姆勒或别克的豪华轿车来接站。在结束了9000多英里的旅程后，这最后一英里半的路必须靠步行。于是，我沿着一条上坡的山路，走向婚后的第一个家。这里的景

乘坐格拉的外祖母和拉文娜姨妈

象让我大为吃惊。到了德班才发现，原来中非地区的大多数房子都是用汽油桶上的铁皮搭起来的，上面还盖着各种颜色的印花布。因此，等走进自己的家，看见地上铺着漂亮的地毯，屋里摆放着家具，我简直太惊喜了。我的丈夫居然在繁忙的工作之余为我打造了这么一个温馨的家。双人床的顶上还有一个架子，挂着蚊帐，可爱极了。屋子很宽敞，有客厅、餐厅、浴室、衣帽间和两间卧室。屋外四周有大大的阳台，可以俯瞰下面的美丽花园。1921年2月，在绕过半个地球之后，我终于抵达了目的地，和我亲爱的丈夫生活在了一起。

在当时，外祖父母无疑选择了一种与众不同的生活。如果他们还留在英国肯特郡的查塔姆，继续做着会计和档案室的文员，生活一定大不相同。外祖母这样描述他们的生活：

布兰太尔风景宜人，幅员广阔。但没有公路，只有一些土路，在漫长的旱季里总是尘土飞扬。现在也还是这样。这里一年有三季：暑季、旱季、雨季。一下雨就涝，满地泥坑，因此外出时必须小心地走道。要知道，蛇和其他小动物最喜欢睡在这些泥坑里！

这里没有英文教堂。每月，中非大学传教会的神父会在北上传教的途中过来给我们做一次礼拜。礼堂就设在杂货店（过去是酒吧）后面的小房间里。此外，当地还有一间非常棒的苏格兰教堂，是19世纪70年代根据大卫·李文斯顿和海泽维克博士的设计建造的。在没有英文礼拜时，我们就会去那里。市里有几间不错的小店、一间俱乐部、一家影院。俱乐部里也会开展各种体育活动，这就是我们的娱乐。

渐渐地，会有一些朋友来家里坐坐，我也会出去串门。每位女士都会在每个月里固定一天邀请大家到家里做客。因此，生活根本就不会无聊，但跟英国比起来还是差别很大。我们没车，也不怎么出门。于是，丈夫给我弄来一辆"格拉"（一种小型的中式人力车），这样我就能到处走走了。

必须一提的是，我们当时没有电灯或煤气灯，只有壁挂式的煤油灯，以及厨房用的防风灯。厨房为砖瓦结构，和我们住的屋子是分开的。所谓炉子，就是把一块波纹铁皮架在砖砌的灶台上。掌勺的小师傅会用它来烤或煮食物，也会烘面包和司康饼，弄得热炉灰四处飞扬。我跟他说，我刚结婚，也刚来到这里，想自己做些蛋糕和果馅饼。结果，这位小师傅很礼貌地用不怎么地道的英语对我说："您是夫人，不能干活。"真是太有趣了。

这里没有水。我们必须去两英里以外的河里取水，再盛在汽油罐里加热，然后拎进浴室，倒入澡盆里洗澡。每天如此。这里也没有厕所，只在花园里砌了间茅房。不过，丈夫特地帮我在浴室里装了个便桶，这样我就不用风雨无阻地往花园里跑了。

这就是我在布兰太尔第一年的生活。虽然得过痢疾和疟疾（在贝拉得的），但政府医院里有一位很好的医生，帮了我很多忙。

1922年1月，我的大姨出生了，取名拉文娜。大家都夸她机灵，不过她一开始只会说非洲土语，直到3岁才能流利地说英语。当时外祖母也决定要学些非洲方言，这样才能和非洲工人打成一片。也正是这样，她家里的佣人才会一直跟了她那么多年。

1925年，他们离开了布兰太尔。外祖母是这样描述的：

> 1925年，我的丈夫被调到了尼亚萨兰湖畔的科塔村。我们乘着卡车走了一段，余下的路就靠马吉拉（machilla）。我们沿山路而下，进入科塔村。非洲脚夫们每天只能走15英里左右，所以我们每晚都要宿在帐篷里，而帐篷就搭在当地的村庄旁。到了科塔，村长带着他的部下出来迎接我们。当看到一个只有4岁的白人小孩儿跑来跑去，还能用当地的土语和人交流时，他们简直惊呆了！村长还给了我们一些鸡蛋和鸡作为礼物。他们也很喜欢我的波美拉尼亚狗，看它长着一身黄棕色的毛发，便叫它为"狮子"。

去科塔的途中，外祖父和外祖母一家睡在帐篷里

在科塔，我迎来了第二个女儿尤妮斯。1926年6月，在政府医院医生和差会护士（来自74英里外的传教站，也是离我们最近的了）的帮助下，我在自家的小土屋里生下了尤妮斯。非洲人从来没见过白皮肤的婴儿，这让村长大开眼界。村长年纪很大，是一个非常好的人。他说自己曾在1897年去过伦敦，参观维多利亚女王登基60周年的纪念礼。村长经常会来家里看看孩子，还会带来些鸡蛋、香蕉等等，其中还有我吃过的最香甜的大米，都是在当地的沼泽田里种出来的。他每次来还会带上一个大大的空药瓶。我问丈夫这是做什么的，他说："哦，你往里面装点儿石蜡，这是给他的回礼。"后来，我们就一直这样交换着物品。

1926年，母亲尤妮斯出生的小土屋

二女儿出生一周后，我们家的院子里坐满了非洲村民。我的心里很是担忧。"他们要干吗？"我问。"哦，想来看看白人宝宝。"于是，丈夫只得把孩子抱出去给他们看。大家不住地欢呼和鼓掌。突然，村长送出一份特殊的礼物——一头公牛和一头怀孕的母牛，可以给宝宝挤奶喝。我的心情一下变得很激动。大旱了一年，我们已经4个月没有牛奶喝了。村长还派了一个非洲小牧童来帮我们看牛。在此之前，教会每天会送一杯牛奶和一杯羊奶给我的大女儿喝。至于我们，就什么也喝不上了。可现在，好心的村长借给了我们一头母牛。奶多得可以用盆装，多余的奶就分给村民。而且我以前还学过瑞士炼乳的做法，只需要将一杯糖和四杯奶混合起来煮就可以了。于是，我就照这个方法，让丈夫在"旅途"中享用到了最美味的炼乳。

尤妮斯出生3个星期后，我的丈夫和其他欧洲人要北上3周，只能把我和孩子留在家里。结果，我就遇到了麻烦，发生了可怕的大出血。该怎么办？我拿出医书查看，上面写：卧床。于是，我孤零零地在床上躺了3个星期，全靠在当地找的几个佣人来照顾我。他们端来一盆水和几条毛巾。于是，我就坐在床上，把宝宝放在膝盖上，帮她洗澡。她的人生还真是"开局不顺"啊。不过，我的工人都很好。他们会给我们送吃的，还帮忙照看我的大女儿。第二个星期，大家把医生叫回来了——医生虽然很年轻，但受过训练，为人也很亲切。不过，他不能进屋，只能隔着铁丝窗问诊，然后让我继续躺满3周的时间。

除了照看两个年幼的孩子，外祖母似乎还有别的事要做：

有时其他人都出远门了，我一个人留下照看村子。走的人里包括医生、地区长官、农业主管、我丈夫，还有4个传教人员。这时候，我就只能带着孩子独守阵地，还要照顾所有生了病的村民。他们相信我拿着本《布莱克医学词典》就能搞定各种小毛病。他们最常见的毛病是胃部不适。只需要一汤匙的石蜡再加一点儿糖，很多情况下是能缓解疼痛的。老村长也来找我拿过"药"，混合液体奎宁（我们随身带着药箱）吃下去之后笑嘻嘻地离开了，满心觉得我能帮到他。

当时没有电话，所以我根本不知道丈夫在哪里，何时能回来。如果听到远处有人大声地喊叫或歌唱，就说明"老爷们儿"从山上回来了。就这样，我的听力被练得很好，能够时刻保持警惕。这项本领可帮了我大忙，哪怕一丁点儿的声音也能将我从睡梦中惊醒。每当我一人在家时，小伙子们（非洲当地人）会带着好几袋钱来。我没法一个人拿着这么多钱穿过走廊把钱放进保险柜里，因此只得把钱塞在床垫下面，压着几百镑

1926年，尤妮斯被抱着渡过库鲁河

的钞票睡到天亮。我从不担心会被袭击或抢劫，第二天数起来一分也不会少（我丈夫数过，硬币足有5000多镑）。

我真的很喜欢科塔和这里一望无际的内陆海景。不知不觉中迎来了暑季，气候干爽而温暖。此时医生正好在家，他建议我搬到科塔的山上去住，那里要凉快些。但我不想走，因为我很喜欢这里，家人也都生活得很好。我说想留下，他却很坚持。正巧此时我的丈夫也接到调令，要去往300多英里外的北尼亚萨兰。看来我们必须要走了。老村长热情地来送我们，不舍地说着再见，临别我们同往常一样互换了礼物。

于是，我们乘着马吉拉出发了。这一路走了9天，每晚都宿在当地人的村庄里。尤妮斯说，她恐怕是世界上唯一在路边喝奶的孩子了。我们一路向北走，所到之处的人们都没见过白人孩子。那是1926年7月，每到一个村子，当村民看到一个5岁的白人孩子跑来跑去，还有一个小宝宝坐在小车里时，都会发出

1930年，外祖父杀死了一头追逐非洲人的狮子

357

惊叹。我们随身带了一个小型留声机，所以每天都有很多人提出要看白人宝宝，听留声机播放唱片。这让他们很开心。

　　途中，我们经过了两处政府的安置点和两处荷兰归正会传教所，它们都由欧洲人（穿着白色长袍，留着长胡须）管理。他们热情地接待了我们，并邀请我们留宿。这个国家里的欧洲人很少，因此不管是什么宗教背景，都显得格外友善。非洲人也给了我们莫大的帮助——事实上，能抱一抱白人小孩儿，在他们看来似乎是一种荣幸。

　　一路上，我们有过很多惊心动魄的经历。有一次，我们睡在小土屋里，丈夫突然听见了粗重的呼吸声。他心想，肯定是哪个非洲人来偷钱了，于是悄悄地把眼睛睁开一条缝，没有动，幸好丈夫没动！那是一头狮子！它正站在屋里看着我的丈夫呢！他一动不动，但是睁大了眼睛，直直地盯住狮子的双眼！狮子一转身，走了出去。不一会儿，一个非洲人冲了进来，大声喊："老爷！狮子在追递送员！"丈夫拿起枪，杀了那头狮子。

母亲的宠物龟的龟壳和外祖父射杀的狮子的悬爪

上面这张照片就是用南非金镶起来的悬爪，还有我母亲在非洲时养的宠物龟的龟壳。这只乌龟在母亲去英国前没多久死了。于是，母亲就取下了龟壳，终生保存着。

就这样，我们到了新站点"姆津巴"。当地人匆匆盖了一间两室的砖瓦房子，房顶铺着稻草，好让我们住。这里还住着一位地区专员和一位助理专员以及他们的妻子。又能和欧洲人在一起，孩子们也能在一起玩，这真是太好

1927年，母亲在屋子的走廊上，穿着外祖父给她做的鞋

了。在这里，所有工作地都叫作"站"，而不是"村子"，虽然这里根本没有铁路。事实上，我们离林贝和布兰太尔的铁路线还有400多英里远呢！

在给我母亲取名时，外祖父选了"尤妮斯"，这源于他在打仗时许下的一个承诺。当年，炸弹袭击了他所乘坐的列车，导致他受伤。照顾他的护士一直不离左右，直到有车把他送去医院。这名护

托马斯和他的妻子

士就叫"尤妮斯"。外祖父对她说，如果有一日自己能生个女儿，一定给她取名"尤妮斯"。不过这个名字后来却给我母亲带来了不少的困扰。

总的来说，母亲在北尼亚萨兰过着质朴而悠闲的生活——整日和姐妹、弟弟，还有当地的小伙伴们一起嬉闹玩耍。他们加入了当地的许多活动。伊莎贝尔姨妈还清楚地记得大家一起外出打猎的情景！早上6点，当地的孩子拍打窗户上的铁丝网（为了防狮子）把他们叫醒，然后带着他们，跟

母亲尤妮斯、舅舅厄内斯特、小姨伊莎贝尔和
大姨拉文娜，摄于1929年

着村里的男人一起去追捕动物。她说，你很快就会知道，必须严格听从命令。比如说，如果别人叫你停下，你就必须立刻停下，因为他们很可能是在前方发现了狮子，必须保持安静才能狮口脱险！

家里雇了许多用人，负责烧饭、打扫和其他家务活。孩子们对于照看自己的托马斯和约翰的印象尤为深刻。他们就来自当地的村庄，因此可以带着里德家的孩子参加当地的各种活动。

孩子们和托马斯、约翰，还有当地的小伙伴们在一起时，都会说非洲土语（齐切瓦语）。根据托马斯所著的《齐切瓦语实用方法》一书，齐切瓦语（湖区语言）属于班图语支。它有多种方言形式，是尼亚萨兰的官方语言。书的序言中提到，这本书旨在为初到此地的农耕者、传教士、文职人员、商人或家庭主妇等提供一些实用的指导。从中也能看出当时都有哪些人前往尼亚萨兰。

外祖父母也都能流利地使用齐切瓦语，这样才能和农场的工

1933年，外祖母在松巴参加"女子步枪俱乐部"

人、用人以及照看孩子的保姆交流。他们在和自己的孩子说话时也会用齐切瓦语。直到今天，里德家的一些成员仍然会在日常语言中夹杂一些在非洲时学会的语句。在母亲、姨妈和舅舅的记忆里，都鲜少有被外祖父母照顾的印象。因为当时外祖父经常要出远门到非洲各地，而外祖母则忙于各种事务，还要去松巴参加"女子步枪俱乐部"、编织缝纫和桥牌聚会等。

尽管如此，我母亲仍然有着非常快乐的童年，在非洲的乡间和当地的小伙伴们无拘无束地奔跑玩耍，说着当地的方言，还不用上学。大家都说她机灵、难对付，还有些叛逆，而这样的个性也给她接下来的人生惹了不少麻烦。

第二章　寄宿学校的生活

（1935—1939年）

每两年，公司就会出钱让外祖父一家回国一趟，待上差不多6个星期的时间。这一段长长的旅行总是让他们记忆犹新。通常回到英国后，他们都会去东南部的肯特郡，包括查塔姆、厄普丘奇和罗彻斯特，同家里的亲戚们待上一段时间。1933年，母亲7岁，她照例随家人回到英格兰，住进了她姨妈多丽丝的家里。这里一定是给母亲留下了很深刻的印象，以至于在我小的时候，母亲一想要我做什么，就会说"多丽丝姨妈说了……"。通常，他们也会去南威尔士看看其他亲戚，顺便度度假。

从非洲远渡重洋回英国，这一路不单是漂在海上，也可以说是在度假。在船上，他们给自己安排了各种各样的活动。伊莎贝尔姨妈回忆道，有一次外祖母要带两个姐姐去厕所，只好将她和双胞胎弟弟厄内斯特拴在

母亲7岁时的照片

1933年，外祖父带着4个孩子去南威尔士度假

栏杆上，生怕他们丢了。可当外祖母回来的时候，却发现这两人不见
了，哪儿都找不到。原来，他们钻过了栏杆，正在海里"划水"呢！
多亏了水手把他们拽上船！在外祖母眼里，伊莎贝尔姨妈是各种调皮
捣蛋之事的始作俑者，因此打了她一耳光，责怪她视弟弟的生命安全
于不顾！

　　1935年，全家又回到了英格兰。这一次，母亲将会留下。1930
年，拉文娜姨妈留在了英国上学，现在该轮到母亲了。这一年，她
也和当年的姨妈一样，差不多9岁。外祖母回忆道，这姐妹俩被送回
英国，其实都算是比较迟的，其他在非洲工作的公职人员，一般都
在子女五六岁时就将他们送回国。因为他们觉得非洲气候太炎热，
而且五六岁也该是上学的年纪了。

　　家里人都记得，每当要将孩子留在英国时，外祖父总会有些
伤感，而外祖母却无动于衷。他们甚至觉得外祖母是高兴的，因为
终于能摆脱这些讨厌的孩子了！当然，外祖母自己并不这么说。
她说，做父母的在这样的时刻总是痛苦的，而被留下的孩子却更痛

母亲（最左边）和
一群孩子在船上

苦。无论怎么说，他们在家庭关系中缺乏情感的交流，这一定也对他们的人生产生了影响。

　　母亲被托付给了她的姨妈凯丝照料，随后前往罗切斯特中学念书。这是一间小型的私立寄宿制学校，由摩根先生担任校长。这对母亲来说，是一段饱受创伤的记忆。因为她习惯了非洲的自由自在，无法适应这个处处受到约束的新环境，也没有一个9岁孩子应该具备的受教育基础。她清楚地记得有一次在课上，摩根先生让她去看一眼过道里的钟，然后再回来报告时间。她却站在这座旧式的大摆钟面前，根本不知道怎么看，于是只好回到教室，告诉全班同学她不知道几点了。在这件事情里，校长作为一个拥有权力的男人，带给了母亲极大的羞耻感，而这也伴随并影响了她的一生。

　　1938年，到了最后两个孩子该回国的年纪。伊莎贝尔姨妈回忆到，当时他们的英语还不如齐切瓦语说得好，而且他们和我母亲一样，在非洲这些年根本没上过学。用她的话说，他们虽然表面上可以读一些英文书，但都是很机械地在读，根本不能真正地理解其中的意思。

1938年，伊莎贝尔姨妈和厄内斯特舅舅也进入了罗切斯特中学。这样，4个孩子都聚齐了。拉文娜姨妈比母亲年长4岁，离开非洲前曾在布兰太尔上过学，因此回国读书的基础略好一些。据伊莎贝尔姨妈回忆，我的母亲太过聪明，总是会向摩根先生提出质疑并纠正他，但场面常常让人尴尬，因而难免和摩根先生发生争执。伊莎贝尔姨妈很喜欢上学，并且认为自己和拉文娜姨妈都深得摩根先生的喜爱。而我母亲却因为摩根先生的缘故，非常讨厌学校。

　　不过在母亲看来，摩根先生倒也做过一件好事：他给母亲的名字正了音。摩根先生的一个儿子彼得当年也在该校上学，据他回忆称，过去同学们都把我母亲的名字念成"尤腻丝"，但摩根先生受过古典教育，立刻指出正确读音应该是"尤妮斯"，于是整个学校都跟着改了过来。别人读不准自己的名字，这是她后来仍常遇到的困扰。因此，等她遇见我父亲时，已经基本不再用"尤妮斯"这个名字了，而改为了更好发音的"苏珊"。

第三章 在威尔士的疏散学校

（1939—1944年）

1939年，罗切斯特中学的所有学生都被疏散到了位于威尔士兰达弗里的兰莱学校。校长想办法租下了这栋楼，把整个寄宿学校搬了过来，以作为战时的过渡。1939年，第二次世界大战爆发。我的外祖父母当时仍在非洲，因此只能把孩子交给学校照看。外祖母说，她和外祖父原本已经定好1940年回国，却因为战争打响，不得不推迟到1944年。

母亲的交际圈很小，有一些朋友还是在非洲的时候认识的。瓦莱丽就是其中之一。在科塔时，她们是门对门的邻居，那会儿母亲才5岁。瓦莱丽还记得她们在长长的走廊上一起玩耍的情景。多年后，她们一起进入了罗切斯特中学，并在大战爆发前夕随着学校搬去了兰达弗里的新校舍，住进了同一间寝室。瓦莱丽说，我的母亲很爱读书，而且不苟言笑。有一天晚上，寝室里的其他姑娘们决定跟她开个玩笑，把她床前挂着的一张照片藏起来。结果还没等藏好，母亲就从澡堂回来了。瓦莱丽赶紧把照片塞在枕头下。姑娘们忙着掩饰，不想让母亲发现她们的计划。结果瓦莱丽忘了照片的事，一脚踩在了枕头上。相框的玻璃碎了！瓦莱丽说，闯祸了！该怎么跟舍管和校长解释？结果还是我母亲想了办法，编了个故事说有只蝙蝠飞进窗户，把照片从墙上撞掉下来了！她们就这样脱身了。不过瓦莱丽觉得舍管根本就不相信她们的话。

玛格丽特·邓恩是我母亲的表妹，也在兰达弗里的兰莱学校上学。她还记得学校有个漂亮的花园，母亲在那儿教她识鸟，甚至教她区分五十雀和旋木雀。

玛格丽特的哥哥大卫·邓恩也在这所学校就读。他还大致记得1941—1944年间与我母亲来往的情景。印象最深的就是母亲教他打毛线。大卫说，当时的女生都想织些东西来慰劳前线的士兵，于是我的母亲、伊莎贝尔小姨和玛格丽特就逼着他帮忙。全校再也找不出第二个打毛线的男生了！她们不会让他帮着织袜子、巴拉克拉法帽这种讲究不同针法的复杂物件，通常只是织围巾。我母亲会先用铅笔一样粗细的针起个20针左右，然后交给大卫一排一排织平针。等织到需要的长度后，我母亲就会来收针，然后起好下一条再交给大卫！大卫说，虽然很枯燥单调，但这么多年过去，他依然能记得

母亲1942年的作画

平针的织法！

　　母亲的缝纫和编织技术在这段日子里练得炉火纯青，日后竟也真的帮上了大忙。大卫给了我一张照片，上面是母亲1942年留在他的纪念册上的画画和签名。看来我母亲的绘画水平也不错！

　　学校里还有一位名叫弗兰克的朋友。母亲很开心地说起过他们在学校的事情。弗兰克有一副麻将牌，常常很骄傲地拿出来教我母亲和她的兄弟姐妹玩。后来，弗兰克和他的母亲玛乔丽在我母亲及我自己的生活中扮演了重要的角色。

　　我母亲在家里是最不合群的一个——她说拉文娜姨妈聪明，伊莎贝尔姨妈漂亮，厄内斯特舅舅男孩子气。遇到自己不喜欢的社交场合，她就会把自己"关起来"。在伊莎贝尔姨妈看来，母亲是不喜欢自己的弟弟妹妹的，因为当年他们可以回非洲，而母亲却被孤零零地留在了英国。不管什么原因塑造了这样的性格，她在学校里确实是一个什么都敢说的叛逆角色。彼得·摩根至今还能记起"她和我争辩时，脸上气势汹汹的表情"，让他一度认为我母亲信奉社会主义。

里德家的孩子们在兰莱学校

第四章　长大成人

（1944—1948年）

厄内斯特舅舅回忆到，1944年，里德家的最后几个孩子陆续离开学校，准备进入大学。此时，外祖父刚从非洲回来，在肯特郡议会的帮助下为孩子们安排好了去处。我母亲去了斯旺利园艺专科学院，而厄内斯特舅舅则去了英国驱逐舰乌斯特号海军训练学校。外祖父和母亲陪着舅舅一起去学校领制服。母亲对舅舅说，他现在穿着伦敦才能见到的军装。这话语里透着自豪：自己的弟弟也要投身战场，为国效力了！

伊莎贝尔姨妈说，虽然我母亲"连草都没除过"，却还是拿到了斯旺利园艺专科学院的奖学金。这种凭借零经验就进入一个陌生行业的事儿，在母亲此后的人生里还有很多。在斯旺利园艺专科学院，母亲认识了玛德琳，不过我一直称她为"兰姨"。她是母亲一生的挚友，后来还成了我最重要的非正式养母。之所以能成为朋友，是因为她们都不愿意参加英国国会每天的礼拜活动。兰姨说，学校要求她们必须待在教堂旁边的小屋子里，就算不去教堂，也得听完整个礼拜！学生们还要参加各种园艺项目，这也是课程的一部分。其中常去的就是位于萨里郡沃金市的威斯利皇家园艺学会花园。

兰姨回忆起在学校时，母亲曾将她介绍给玛乔丽和其他一些朋友。这些人当时住在伦敦的维多利亚区，看起来很像是共产主义者。虽然兰姨觉得他们的政治观点有些狭隘，不太能够接受，但当他们提出应该将一些无人居住的屋子清理出来，让给维多利亚区一些生活环境过分拥挤和恶劣的居民及欧洲难民居住时，兰姨表示了支持。

后来，母亲和兰姨仍常去伦敦，不仅为了见朋友，还为了看戏。兰姨说，母亲带她去过尤斯顿附近的统一剧院，那里经常演出政治剧。她们一起看了呼声很高的爱尔兰舞台剧《朱诺与孔雀》，兰姨说她基本没看懂。剧院很冷，座位很硬，进出也很困难。兰姨后来再没去过，不过我母亲去过。

从斯旺利园艺专科学院毕业后，母亲和兰姨合租过各种公寓。这样的生活持续了许多年。其中就包括位于克劳利附近的盖特威克大会堂酒店（Gatwick Hall Hotel）。这座建筑现在已经拆除了，不过它也曾有过一段特殊的历史。这里住过臭名昭著的"酸浴杀手"乔治·黑格。兰姨回忆道，她们曾注意到乔治·黑格，因为他"养了"一条看起来不太快乐的红色塞特犬。后来才知道这条狗的真正主人就是被他残忍杀害的两名死者。母亲和兰姨原本都只觉得乔治是个衣冠楚楚、自视很高的人，而且很少听他谈论自己的事情，当得知这位邻居的真实身份后，她们才着实被吓得不轻。

离开斯旺利园艺专科学院后，母亲和兰姨都来到苏塞克斯郡克劳利附近的迪尔加特，进入了园艺研究所的伯克公司工作，但母亲只从1945年11月工作到次年7月就辞职了。兰姨说，不知道母亲为何要辞职，但估计是因为母亲觉得男领导脾气太差。兰姨也深有同感。

1946—1947年间，母亲和兰姨在当地做了很多园艺工作，这才付得起房租。1947年10月，母亲在位于萨里郡雷德希尔市的鹈鹕书店找到一份工作。兰姨说，我母亲很喜欢这份工作，觉得皮齐先生是一个很好的老板。

在鹈鹕书店工作期间，有一天母亲走进当地的一间工合社，看到一张论文竞赛的宣传单，题目是关于"国际合作"。于是，母亲就写好论文，寄出去参加评选。之后的某一天，皮齐先生喊她去办公室，说有她的电话。这在当时肯定是非常稀罕的事，所以她接起电话时还有些紧张。电话是工合社打来的，通知她论文获了一等奖！作为奖励，她可以去斯坦得工合学校免费学习一年，学校将提供膳宿和一些基本课程。母亲很高兴，皮齐先生也表示非常支持，鼓励她好好利用这一年。

母亲说，她已经习惯了不断地离开旧环境，再重新开始新生活。这种选择在她的生命中出现过很多次。而这一次，她立刻就抓住了机会。于是，已经基本与家人断了联系的她，又不得不离开朋友。在和伊莎贝尔姨妈的聊天中得知，离开学校后，家人和母亲的接触非常少，只偶尔见面，也不太清楚她的生活里究竟发生了什么。

第五章　和孙光俊在一起

（1949—1950年）

1949年，在斯坦得工合学校，我的父亲和母亲相遇了。

工合学校于1919年由工合联盟创建，设于曼彻斯特的霍利约克大楼（Holyoake House）。1943年，这里成为一个慈善基金机构。

1945年，霍利约克大楼在轰炸中被摧毁，工合学校只得迁往斯坦得，并在这里度过了近半个世纪的时间。在此期间，学校向成人开放各种社会类、经济类的寄宿制课程，并为工合员工提供一系列的零售和管理培训。1946年，荣获大英帝国官佐勋衔的罗伯特·马歇尔博士出任了工合学校的校长和首席执行官，使学校在国内外声名远播。

斯坦得位于英国诺丁汉郡拉夫堡以南的城市。这是一座受到保护的18世纪英国乡村建筑，由红砖砌成，占地面积很大。建筑共分两层，主楼和侧楼的7个正面都是临街而建。建筑保存得很好，花园、湖泊、游泳池、剧场等设施一应俱全。

从工合学校当时开设的课程来看，母亲参加的商业研究课程实际上是针对从事零售业的工合社员工的。她说自己很喜欢上"国际合作"课，并且在这里遇见了来自世界各地的同学。母亲描述过她和父亲散步的美丽花园，以及从休息室一直到湖面的景色。因为她和父亲的身材都不高大，所以每次散步回来，都会坐在同一张大大的扶手椅上，一起欣赏湖面。她还记得同学们会唱美国作曲家弗兰克·罗瑟写的那首《在开往中国的慢船上》。而这首歌就发表在她和父亲相识的那一年。

很显然，他们在斯坦得度过了一年悠闲自在的生活。对母亲而言，进入工合学校是又一个新的机会，可以开启又一段新的人生。这样的机会在她的一生出现过很多次，但重要的是，这一次终于没有人跟她争夺男孩子了！以前，她总觉得在和姐妹们竞争——她觉得拉文娜比自己聪明，伊莎贝尔比自己漂亮，而且她们俩都长着一头金色的卷发，比自己的棕色直发要好看多了！母亲说，学校里有100个男学生，但只有寥寥几个女生，所以她可以结识到世界各地的同学。从下页的"1949年工合学校年鉴照"中不难看出，学校里绝大多数都是男生（在讲述我父亲的上半部书中也用到过这张照片）。兰姨还记得，母亲曾向她说起过一个冰岛的男孩，但最吸引她的还是我的父亲。很快，他们就坠入情网，形影不离。

2005年9月母亲去世后，我曾给一些认识她的人寄去空白的便条，请他们写下记忆中的苏珊。于是，我根据照片和收回的便条，编写了一本记述母亲一生的纪念图书。父亲也答应

孙光俊在游泳池畔

1949年工合学校年鉴照：最后排左起第三为父亲孙光俊；
第一排左起第二为母亲苏珊

了我的请求，（用中英文）回忆了一些往事。这些内容均被我收入了有关父亲的前半部书中。我将摘录他信里的部分内容，从一个侧面来展现我母亲的性格以及他们往日的情意。我将父亲写在便条上的内容原封不动地呈现出来，为的就是更好地体会他对我母亲的感情。他回信时一定也经过了深思熟虑，知道所写内容会被收入书中，被大家看到。所以，他一定是希望通过这些故事，折射出他眼中的苏珊。

以下3则故事记述了他们在斯坦得共同度过的时光：

我们第一次聊天是在工合学校的客厅里。那是1949年的春假，本地学生基本都回家了，国外学生也去了其他地方旅游，只剩少数几个人还留在学校。有一天傍晚，我坐在长沙发上看报纸。这时，苏珊走了进来。"我可以坐在这儿吗？""坐吧。""我叫苏珊。""哦，我叫孙光俊。"我们握了握手。苏珊（苏三）这个名字很耳熟，因为这在中国是一个家喻户晓的戏剧人物。就这样，她给我留下了很深刻、也很亲切的第一印象。后来我们见得越来越多。第二天下午，苏珊邀请我一起走走。我们穿过树林和草地，走到湖边。湖面并不算宽广，但上面有一对大大的白天鹅，非常美丽。我经常去喂它们。湖的四周是郁郁葱葱的草地。突然，我们的手牵了起来，围着湖边走。那种感觉说不清是开心还是陌生。我们的手越握越紧……经过一片绿草地时，我们躺了下来，拥抱着，亲吻着……

孙光俊于兰州

2005年11月7日

伦敦的暑假（1949年）

暑假的前两周，学校没有安排任何功课，我们可以彻底放松。于是，我让苏珊带我去伦敦转转，待上一周。苏珊答应了。她伦敦的朋友正好外出度假，空出了屋子可以给我们住。有一天晚上，她带我去听了著名歌手保罗·罗伯逊（非裔美国人）的演唱会。我们坐在最后一排，离歌手远得根本什么也听不清、看不清，她很不高兴。于是第二天晚上，她又买了第一排正中的两张票！我们甚至还能摸到歌手和他的小提琴手！就在那一刻，我突然意识到，她是一个意志很坚定的人，很棒！

孙光俊于兰州

2005年11月8日

1949年的秋假，我收到史蒂芬夫妇的来信，邀请我去家里玩一个星期，还希望我能给当地妇联做演讲。我的心情很复杂。虽然觉得困难，但又无法拒绝，因为他们对我实在太好了。该怎么办呢？这时，我想到了苏珊"老师"。她既是我的女朋友，又是我的"良师"，一直在教我学英语。在我看来，她非常聪明、善良、乐于助人。我对她说，大家希望我谈谈中国的共产主义。于是，苏珊就看了《红星照耀中国》，写了一篇非常出色的演讲稿，并且打印出来给我。我在演讲时直接照着读就行了。这以后，我们在一起的时间更多了，我真的非常仰慕她。

孙光俊于兰州

2005年11月9日

以下2则故事发生于孙光俊在北威尔士的霍利韦尔工作时期：

　　到了霍利韦尔后，苏珊在诊所里找了份临时工作。有时候白天上班，有时候晚上。她待在这里差不多有一周的时间，我们每天都会见面。最后一天的晚上，她问我："去徒步怎么样？""'徒步'是什么？""就是走走，没有目的地，也不看时间。觉得累了就休息休息，坐着、躺着，都行。""听起来不错啊！"于是，下午6点左右，我们约在炸鱼和薯条店门口见面，买了两包薯条，和平时一样撒了点儿盐和醋。我喜欢醋的香味。我们沿着通往罗彻斯特的路开始走，途经一座桥时，发现桥下有一片沙滩。她说："下去看看吧？""好啊。"于是，我们就在桥下过了一夜。第二天早上很快就到来了，我们都觉得时间过得太快，不舍得分开。

孙光俊于兰州

2005年11月9日

1950年6月或7月的一个周末，苏珊来霍利韦尔看我，当时我还在纺织厂工作。她带我去莱尔游泳。从霍利韦尔到莱尔，大概有10~12英里的路程。我们乘着巴士，公路看起来离海边并不远，沿途景色如画。她不时地指向窗外，说："看，这是大海，这是……"我们彼此靠得很近，一路上谈笑风生。到了泳池门口，发现全是人。"为什么今天会有这么多人？""来看跳水表演的（各种花样跳水）。"她回答。那天我拍了很多照片，但现在一张也不剩了。其中有一幕，两个跳水运动员站在高台上（非常高，大概有15米），其中一人跳下，另一人紧跟其后，双手拽着前一个人的双脚。两人一前一后落入水中，很好看，但也很危险。我确实觉得非常危险。我们一直看到表演结束，然后我下水游了一会儿。在回程的巴士上，我问苏珊："你怎么知道今天有表演的？""报纸上看的。我知道你会喜欢的。我经常看到你在学校的泳池游泳，你也喜欢跳水。所以就来啦。""谢谢，你对我真是太好了。爱你。""我也爱你。"

孙光俊于兰州

2005年11月9日

　　兰姨清楚地记得，母亲曾把自己在工合学校认识的一位帅气同学带给她认识，而这位同学后来成了我的父亲！此外，兰姨还很无奈地陪着父亲的朋友，那人可比我父亲无趣多了。去伦敦时，厄内斯特舅舅和伊莎贝尔姨妈也和父亲匆匆见过一面，而这也是父亲和母亲的家人唯一的接触。此后的日子里，母亲很少提及自己的生活，继续享受着这段特殊的关系。

到了晚年，母亲开始向我说起她的过去，包括与父亲在一起的日子。在我印象中，父亲最后是很想回中国的，但母亲却希望他们能有机会在一起生活——不是立刻就在一起，但希望总有一天可以。但她知道，这并不是父亲想要的生活。母亲回忆说，她和父亲的最后一次见面是在克鲁火车站，两人不欢而散。很快，父亲就乘船回国了。我一直觉得母亲应该跟着父亲回中国，开始新生活。她总是很激动地说，解决全球矛盾最有效的途径就是生出一整代的混血儿，创造"一个全是咖啡色人种的世界"。

　　1950年11月，父亲离开英国，一去不返。而那会儿，母亲已经怀着我5个月了。

第六章　一个单身母亲的求职生涯
（1950—1951年）

　　当时，我的母亲正在惠特福德市的弗林特郡议会儿童福利院工作，任高级舍监。这里离霍利韦尔很近。然而，随着她的肚子越来越大，最终还是丢掉了这份工作。那一天，舍管把母亲喊进办公室，问她："姑娘，你的肚子怎么了？"然后，意味深长地看了看她的肚子。"你被辞退了。"在那个年代，这是最惯常的做法。

　　于是，同那个年代大多数未婚先孕的女性一样，我母亲去了伦敦。她也没想好要去做什么，只知道自己成了一个没有工作、无家可归的人，必须得找点儿事做。她说，列车直到深夜才抵达尤斯顿站。她下了车，却不知道接下来该往哪儿去。她坐在一张长凳上。终于，来了一名警察，主动提出帮她找个地方过夜。于是，我母亲住进了一家专门接待女性的招待所。从1951年1月月初到29日，她一直住在国家未婚母亲委员会之家，地址就在密德萨斯郡山上的哈罗（Harrow-on-the-Hill）地区洛克斯伯勒大道5号。

　　我母亲很聪明。父亲之前在英国时常常提起和探望李约瑟。于是母亲决定写信给李约瑟，寻求他的帮助。我父亲后来自称"K.C. Sun"，而我母亲在信里的称呼还是"光俊"。2004年6月1日，我和丈夫理查德前往剑桥大学图书馆查阅李约瑟博士的资料时，发现了母亲寄给他的信件，并根据信上的地址和日期了解到母亲当时的住所以及居住的时间。我们浏览了馆内所有关于李博士的档案和文件目录，并且调取了其中的3件，标题分别为"男孩儿们"、"佐伊·俊·里德（原文如此）"和"收养卷宗"。看完这些档案我才知道，母亲曾考虑过将我送给别人收养。在那个年代，这依旧是未婚先孕的女性最惯常的做法。

母亲寄给李约瑟的第一封信是在1951年1月17日，寄出地就是哈罗。信中陈明了她的困境，以及需要向李约瑟寻求的帮助。

亲爱的李博士：

不知您是否能够或愿意帮助我？您肯定还不认识我吧。先自我介绍一下，我就是几年前和孙光俊谈及婚嫁的苏珊·里德。当然，我们后来分开了，而我却突然发现自己怀了他的孩子，今年3月就要出生。去年6月，我开始在霍利韦尔附近的一家儿童福利院工作。但到现在，我和他至少4个月没有再见面。听霍利韦尔的阿瑟顿夫人说，他已经回了中国。

我本不该来打扰你，因为我知道这件事自始至终都是我自己的错。无奈生活中遇到了太多困难，远远超出我的预料。

我向国家未婚母亲委员会提出过申请，满心以为他们能帮我找一份工作，直到孩子出生。但让我非常失望的是，根本没有人愿意聘用一个怀孕的女人。无论是他们，还是福利工作员，最多也只能帮我找一间专门接待女性的招待所而已。眼下，我准备先住在这里，等到预产期前6周再搬入母子之家，一直住到孩子出生后6周。

现在最重要的是，我急需一份工作，以求稳定的收入和内心的安定。不知道您是否能帮帮我？我很强壮、健康、聪明，适应能力很强。我什么都可以做，缝纫、烹饪、打字……其他不会的我也可以学。如果这几个月继续闲着无所事事，我会发疯的。请您帮帮我吧。一定有什么工作是我能做的，去任何城市都行。我只要有口饭吃。

还有另一件事想拜托您。我不想要这个孩子。但我听说，英国家庭都不愿意收养混血的孩子。光俊曾说，他很希望自己今后的孩子能在山丹生活。能这样当然是最好，但政府不会允许我们"出口"孩子的！所以想拜托您帮我打听一下，有没有出生在中英混血家庭的中国人愿意收养或领养我的孩子？如果需要的话，我也可以出一些生活费。此事了结之后，我想去考注册护士，所以我确实无法留下这个孩子。

希望我们能有机会面谈此事。但无论怎样，希望您能在百忙之中尽快给我回信，告诉我能不能给我一些帮助。我现在很焦虑、很沮丧，简直陷入了绝望。我知道您是很关心光俊的。

此致

敬礼

尤妮斯·大卫·里德（苏珊·里德）

显然，李约瑟夫妇很快就回了信，因为下一封信的日期是1951年1月30日，收件人为李约瑟夫妇。信里表达了母亲对他们寄来的一英镑的感谢，并表示将接受他们的邀请去剑桥拜访。信中还提到她换了地址。她成功地说服老板给了她一份厨房女工的工作，现在的新地址为伦敦伊灵区阿姆赫斯特路47号阿姆赫斯特旅店。在这里，她会待上一个月左右。

1951年2月26日，母亲又给李约瑟夫妇去信，称自己已经转到了英国红十字会的临时收容所，地址在伦敦格德斯绿地区公园路16号，将在这里等待孩子出生。母亲在信中说，她一直没有收到李约瑟夫妇的信，想必是领养一事无果。她还说，自己不喜欢这间收容所，因为"护士全都凶神恶煞的；同住的其他人也都傻里傻气的，头脑空空；这里毫无隐私可言；最惨的是，从来没有一天能吃饱"，真希望孩子能提前降生。在信的最后，她说，像她这样的女人似乎也不可能有更好的出路了，抱怨也没有什么意义。

下一封信写于1951年3月6日，篇幅很短，主要是感谢李约瑟夫妇的邀请和寄来的食物。母亲还说，她已经用李博士给她的回邮信封给光俊写了信，烦请李博士在方便时再给她一些写好地址的回邮信封，她希望光俊能够知道孩子出生的消息。

档案里的下一封信来自国家儿童收养协会，同样写于1951年3月6日，来信地址为伦敦骑士桥71号。收信人为"剑桥大学冈维尔与凯斯学院李约瑟"。信中写道，感谢李博士的来信，但很遗憾无法帮到他的朋友，因为目前没有人愿意考虑有中国血统的孩子。他们建议李博士联系有色人种同盟。

1951年3月7日，全国领养学会也给李博士回了信，来信地址为伦敦贝克街4号。信中说，他们觉得像这样有一半中国血统的孩子不太可能找到领养家庭，但愿意试试看，不过能否成功还要看有没有合适的有混血背景的家庭出现。

1951年3月27日，李约瑟的一位医生朋友用密德萨斯郡史丹摩地区皇家国立整形外科医院的信笺回信，说他不认识任何愿意收养这个孩子的人，而且"刚从中国回来的人手头都很紧"。他说不知道

The League of Coloured Peoples

Telephone & Telegrams:

WHItehall 6591   FOUNDED IN 1931

19, Old Queen Street,
London, S.W.1.

President : *R. S. NEHRA, Esq., B.A.

SOLICITOR AND PRIVY COUNCIL AGENT LONDON. (RETD.)
Formerly M.L.C. Kenya Colony

Objects:

To promote World Peace by
fostering good relations among
all peoples.
To promote and protect the
social, educational, economic
and political interests of all
Coloured Peoples.
To interest members in the
welfare of Coloured Peoples in
all parts of the world.
To co-operate and affiliate with
organisations sympathetic to
Coloured Peoples.

Patrons:

The Right Rev. The
Bishop of Lichfield.
Commander Stephen King-Hall,
R.N. (retd.).
J. B. Priestley, Esq.,
M.A., LL.D., D.Litt.

Past Presidents:

Late *Dr. Harold A. Moody,
M.D., B.S. (Lond)
Learie N. Constantine, Esq. M. B. E.
R. B. Wellesley Cole, Esq. M.A.,
M.D., F.R.C.S.

Executive Committee:

Vice-Presidents:
J. C. T. Bailie, Esq.
David Pitt, Esq. M.B., Ch.B.,
D.Ch.

Hon. Secretary:
Samson U. Morris, Esq.

Hon. Treasurer:
Miss Marjorie O. Griffith.

James S. Clark, Esq. M.C., M.A.,
barrister-at-law.
Colin A. Jones, Esq.
Albert A. Hyndman, Esq.

*FOUNDATION MEMBER

SM/AF   29th March, 1951.

Dr. J. Needham, FRS,
Reader in the University of Cambridge,
Gonville & Caius College,
Cambridge.

Dear Dr. Needham,

Thank you for yours of the 11th inst., concerning this unmarried woman who is shortly to become a mother.

There is little hope that we can do anything for her because we find great difficulty in placing our children, as you will understand, and as a consequence we have a large waiting list.

It does happen sometimes that one case may jump the list if the request made favours the specification of a particular case.

In the circumstances it may be advisable for us to know of the sex of the child at birth.

有色人种同盟寄给李约瑟的信。照片由李约瑟提供，转自李约瑟研究中心在《新政治家》上登条广告会不会有用，还说会帮忙问问施赈所的朋友。

档案里的下一封信写于1951年3月29日，寄信人是有色人种同盟，地址为伦敦老皇后街19号。信里称希望很渺茫，因为等待被收养的孩子很多，很难帮我们的孩子们找到家。不过，他们说一定会帮着留意，也说不定什么时候机会就会突然出现。

从这些信中不难看出，李约瑟已经尽了全力来帮助母亲寻找领养途径，但"有一半中国血统"的事实导致无人愿意领养。1951年3月29日，母亲写信给李约瑟夫妇，称"有件事很难开口，我猜想你们听完也会非常生气。但经过深思熟虑，我还是决定留下这个孩子。我一直在思考这个问题，尽可能地理性、全面、不掺杂感情。最后，出于以下几点考虑，我决定留下孩子：很难找到领养家庭；就算能被顺利地领养，也不能保证孩子可以在一个安全、被爱和幸福的环境中成长；独自养大一个女孩儿，会比男孩儿要容易些；这么说或许很可笑，但我确实很爱她"。

这封信是从密德萨斯郡埃奇韦尔地区埃奇韦尔总医院产科2号楼寄出的，信里说："分娩的过程很痛苦，但愿今天能下得了床。"我出生时重6磅6盎司，体长20英寸，非常结实、健康。母亲说，她给孩子取名"佐伊·俊"。"俊"取自光俊，是母亲和朋友们对父亲的称呼。母亲说，孩子很像光俊，也有一点儿像她，"她真的非常漂亮，护士们都不住地夸她"。母亲曾告诉我说，分娩的过程很长，很困难，很痛苦。好不容易才将我生下来，母亲连看都不想看我一眼。但接生的医生一直在对着我说话，说我好漂亮，说他确信我母亲一定会想留下我——终于，她被说动了，伸手把我抱在怀里，然后一下就改变了主意，决定将我留下来！分娩时肯定出了些严重的问题，导致她术后第一次下床时大出血，最后在医院治疗了差不多一个月的时间才出院。

在给李博士的信中，她分析了眼下的难处，觉得自己带着个孩子很难找到工作，也不太可能再回到郡议会下属的福利院了，只能去私人机构或学校试试运气。信的最后，她感谢李约瑟夫妇为自己所做的一切，并说："我准备给光俊写封信，希望他会有兴趣了解自己的女儿。给女儿写写信，寄些小东西。只要女儿问起，我就不会隐瞒她的身世。我仍希望她长大了能去山丹看看。"

1951年5月7日，母亲写信给李约瑟夫妇，说自己从4月底开始就已经搬入了位于伦敦卫斯顿巷167号的密德萨斯郡议会母子之家。在此之前，也就是产后近一个月的时间里，她都一直住在医院。她描述了母子之家的情况，说比之前的收容所要好多了。我也在茁壮成长，简直和光俊一个模子，甚至笑起来都一模一样。她说自己还在等光俊的回信。信的最后，她问李约瑟夫妇能不能在找工作时填写他们的名字作为推荐人，还说想找一份能带着孩子上班的工作实在是越来越困难了。

1951年5月30日，她又从同一地址寄出一封信，感谢李约瑟夫妇的回信以及送给我的上衣，还说白色是最适合我的颜色，因为通常大家都会给女孩儿选粉色衣服，可这并不衬我的黑皮肤。母亲还说，前一天晚上她参加了英中友好协会在霍尔本厅举办的见面会，但还来不及等到李博士发言就离开了（因为母子之家晚上9点半要查房）。她很高兴地说，自己终于在一间寄宿制的育儿所找到了工作，可以带着我一起上班。下周六就开始。母亲还说已经让我完成了受洗礼，这倒不是因为她特别想让我受洗，而是为了让教会姐妹，也就是负责她的福利工作员高兴。有趣的是，受洗之后，他们

Maternity Block 2,
Edgware General Hospital,
Edgware,
Middlesex.
March 29th 1951.

Dear Dr. & Mrs. Needham,

My baby was born on March 21st & was a girl. She was 6 lb. 6z & 20 ins. long at birth & is very strong & healthy. The confinement was ghastly — doesn't bear thinking about even now! — but I feel quite fit again & expect to get up to-day for the first time.

Now I come to the hardest part of this letter & I feel you may both be rather cross with me!

I have after much thought decided to keep the baby myself. I have tried to think it all out as logically

1951年3月29日，母亲写给李约瑟的信。
照片由李约瑟提供，转自李约瑟研究中心

387

给我取名为"佐伊·俊·安妮",最后的"安妮"硬是母亲这位善良的姐妹给加上的,因为她觉得"'佐伊·俊'听起来一点儿都不虔诚"。信的最后,她再一次感谢李约瑟夫妇在这几个月里给予她的帮助和鼓励,她永远也不会忘记。

第七章　跟随工作走

（1951—1957年）

1951年6月，母亲进入了寄宿制育儿所布鲁克屋工作，担任护士。这里靠近苏塞克斯郡的克罗伯勒市。但只过了两个月，女老板就辞退了我的母亲和其他员工，理由是育儿所付不出工资给他们了。母亲在给李约瑟夫妇的信中说，她一点儿都不觉得难过，因为这里怎么看都很差劲。

后来，母亲又在汉普郡安德沃市附近的一间家庭式育儿所里找到了一份高级护士的工作。她很认同这里的女老板和她的经营理念，将育儿所就保持在一个很小的规模，也不需要那么多的制度约束。不像前一家育儿所规模那么大，导致经营不善。

1951年10月19日，母亲又在这间新的育儿所里给李约瑟夫妇写了一封信。信上说，她希望趁着孩子尚小，就在这里一直待下去。不过哪怕是朋友，恐怕也不可能帮她这么多。对于李约瑟夫妇上一封信中提到的问题，她表示自己心意已决，一定会将我养大。她强调说，自己再也不会改变主意了，不管发生什么，都不会与我分开。但她仍很感谢李约瑟夫妇费心帮她找到了可能愿意收养孩子的人家。接着她又说了说我的近况，说我脾气很好，也很听话，"非常可爱、聪明，有趣极了"。母亲说，她正在给我断奶，开始喂些素食，因为她自己就是个素食主义者。信中，她还应李约瑟夫妇的要求夹入了几张照片。她说自己不太会照相，如果李博士能像当年给光俊照相一样，也给我照几张就好了。

信的最后，她说她一直没有收到孙光俊的回信，她准备再写一次（第三封），并且让孙光俊回信时寄到剑桥，由李约瑟夫妇代收。她还说，如果第三封信仍然石沉大海，她就不会再写了。

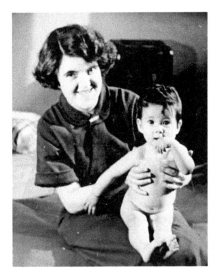

母亲和我，摄于1952年

她写信是为了他和孩子好，如果他选择对这个女儿不闻不问，那她也没有什么可说的了。但母亲觉得，最好还是要让孩子感到，即使自己的爸爸远在世界的另一端也仍然爱着自己。

1951年10月3日，李约瑟夫妇提到的那个"可能愿意收养孩子的人"从伦敦巴恩斯区给李博士寄来一封信。他们得知有这样一个孩子，想要再详细了解一下情况。1951年12月9日，还有另一位有收养意愿的人从伦敦的某一处地址给李博士写了一封信。他们表示从有色人种同盟处获知，有一个有一半中国血统的婴儿等待领养，他们愿意做这个孩子的父母。读李博士收养卷宗里的这些信件，很有意思。我也不住地会想，如果当时真的被收养了，我的人生又会是怎样？

就在安德沃市的这间育儿所里，母亲遇见了西尔维亚，两人很快成了朋友。1952年1月，西尔维亚曾在结婚之前来育儿所打了一个月的短工。她还记得那年2月的一天，她刚哄完孩子睡觉，正忙着给小宝宝洗尿布，门猛地一下推开了。只见"苏珊站在门口，冲着我喊：'哎！西尔维亚，国王死了！'"。西尔维亚说，母亲的反应很强烈，就好像这是什么大新闻一样，甚至都忘了她们还有工作要做！西尔维亚离开育儿所后，还一直和母亲保持着联系。有一天，她收到了母亲的信，说自己的颈部有点问题，需要住院几天，问她能否帮忙照看我。

母亲所说的"颈部问题"其实是颈淋巴结结核。后来，母亲在位于萨里郡沃金市梅伯里山圣彼得修道院的"罗斯利亚"疗养院住了3个月，在此期间一直是西尔维亚和她的家人在照看我。

此时，母亲和李约瑟博士以及他的妻子李大斐博士都已经非常熟悉，无论给他们夫妇二人还是其中任何一人写信都不算失礼了。于是，1952年7月14日，母亲从疗养院给大斐写了一封信，感谢她邀请自己和我一起度过了一个愉快的周末。由于李博士当时正在中国，母亲还问到他是否传回什么消息，尤其是和孙光俊有关的消息。母亲在给大斐的信中，夹入了一封写给光俊的信，里面还有一张我的照片。母亲问大斐可否在给李博士寄信时顺便把这封信也一并寄去，或许李博士会转交给光俊。

母亲还在信里对白天发生的政治事件表达了自己的看法，看得出她的左翼倾向。"许立脱是主动将自己置于风暴之中，不是吗？脱离了工人的'媒体'会故意歪曲他所说的话，这都是意料之中的事。他一定是个非常勇敢和真诚的男人！"

母亲还说，总的来看，能在这间疗养院闲躺3个月已经算是好的了。这间英国国教的疗养院专门负责培养教团的新人，以照顾年迈病弱的修女们，而且就靠收治处于结核病恢复期的病人来赚些钱。母亲说，修女们都非常亲切，而她的床位就在结核病人专属的阳台上。整个外墙上布满窗户，不分昼夜地开着，感觉就好像睡在户外一样。母亲一直要在床上休息，直到午饭过后才能穿好衣服出去活动活动，然后7点吃晚饭。探视者每天只有下午可以短暂探望，并且只能待在院子里，不能进病房。母亲说她很想我，西尔维亚过几天会把我从索尔兹伯里一起带来看望她。

在最初的这几年里，李约瑟夫妇给了母亲莫大的支持和帮助。他们不仅给我寄来衣服，还邀请我们母女去剑桥的家里小住。档案里有一封1952年12月8日母亲写给大裴阿姨的信，感谢她在自己住院期间借来一些书读，并对尚未还书表示歉意。她说之所以推迟还书，有一部分原因是几个朋友把《中国科学》这本书借走看了一阵，并且都很喜欢。她还说，在报纸上看到了李博士对在中国发生的生物战的报道，对此很感兴趣，也深表同情。她说，从李博士的文字来看，"他绝对是个很诚实、很真诚的人，我相信所有思维正常的人都会认同我的观点"。她接着说，相信李博士在中国一定发生了一些有趣的故事，下次去剑桥拜访时愿闻其详。

这封信写于1952年12月，但来信地址已经换成了大霍兰德育儿所，靠近肯特郡的七橡树镇。母亲在信里解释说，自己已于一个月前离开了疗养院，现在正在这间育儿所工作。之前在安德沃市工作过的那间育儿所因为生意萧条而关门大吉了，而这间新的育儿所恐怕月底也要倒闭了。母亲说，眼看这么多家私营育儿所都经营不下去，她真不知道这个行业还稳不稳定，并且觉得"总这样换来换去对佐伊不好。要能安稳下来就好了！"

我在为这本书做资料研究时发现了一个有分歧的地方，那就是父亲在1950年回国之前到底知不知道自己要当父亲了。我一直认为他根本不知道母亲怀孕的事，而其他几个人的说法也都证实了这一点。举例而言，黄博士（后面会提到）在他出版的生平故事《跨越三大洲的生活：一部回忆录》中写道："1943年前往西北的途中，路易·艾黎带着他在双石铺培黎学校的两个学生同我们一起去了敦煌……后来，这两个学生被送去英国，接受纺织技术培训。其中一人名为孙光俊，他爱上了一个名为苏珊的英国护士。在他离开英国后，苏珊生下一个女儿。但光俊从来就不知道，自己有一个在英国的女儿……"

然而母亲在1951年1月写给李约瑟的信中似乎已明确说明，父亲知道此事。为了保证这本书的准确性，我认真地阅读了原始资料，力求清楚无误。我的妹妹孙坤和外甥女娟娟都认为，如果父亲早就知道母亲怀孕的事情，一定会感到非常的羞耻，因为在中国文化中，一个男人让自己的女朋友未婚先孕是非常恶劣的行为。但他的内心也一定不知所措地挣扎过。因为英国联合援华会和李约瑟博士都已经说得很清楚，这两个男孩儿都必须回到中国，为新社会的建设添砖加瓦。父亲的姐姐孙兰芬说，父亲在刚回国时确实跟她提过英国的女朋友，也承认他们发生过关系，并且担心女朋友会怀孕。1996年，当我第一次问到父亲是否还记得苏珊时，他说当然记得。而在说到他们有一个孩子时，父亲却没有表示怀疑。然后，他告诉凤云阿姨和孙坤，自己在英国有过一个孩子。他说，苏珊是不会对他说谎的，听到这个消息他很安慰。所以，我们大概永远也不会知道真相，不过这恐怕也没那么重要。

还有一个很有趣的争论点在于，既然母亲当时的处境那么困难，为什么不向家人寻求帮助？母亲很坚决地说，是因为家里人都将她拒之门外，还向我讲述了当时的情形。据母亲说，外祖父母当时去医院看过她，那也是第一次见到我。他们要求母亲放弃我，送给别人收养。他们之所以那么坚持，至少有部分原因在于我有一半的中国血统。母亲拒绝了。于是，外祖母转过身对外祖父说，"走，厄内斯特。我们没有这个女儿！"我的小姨伊莎贝尔又补充了一些细节。主要是说，当时外祖父母和她住在一起。在外祖父母去医院看望母亲之前，她和他们谈过，让他们转告母亲，欢迎她有机会来家里。外祖父母去医院看过我母亲后，对小姨说，母亲听到小姨邀请自己去家里的消息后说："如果她想满足好奇心，让她自己来看我。"小姨说她没有去，而且她觉得母亲总是和别人保持距离，把自己藏起来。舅舅厄内斯特则说："我青年时期（1944—1957年），还在皇家商船队，对尤妮斯的事一无所知。我常年在海上漂着，没有参与过这些事，只听过一些'三手'的转述而已。"

不管真相如何，事实是在我11岁之前，母亲和她的家人没有任何联系。后文会再细述。

家庭成员中曾有一个人试着联络母亲，那就是梅西姨妈——伊丽莎白·格里菲思小姐，她住在皮姆利科区剑桥街1号。据母亲的表妹玛格丽特·邓恩回忆说，梅西姨妈曾让她去母亲的一位朋友家打听下落，而这位朋友就住在不足5分钟路程以外的伦敦圣乔治大道。梅西姨妈觉得自己曾在街上见过母亲，因此推测母亲可能带着孩子住在这位朋友家。玛格丽特·邓恩说，梅西姨妈很急切地想要找到并帮助母亲和宝宝，但可惜那位朋友家无人应门。在我11岁之前，我也从未见过梅西姨妈。

我确实记得和玛乔丽以及小她几岁的情人（按照当时的称谓）大卫一起住在圣乔治大道的情形。玛乔丽的儿子弗兰克和我母亲是同一所学校的同学。兰姨说，玛乔丽就是母亲那群信奉共产主义的

我的3岁生日聚会

1953年,穿着母亲做的外套在邱园游玩

朋友中的一员。玛乔丽还将另一位激进派朋友雷介绍给母亲认识。她还说,母亲很聪明,兴趣非常广泛,出于对女儿的爱而选择了护士职业。她说我母亲总是雄心勃勃的,一心想要开一间属于自己的私人疗养院或育儿所,并且一定会经营得有声有色,绝不会像过去工作过的几间育儿所一样。我也不确定自己是真的记得孩提时期与这些有趣的激进人士在一起相处的情形,还是只是看过照片而已。不过,大卫非常擅长摄影,我至今还保留着某年生日时在他们家拍的照片。照片里,我玩着小推车里的布娃娃,还在邱园里散步,就和我记忆里的场景一样!在这些快乐的

1953年，玩着小推车里的布娃娃　　　　母亲和玛乔丽

时光里，母亲和我被朋友们的爱紧紧包围着——有一种被照顾的感觉。大卫和玛乔丽把我们当成了自己的家人。

1953—1957年，母亲的工作和住处终于相对稳定了。她仍然从事私营育儿所或福利院的工作。1953—1955年是在萨里郡欣德黑德村的格兰奇，之后的1955—1957年是在萨里郡沃金市海滨路的鲁斯凡之家。印象中，这两处是同一个老板开的。他给带孩子的员工提供住的地方，还很慷慨地帮助照顾这些孩子们。我相信是他出钱让大家去上了欣德黑德村的格罗夫学校——一间规模不大的私立学校。1953年秋天到1955年春天，我也在这里就读。当时我刚两岁多，从1953年秋天拿到的第一份评价表来看，"佐伊一出现就赢得了大家的喜爱，她很可爱，并且掌握的词汇量远大于同龄人"。

没有大人的管束，我们在育儿所的屋子里和操场上过着"放养"的生活，其中一些片段至今我都还记得。送到这里来的孩子一般都有些精神或身体上的残疾，可我们当时并不懂，一个劲儿盯着屋

1953年，我在学校的照片（前排）

里的孩子看，还会刻薄地指指点点。其中就有一个头很大的孩子（脑水肿）。我们还常常在操场上跑来跑去。记得有一天下着大雨，我们开心地在雨中狂奔。有一次，我们在窗户的安全栅栏下嬉笑追打。突然，我用力一拉，一根栏杆掉了下来，我就这么摔在地上。直到现在我的下巴上还留着疤呢。

这些地方有我和母亲在一起的快乐回忆。我经常一个人待在房间里，母亲会时不时地过来看看我的情况。我酷爱读书，也擅长自娱自乐。因为得了扁桃体炎，我有好一段时间没有去上学（后来我把扁桃体切除了）。不上学时，我喜欢到母亲工作的地方，不仅有得玩，还有人照顾我。我到现在还留着母亲和其他人送给我的一些书，看见它们就会想起我那孤单而又快乐的童年。这里面有艾莉森·厄特丽的系列故事书，包括《小灰兔》和其他动物朋友的豪侠历险记；西塞莉·玛丽巴克的"花仙子"系列等等。第一本书是1953年3月大卫送给我的，他还在书上题字，祝我两岁生日快乐。而后一本书上有我母亲的题字"送给我的乖女儿佐伊·俊——妈咪，1957年5月2日至5日"（我不记得是为什么了）。此外，我还有毕翠克丝·波特的"小书"系列。能拥有这些小书真是太棒了，读着读着就可以钻进故事里。6岁生日那天，母亲送我一本标准尺寸的施皮里的《海蒂》。直到今天我仍能清楚地记得，读书时那种身临其境的美好感觉。

后来，母亲又和另外两位单身妈妈成了朋友。她们也带着孩子

（玛丽和她的儿子大卫，菲茨和她的儿子彼得）在福利院工作和生活。这两位朋友在母亲日后的生活中也出现过。此外，母亲还和福利院里一个孩子的父母（弗雷德和格拉迪斯）以及厨师（弗雷达）交了朋友，后来也常和他们在一起。在那段时间，母亲还带我去拜访过其他朋友，还一起去过伦敦。我清楚地记得1957年6月13日，为庆祝女皇陛下寿辰，去伦敦欣赏军旗敬礼分列式的情景。

母亲苏珊和我

第八章　终于成了一名合格的护士

（1957—1962年）

　　就像父亲一心想成为工程师一样，母亲也一直希望自己在专业上能够有所建树，得到别人的认可。未婚妈妈的身份使她走入了护理行业，因为照顾别人的孩子是唯一能够既提供住宿，又可以照看自己孩子的职业。现在，她的志向是成为一名合格的护士。她曾和我讨论过她的座右铭——7岁前把孩子交给我，我还你一个真正的大人。换句话说，她已经陪伴着我、养育了我7年，现在是时候施展她自己的职业抱负了。如此一来，我们就必须要分开了。我记得她曾跟我商量过，是愿意去寄宿学校，还是去她的朋友家住，我最终选择了后者。

　　母亲一直希望自己在学术上不断精进。认识她的人也说，她很聪明，但并不得志。后来，她发现通过四年制的综合培训计划就可以获得精神科和全科护士培训资质（我在她的文件里找到了1956年5月11日发表在《护理镜报》上的一篇文章，上面介绍了由弗吉尼亚沃特的霍洛威疗养院和帕丁顿区的圣玛丽医院共同开展的实验性培训课程）。她知道，这正是她想要的。

　　1956年6月21日，西南大都市地区医院董事会寄来一封信，回答了母亲有关综合培训课程如何申请的咨询。1957年11月14日，位于萨里郡弗吉尼亚沃特镇的霍洛威疗养院来信，确认母亲已成功申请护士学员一职，并列明了条件和条款。她的年薪将在362~420英镑之间，还需要再扣掉124英镑的食宿费。此外，她每周需要工作48小时。医院将提供统一制服，但每人还必须自己准备黑色长袜以及塑料跟的纯黑色鞋。培训将从1957年12月30日开始。

在护士学员的基础上，她又进一步申请并进入到了霍洛威疗养院和帕丁顿圣玛丽医院共同开展的四年制精神科和全科护士培训项目。1958年3月25日寄来的一封信中确认了此事。1959年6月30日，她转入了位于伦敦帕丁顿区的圣玛丽医院，接受为期两年的全科护士培训。

在这段时间，母亲一直和她在格兰奇和鲁斯凡之家认识的朋友们保持着联系，其中就包括菲茨。她曾在里士满山的一家大酒店（当时叫斯图亚特酒店）工作，我还记得我去酒店顶层的员工宿舍找过她。我之所以记得这么清楚，是因为她当时住在阁楼里，用一个小煤油炉取暖，我的胳膊就被这个炉子烫伤了！我们还探望过住在诺福克郡西朗顿村的西尔维亚和她的家人；住在沃金市希尔渥特的弗雷达和她的家人；住在伦敦新莫尔登区酷比花园的弗雷德和格拉迪斯，以及他们的女儿茱莉亚。我清晰地记得和兰姨的父母一起生活的情景。他们的家就在萨里郡吉尔福德小镇上的温什地区。兰姨的父母待我如同亲孙女一样，总会把好东西留给我，比如把大棚里的第一颗小草莓和番茄留给我摘，等等。兰姨的丈夫彼得还会教我玩小型的金属牵引机。

1957年，母亲开始在霍洛威疗养院工作。所有的护理人员都必须住在医院里，这就意味着我不能再和母亲住在一起了。于是，我被送去诺福克郡的西朗顿村，住进了西尔维亚的家里。西尔维亚的

母亲和我；西尔维亚和她的孩子；
摄于1961年

丈夫泰瑞是一家肉店的经理。可想而知，我的素食生涯就这么突然地结束了！他们家有两个孩子，大女儿缇娜比我小几岁。我们都在东朗顿村的学校读书，据西尔维亚所说，我们都很讨厌上学。由于这里距离伦敦很远，母亲不能经常来看我。西尔维亚说，我在学校一直都没能定下心来，最后只好搬去离母亲近一点的地方。

在培训期间，母亲一直用玛乔丽和大卫在圣乔治大道的公寓作为自己的家庭住址。我们是那里的常客。此外，我们还经常去哈罗伦敦自治市的肯顿地区看望雷、哈里姨父和他们的家人。

1959年，我搬入了东伦敦的一栋市政公寓大楼，与玛乔丽的儿子弗兰克和儿媳黛比同住。在这一间小小的屋子里，蜗居着弗兰克夫妇和他们的几个孩子，还有黛比的妈妈，我们都叫她奶奶。奶奶很喜欢陪孩子们玩。我们会把煮好的鸡蛋吃掉，然后留下蛋壳，反过来扣在蛋杯里，再递给奶奶。等她撬开蛋壳，就会发现里面是空的！我们在一起的每一天都充满了快乐和欢笑。后来，我去了鲍区的奥尔加初中小学一贯制学校读书。我至今还保留着1959年班尼特校长奖励给我的一本书——拉夫·安诺写的《佐伊的动物园》。

雷说，母亲在外苦读，这里对我来说就是一个充满温暖和爱的家。相比诺福克郡，母亲现在来看望我的次数多多了。弗兰克和母

孙如意于伦敦

亲过去是同学，也是很好的朋友。而我和弗兰克一家住在一起之后，这份友情重又点燃、升华，甚至已经超越了友情。我并不了解其中的细节，但现在看来是为了保住弗兰克夫妇的婚姻，大家决定不再让我和他们住在一起了，这样母亲才不会有机会再去见弗兰克。我找到了一封由班尼特校长在1960年7月13日手写给我母亲的信，说听到我不再去上学的消息，感到非常遗憾。我本来下个学期就可以升入奖学金班，这样以后就能进入公立的文法学校了。

于是，在1960年假期结束后，我就离开了弗兰克和他的家人，搬到苏塞克斯郡的东格林斯特德市，和兰姨以及她的丈夫彼得同住。当时，他们和另外两个朋友克里斯丁、莱斯利合租在一栋小房子里。与此同时，我也转去了当地的鲍德温希尔学校（Baldwins Hill School）。除了记得玩过简化曲棍球（一种源自苏格兰的曲棍球项目），证明我毫无体育天赋之外，我对这所学校就再没有别的印象了。我还曾跟维尔夫、宝拉以及他们的女儿，还有他们家的拳师犬住过一阵，但结果不太愉快。所以很快我又回到了兰姨和彼得的家里。我猜想大人们一定觉得我会喜欢有孩子的家庭，但其实我从小就跟着母亲一起生活，更习惯于只有大人的世界。当然，还有一个原因就是，这些家庭里的孩子也不太愿意看到家里突然冒出个年纪

我和晚年的兰姨

相仿的外人。等我再回到兰姨、彼得，还有他们的小狗身边时，已经是在东格林斯特德市内的另一处小公寓了。我对那里印象很深。每天听着艾拉夫人和其他歌手的爵士乐，享受着我的新生活。兰姨回忆说："佐伊给了我和彼得太多的快乐，这让我对尤妮斯一直心存感激。小佐伊出生没几天，我就见过她了。在她成年之前，我们一直都是她的监护人。我不想说太多细节，显得我太多愁善感。但总之，直到现在我仍把她当作自己的女儿。"后来，我和兰姨一家一直很亲近，经常去看他们，直到2011年兰姨去世。而在此之前几年，彼得就已经去世了。

1958—1962年，母亲正在苦攻护士培训的课程。兰姨回忆说："苏珊经常要去看佐伊，很多时候只能在'绿线大巴'上学习。"但她却总有办法以很高的分数通过考试，这种本事真是让人羡慕。

举个简单的例子，在圣玛丽医院的初级考试中，母亲以79分的成绩得到了第二名（第一名是80分）；1959年，她又在霍洛威疗养院的初级考试中取得了第一名，并获得了奖励。1961年11月3日，她在一个颁奖典礼被授予一项特殊的精神病学奖。1962年11月5日，她圆满完成了为期4年的一贯制培训课程，得到了伊丽莎白女王陛下颁发的奖励和护士长的祝贺。

就在此时，大姨拉文娜和小姨伊莎贝尔决定要来寻找我们的下落。对此，我们一无所知。据说大姨联系了救世军组织，现在看来还真的帮上了忙。小姨记得，在母亲和大姨约好的地点——剑桥靴子商店门口的台阶上——她第一次见到了我。直到那时，我才知道自己还有这么一大家子亲人。在很短的时间内，我见到了拉文娜姨妈、哈里姨父和他们的3个孩子：苏、克里斯多佛和马丁；见到了伊莎贝尔姨妈和菲利普姨父；也见到了厄内斯特舅舅、凯思琳舅妈和他们的孩子迈克尔、萨莉和海伦。我还记得，在我最早见到的亲人中就有表姐苏，地点就在伊莎贝尔小姨的宿舍里。当时小姨正在赫特福德郡莱奇沃思市的圣克里斯托佛学校里管理着一间寄宿公寓。很多名人都把自己的孩子送来住校，其中就包括女作家多丽丝·莱辛的儿子彼得·莱辛。小姨很喜欢照顾他们。后来，小姨不再负责公寓的管理，转而接手了学校的缝纫和手工制作课程。

第九章　开办私人疗养院

（1962—1973年）

1962年，母亲终于完成了护士培训课程，前往她朋友玛丽（当时已结婚）买下的罗斯莫尔老年疗养院工作，地址就在约克郡赫尔市阳光之岸66号。母亲之所以决定搬去赫尔市，有一部分原因在于我未能通过小升初考试。这就意味着，11岁以后我只能去中等职业学校学习，而不是文法学校，也就是说我不太可能上得了大学。可母亲坚持认为，只有接受过良好的教育，将来才可能有好的生活。此时她正巧发现，在赫尔市上中等职业学校的孩子可以有"第二次机会"，只要通过考试就能升入文法学校。

于是11岁那年，我又回到了母亲身边，进入了赫尔市的一间中等职业学校——韦尔顿高中。我们搬入阳光之岸的一间公寓，而隔壁的100号里就住着玛丽和她的丈夫艾伯特，以及4个孩子：大卫、迈克、帕特里克和安德鲁。我们两家的关系一直很好。其中帕特里克是一位全科医生，母亲和他成了一辈子的朋友。哥哥大卫比帕特里克年长许多，负责经营疗养院。20世纪50年代初时，和我一起在格兰奇和鲁斯凡之家跑来跑去的孩子里就有他一个。大卫告诉帕特里克，苏珊和他们的母亲一起在罗斯莫尔疗养院工作，多亏了有苏珊，疗养院才开始专注发展高级护理业务。

1963年，我参加并通过考试，获得了"第二次机会"。9月，我转校到了当地的文法学校——金士顿高中。我还清晰地记得站在学校操场上，从迎面扑来的风中嗅到的那一阵鱼码头的味道。不知道是什么原因，1964年我们又搬家了。这一次是要去沃金市拜夫利特的希尔渥特，投奔弗雷达、亚瑟以及他们的儿子克里斯托

穿着护士服的母亲在罗斯莫尔疗养院的后院里

弗。弗雷达也是母亲50年代初时在格兰奇和鲁斯凡之家认识的同事和朋友。她有一栋很漂亮的屋子，背靠着运河。当时，弗雷达正在一所小型的私立女子学校做厨师，所以我只在沃金市的奥克菲尔德学校上了一个学期。

1965年3月，我搬去了伦敦新莫尔登区威斯伯雷路51号，和拉文娜姨妈、哈里姨父以及他们的孩子同住。与此同时，我也转入了温布尔登女子学校就读，印象最深的就是家政课——学会了如何刷牙，还做了一锅难吃的蔬菜炖肉（多年后我在储藏室里发现了它，还密封在大保鲜瓶里呢）。大姨的家虽然很大，但东西堆得杂乱无章，大大的花园也基本都被她养的牛头梗占领了。在与厨房相连的早餐间里（厨房的另一头是储藏室），我们几个孩子坐在长桌上，聊着学校里发生的事情，以及自己的打算和想法等。这一幕场景至今还清晰地印在我的脑海里。我们的房间里有一个取暖的炉子。我还记得有一天深夜，大家都睡着了，我一个人坐在房间里织毛背

心，看着银色小鱼游向炉子方向取暖的情形。克里斯多佛在年龄上与我最接近，他和他的朋友都很爱开玩笑，我和他们在一起总是笑声不断。可他却在80年代的一场滑翔机事故中失去了生命。此后，我与马丁和苏还一直保持着很好的关系，直到苏2010年去世。

后来才知道，我之所以会搬去南方住，是因为母亲不打算留在赫尔市了。她要去赫特福德郡的希钦市，应聘本思路疗养院副护士长一职。1964年10月17日，疗养院给她发来了录用通知书。她的起

始周薪为16英镑。除了悉心照料病人，管理护理人员外，还要在老板雷纳姆夫人外出时全权负责整个疗养院的工作。她每周要工作44小时，如果夜班护士需要帮助，她还得随叫随到。

1964年的本思路疗养院

母亲在这里结识了楠姨。据楠姨的女儿露西回忆：

> 60年代的时候，苏珊开始接手本思路疗养院。作为师姐，我母亲（楠姨）去给她做副手。这对搭档相处得极好，感情笃深。苏珊是一个关心下属、待人慷慨的老板。我母亲非常喜欢她。

母亲的新工作刚开始没多久，老板就宣布要转让疗养院，然后退休。她问母亲有没有意向盘下来。要知道，母亲这么多年来一直想拥有一家属于自己的疗养院，于是她果断地抓住了这次机会。她

叫上了50年代初时认识的朋友菲茨，两人想办法凑够了钱，把疗养院买了下来。但母亲和菲茨的经营理念有很大分歧，菲茨觉得财务上应该抓得更紧一些，于是两人很快就散伙了。菲茨很快又在当地成功地经营了一家养老院。同时要求拿回原先用于购买本思路商誉和租赁权的本金，这笔钱必须要做出安排。

母亲接手本思路疗养院后不久，就在镇上租了一间房子，地址就在帕克之家的4号公寓。1966年，我搬去与母亲同住。在此之前，母亲曾让我选择，是前往相邻的莱奇沃思市的圣克里斯托佛学校——也就是伊莎贝尔姨妈和菲利普姨父工作的地方——还是去读希钦继续教育学院。我选择了后者，并且在那儿读完了初中（O-level）和高中（A-level）课程。初入这所学校时，我才15岁，在那里结交的很多同学直到今天仍是很好的朋友。西奥就是其中之一。当时他的父母都在军队，于是他就搬来与我们同住，好继续在希钦读书。正因为这样，他对母亲的生意也有所了解。他还清楚地记得那些逸趣横生的日子。当时，母亲下定决心要经营好疗养院。她一心注重护理的质量，认为最重要的事情就是让病人、员工和身边人享受到快乐。至于财务问题，就顺其自然了。

母亲真的非常关心疗养院里的那些老人们。不管发生什么，都坚持给他们最全面的护理，一点儿不会将就——即便是那些已经完全不行的人；医生未尽最大的努力来挽救一个虚弱的、神智不清醒的老妇人，对此她绝对不能接受。

我可以很自信地说，我们这两个孩子（托尼和我）什么都能修；正是因为苏珊允许我犯错，我才能有今天的动手能力。

1967年，我们搬到了希钦市的小平房。这里离疗养院更近，顺便也能离我的学校更近些。这里也属于本思路疗养院的一部分，因此无须再多付房租。西奥的话也表达了这层意思：

> 搭好折叠床，住在小平房的地窖里；苏珊最常说"走一步看一步吧"；睡前来一杯"缇欧佩佩"，我到现在还是好这一口。

我之前说过，管钱不是母亲的长项。当初借钱给她盘疗养院的人对此颇为不满。还有一些人虽然与这间养老院没有经济利益关系，但很喜欢挑刺，也会指责母亲过于铺张浪费。但对于母亲来说，人生原本是那么的艰难，现在好不容易能有这么一个属于自己的地方，做着自己热爱的事情，能为病人提供高品质的护理服务，而且也不愁资金……她是不会放弃的。她并不是故意要挥霍浪费，只是觉得钱的问题总会迎刃而解的，没必要把每一分都算得那么清楚。西奥的回忆也很好地反映了这一点：

> 到了年底，要计算疗养院的零用现金；上百张的账单、单据和钱根本对不上。最后，苏珊只能撕掉几张单据，再自掏腰包往钱箱里塞点儿钱——喏，账都平了！吃个大餐庆祝一下吧！

帕特里克小时候也来希钦和我们待过一段时间，看看他是怎么说的：

> 电影院餐厅——我记不清名字了，只记得苏珊让我尝尝苏赛特可

帕特里克和母亲在邮政塔顶上的旋转餐厅

409

丽饼（Crepe Suzette）。这道菜非常特别，不仅由厨师亲自上菜，而且上桌时还带着炫目的火焰。苏珊懂得如何把一个难忘的时刻打造得非常特别——一顿饭吃出了盛宴的感觉。从这样的事情里，不难看出她的热情和大方。

苏珊懂得享受伦敦人的生活。我非常清楚地记得，她带我去伦敦邮政塔顶上的旋转餐厅吃饭。我们坐在窗前，看着身披夜幕的伦敦在脚下旋转。我永远都忘不了那一晚——连伦敦眼都得羡慕我！

自从几年前团聚后，母亲一直与家人保持着联络。另一位家庭成员布莱恩说道：

> 如果你问我们这一代的人，得知肯尼迪遇刺的消息时你在哪里？大多数人都能答得上来——我也可以！我同样可以记得第一次见到苏珊的具体日期——1968年3月18日，周日。因为就在前一天，我刚去位于格罗夫纳广场的美国大使馆前，参加了著名的"反越战"游行活动。周日，我和梅西姨妈一起前往苏珊在希钦的家。苏珊给我泡了一杯非常好喝的奶茶。我还记得，苏珊温柔地责备我不该去参加游行，因为电视新闻里放出了示威者弄伤骑警的照片（那可不是我干的）。

兰姨也提到过母亲的热情好客：

> 这几年，我们见面的次数并不多。但无论在赫尔、希钦还是伦敦，见面时她对我都非常热情——想尽一切办法来款待

我。她的公寓和小平房里的色彩搭配、家居摆设都很有品位，很吸引我。

而此时的我正在希钦的学校里苦读，努力通过了O-Level和A-Level的考试，终于可以升入大学了。上大学是母亲在学业上为我设定的目标，看到我有此成绩，甚为高兴和欣慰。于是，我进入了切尔西学院（现在并入了伦敦国王学院），在那里结识了我的好朋友安妮特。安妮特来自特立尼达，大学毕业后就回国了。据她回忆：

> 我的记忆很模糊，但也很甜蜜。我喜欢苏珊的样子。她总是自信满满地大步走着。她招待我的方式让我很舒服——仿佛从她见到我的那一刻起，我就不再只是佐伊的朋友，而是也进入了她的生活。我很后悔她在巴罗的时候没有写信给她。她不知道，其实我经常想起她，也很珍惜在希钦的快乐时光。

1972年，母亲决定回伦敦，做回一名专业护士。她发现，自己越来越难搞定疗养院的业务。而且，做了老板之后，她也不再像以前一样享受希钦的小镇式生活了。过去，她一心想挣脱传统束缚，成为一个自由的灵魂；可现在，她和我的大学同学——一个比他小25岁左右的男人——有了来往，再不希望被别人看作"一个可靠的中年妇女"。她想摆脱这样的形象，重新找回失去的青春，再度成为一个无忧无虑的护士。我记得曾经苦劝过她，在疗养院安插一个经理，这样或许以后还会再回去。但我的话丝毫没有起到作用。她还跟以前一样，希望和过去有个清楚的了断，然后在新的环境下，开始新的职业。

母亲去世后，我在她的遗物中发现了一个大纸盒，里面装着她经营本思路疗养院时的各种文件。这些文件基本上都与生意有关，看得出来，经营一家有着如此多债权人和债务人、业务复杂的小企业实在不是一件容易的事情。我还发现一张邀请函，请她去参加1969年剑桥大学格顿学院的百年庆典。这所女子学校在建校之初为了远离剑桥的男生，而将地址选在了本思路疗养院的房子里。庆典仪式的受邀嘉宾中就包括国会议员雪莉·威廉姆斯。

从文件中不难看出，虽然母亲也和一些会计师、律师、银行经理有过票据和书信往来，但她并没有得到想要的支持，她没法经营好这么复杂的生意，而且财务上也出现了问题。文件中有一张利润评估表，里面写着5年来的经营数据，估计是当初母亲和菲茨盘下养老院时用的。但这张用铅笔手写的文件上并没有任何证据来支持这些数字，让人不免质疑这间养老院是不是根本没有盈利的可能。看上去，养老院一方面在不断地筹钱，另一方面又尽量推迟给债权人付款。这种局面一定很让人操心。一开始，母亲雄心勃勃地想要做成一件有意义的事，提供尽可能好的护理服务。但很快，美梦就变成了令人不安的噩梦。难怪母亲会选择卖掉养老院，重新做一名护士。

1973年年初，养老院的商誉和租赁权被成功出售。文件中还有1973年2月对养老院售出时欠下的资本收益及增值税的评估；1973年10月签署的透支协议；1974年3月收到的资本增值税追讨函。显然，虽然母亲卖掉了生意，但债务并没有还清。而这也成为此后10年多间，母亲每一次做决策时不得不考虑的一项因素。

第十章 晚年生活

（1973—2005年）

1972年4月1日，母亲又回到了位于伦敦帕丁顿区蒲雷德街的圣玛丽医院。1958—1962年，母亲就是在这里完成培训的。回到医院后，她被分到赫希病区（De Hirsch Ward），这段愉快的工作时光一直持续到1973年3月31日。在此期间，她从希钦的小平房搬到了伦敦麦达维尔地区的埃森代恩路。大部分时间里，她都和她的小男友，也就是我的大学朋友，一起生活在这间租住的公寓里。

后来，母亲接到她的朋友玛丽的求助，便赶回赫尔，陪她住了一阵子。据帕特里克回忆，当时他的父亲病得越来越重，常常酗酒赌博。他患上了躁郁症，在我母亲的劝说下同意入院治疗。帕特里克非常肯定地说，是我母亲挽救了他父亲的生命。

1973年5月7日，母亲加入位于伦敦皇后广场的国立医院，担任普通护士。年薪为1191镑，外加126镑的伦敦地区额外津贴。这是一所专科医院，专门收治精神疾病患者。母亲非常喜欢这份工作！因为要运用高科技手段来治疗病重的患者，还要迅速地做出决策，正好可以发挥她的智慧，也符合她的趣味。

1974年，母亲又回到了圣玛丽医院。她住在伦敦吉尔福德街的护士宿舍，每天去林都翼上班。其间，她还在伦敦海布里（N5）区住过很短的一段时间。林都翼是圣玛丽医院下属的私立分院，许多皇室成员都选择在这里生孩子。据伊莎贝尔姨妈回忆，母亲曾跟她说，其实自己更喜欢为弱势群体服务，比如她在精神病医院培训时接触到的那些病人。

1974年，母亲又在埃森代恩路上租了一间公寓，和几年前租的房子位于同一条街。1975年，她通过房东买下了这间公寓，每天从埃森代恩路的家里去林都翼工作。为了增加收入，她还在其他医院当机动护士，有时还上晚班和夜班（因为她从未忘记自己有债要还，其中就包括本思路疗养院欠下的资本增值税）。她的病人里常常有一些名人。母亲还读了一个开放大学的学位，在不停地学习中度过余生。在做护士的这些年里，母亲还会接些缝纫活来贴补家用。就像大家所公认的那样，她非常有才华，同时也非常勤奋！

1977年6月，母亲开始担任伦敦哈默史密斯区的救助副干事，直到第二年的8月辞职。她的雇主哈默史密斯区社会事务部说，非常感谢母亲愿意辞掉原来的工作，全然不在意这份工作的难度之大而来到这里。后来之所以离开，也是因为豪恩斯洛区社会事务部给她提供了救助主管的职务。一开始是在密德萨斯的赫斯顿区工作，起始年薪为3621镑。1979年，她又到了坐落在威斯敏斯特埃尔金斯大道上的老人关怀日间护理中心担任经理。当时，经常来护理中心的老人们都叫她"女掌柜"，大家都很欣赏她。

1980年，我和理查德结婚了。在理查德的母亲眼中，我母亲是一位非常孤僻的人，但一直以自己的家庭，尤其是女儿为傲。对于母亲同意我们在沃尔索尔结婚，理查德的父母非常高兴，因为这是他们一直生活的地方。我的朋友黛安评价我母亲是一个独立的灵魂，她喜欢穿着上衣加长裙，打造出嬉皮风格。而且，她也不是一位传统的母亲。所以黛安更喜欢跟我母亲探讨问题，感觉就像同龄人一样。她的穿衣风格不循规蹈矩，往往能吸引别人的眼光。但在当时，人们对于传统中年妇女的穿着都有比较刻板的定义，母亲因此显得有点儿格格不入。

1980年，我和理查德的婚礼

1981年8月3日，母亲出任了伦敦卡姆登区社会事务部的救助副主管一职。1982年2月1日，她又担任了英格斯特里路老人之家的主管，年薪约1万英镑。这是她在公立机构的最后一份工作。因为身体状况一直不好，她在1985年11月选择了退休。1986年，她接受了几次背部和膝部手术。手术费用有一部分可以报销，剩余部分则要自行承担，导致她经济上出现困难。与此同时，男友也离开了她。她当然非常伤心，但她更清楚，必须要靠自己的力量走过来。

退休生活

母亲曾经去伦敦参加过一个营销展，那里正在出售全国各地的小型移动式度假屋。想到自己还有很多债要还，而且也没有工作或男朋友，不需要固定在某一个地方过日子，她突然萌生一个想法：可以把麦达维尔的那套公寓卖掉，还清一部分债，然后再重新开始新生活。我和以前一样，质疑这样极端的做法到底明不明智。可母亲并不听劝。她一旦拿定主意，就会立刻付诸行动，绝不会再回头。

于是，1988年8月，母亲搬去了坎布里亚郡巴罗因弗内斯的沃尔尼岛。理查德的兄弟安迪帮她收拾好公寓，然后开着货车把她和她的家当送到了坎布里亚郡。安迪说自己在那之前从来没有开过货车，更别说赶上了银行假，在西伦敦拥挤的车流中穿行了。但母亲却非常有耐心。在这样的状况下能听见别人说"你做得很好"，确实觉得很安心。母亲的话稳定了他的情绪，这种感觉让他一直记忆犹新。他们前往的沃尔尼岛西海岸公园235号在夏日的阳光下展示出一派诗情画意的风光，海景尽收眼底，还能看见沙丘上的野生动物。厄内斯特舅舅还记得放假时来看过母亲，住在她"位于沙滩上的可爱的度假屋"里，还跟她一起去了邻近的湖区游玩。到了圣诞节和暑假，我也会带着家人去看她。

但是每到冬天，这里都会经历几个月的狂风暴雨，导致移动屋严重磨损，外出也变得十分困难。碰巧有一天，有个人来敲母亲的房门，问她有没有兴趣和自己换房子。他在巴罗镇上有一栋房子，现在想搬到沃尔尼岛上来。母亲请人调查了那栋房子，结果认为这

桩交易很划算。于是，双方经过法
律手续交换了房子，母亲搬去了
坎布里亚郡巴罗因弗内斯教堂街39
号。她很高兴自己能够住在实实在
在的排屋里，而且还紧邻市中心。
在这里，她可以用上岛上没有的各
种设施，还能交上几个邻居做朋
友，打发一下时间。

报答李约瑟的恩情

1992年5月2日，母亲的生活又
要发生改变，而这一次又是因我而

母亲、凯特和赛梦在沃尔尼岛的沙
丘上

起。那天我正在参加李约瑟博士的第二任夫人鲁桂珍的追悼会。当
时，李博士已经92岁高龄，身体虚弱。在追悼会后的茶会上，李博
士介绍我认识了共事多年的黄兴宗博士。1943年，黄博士也和我父
亲一样，陪同李博士一起前往了敦煌。茶会过后，我随李博士回到
了他的研究所办公室，听到他与别人谈起日后的护理问题。从谈话
中不难听出，对方提出要派一个中国学生来照顾他，但李博士对此
显然是不满意的。我走上前，问他需不需要我母亲过来照顾他。母
亲和李博士一直很熟，她擅长照顾老人，而且已经退休了，随时都
能过来帮忙。再加上母亲也总说要报答李博士的"恩情"。就像她
自己在1951年5月30日写给李博士的信中所说，在我出生前后的几个
月里，李博士夫妇给了她莫大的帮助和鼓励，对此她永远也不会忘
记——这就是她常常跟我说到的"恩情"。李博士听到我的话，表

示非常感激，于是我当即给住在巴罗因弗内斯的母亲拨通了电话。我对她说明了情况，告诉她李博士需要她。她毫不犹疑地应了下来。我们为她做好安排后，她来到了剑桥，开始照顾起李博士。

1992年6月，母亲搬到了剑桥市的夕维斯特路2号。李博士的家位于研究所内，是一间很大的底层公寓，其中有一间专门留给看护人员住的房间。楼上一层是给研究所的长期客人住的，其中就包括黄博士。黄博士回忆起与我母亲的第一次见面：

> 我第一次见到苏珊是在1992年6月。当时，她刚来剑桥给李约瑟做看护。李博士之前经常跟我说起她，所以我感觉自己是在见一位久未谋面的老朋友。她是一个很有魅力、充满热情和活力的女性。住在研究所时，我经常在周日与她和李博士一起喝茶，给我留下了很多快乐的回忆。我带他们去玉泉酒家吃过几次饭，大家都吃得非常开心。

母亲竭尽所能地满足李博士的一切要求——比如帮他把吐司和脆饼烤煳，因为这是他喜欢的吃法！当她发现李博士需要24小时不间断的护理时，又帮着招了些人，以便轮流照顾。如果精神不错，李博士就会去研究所的办公室转转，那就需要有人帮他推轮椅。他还会去拜访朋友或者在家招待客人，其中不乏一些非常有名的人。

伊莎贝尔姨妈住的地方离剑桥很近，所以她时不时会来看看母亲。她记得曾在李博士家中碰见前来拜访的特里·韦特。特里·韦特在20世纪80年代曾任坎特伯雷大主教的助手，负责圣公会教区事务。他曾以特使的身份前往黎巴嫩解救4名人质，但却于1987年不幸被俘，被单独囚禁近5年，直到1991年才被释放出来。谈话中，李博

李约瑟、李大斐和鲁桂珍的合影，照片的背面写着"苏珊·大卫·里德惠存——爱你的李约瑟，1993年于剑桥"

母亲在李博士的家中照顾他

研究所内，母亲和肯尼斯·罗宾逊在李博士的公寓门前合影

母亲、李约瑟博士和黄兴宗博士

士突然让我母亲去车库里把他母亲的自行车取出来给特里。于是，特里花了5镑将车子买下。后来，特里把车修好擦干净之后又拿回来给李博士看，李博士说，这车不止值5镑了，得问特里再要5镑！我母亲开玩笑似的责备李博士说："希望你觉得为5镑失去特里这个朋友值得。"

黄博士回忆和名人的一次见面：

> 多谢苏珊的好意，我才能有幸和史蒂芬·霍金一起喝茶。1992年秋天，霍金邀请李博士去家里喝茶。他的家离研究所不到一英里。苏珊特意问霍金夫人，李博士可不可以带个朋友来。这样，我才有了机会和霍金一起品茶、吃烤饼！

李博士本来很高大，但被帕金森病折磨得日渐虚弱。而此时我母亲的膝盖和背部却出了问题，需要再做一次手术。李博士摔倒的次数越来越多，可我母亲力气不够，于是经常需要喊消防队来扶他。我不知道当时究竟是谁在负责李博士的一应事务，只知道大家对于他需要哪些护理以及该在这方面花多少钱存在分歧。最终，我母亲于1994年离开了李博士的家，回到了巴罗因弗内斯。

最后的日子

母亲生命的最后几年几乎都是在独处中度过的。脊柱融合术和膝关节置换术的效果不太理想，并未让她真正摆脱疼痛的折磨。后来，她还患上了乳腺癌，必须接受长时间的治疗。这些原因使得她只能待在巴罗因弗内斯的家中。她越来越不喜欢和其他人待在一起，她说自己一辈子都住在别人的屋檐下，现在只想在自己家里随心所欲地生活。她习惯了晚睡晚起，因此总担心如果有一天不得不进养老院了，这种作息习惯是不会被允许的。她还在继续攻读开放大学的课程，虽然难度越来越大，却一直未放弃。此外，她还不断地给《读者文摘》投稿，指望这样能增加她抽中大奖的机会。她从未放弃过希望，一直到最后都在想如果中了奖该干吗。

我的丈夫理查德描述了我母亲的晚年生活：

我和岳母第一次见面是在1977年夏天的一场民间摇滚音乐会上——听起来似乎很奇怪，但我很快发现，这样的场合确实跟她很相配。那时候的她就是"朋友苏珊"——友好、热情、慷慨、睿智，难以捉摸，也容易激动上火。她当时的工作是照顾老人，很关注他们的津贴问题。她觉得正是因为管理层的无能，才会导致津贴无法发放到位，为此经常恼怒不已。我们过去常常探讨这类问题！

在麦达维尔的家里，我发现她简直沉浸在启蒙时代和开放大学的其他课程里。

1988年搬到巴罗，意味着她退休了。于是，"朋友苏珊"变成了"岳母尤妮斯"，至少我们的感觉是这样。她隐居到了沃尔尼岛。那是真正意义上的海边，一片未曾受到过任何破坏的原始海滩，很壮观。几年后，为了生活方便，她又搬到了巴罗镇的中心。在其他方面，也看得出她在躲避。到了后来，我和她之间的联系就只能通过佐伊了。我觉得岳母和巴罗这个地方很像：它以一种奇怪的方式将谦虚务实的气质和原始粗犷的美糅合在一起；它在历史上曾属于兰开夏郡，现在又归入了坎布里亚郡；它确实就像当地人所说的那样，位于全英国最长的一条死胡同深处。但我们又有什么资格去评头论足呢？

在独处的日子里，母亲的精神和身体都日渐虚弱。好在周围有一些很好的邻居和朋友会去照看她。当初她决定要远离我们生活，我想是因为她知道如果住得近，她就会失去独立的能力，最终也会失去尊严。她决意要死在自己家里，坚决不接受任何社会关怀，也不愿搬入任何形式的养老机构。她真的做到了。而我也深深地感激她身边的朋友和邻居在她风烛残年之际给予她的关照和支持——我住得太远，这些事情我都做不到。母亲常常和我提起他们，所以我想在本章的最后附上他们的话。

爱德加写道：

> 关于苏珊——我们是在1990年认识的。当时我刚退休，搬到西海岸公园来住。苏珊搬去巴罗一段时间后，需要到剑桥待一阵儿。于是，她就叫我帮她照看教堂街39号的房子，生怕会有窃贼。后来等她再回到巴罗，我又去看望过她——通常都是6月6日她过生日那天，还有圣诞节之前。

戴夫写道：

> 苏珊跟我说过，她照顾了李约瑟博士一段时间，并且对他的工作非常感兴趣。她说他们曾谈及婚嫁，但最终并未走到一起。我觉得很遗憾。不过真要在一起，苏珊就得离开巴罗，去剑桥和李博士生活了。

苏珊很健谈，也很善于聆听。我有什么问题都会找她说，这可不是跟谁都能做到的。她总会给我一些很好的建议，是一个值得永远信赖的朋友。

我很欣赏苏珊的性情和生活态度。她和所有人一样，也会遇到住房等各种问题，但她绝不会为此而烦心。问题出现了，那就解决问题，然后事情就过去了。她也几乎不会抱怨。她身体不好，但除非你问她，否则很少听她提起。她很懂得如何处理生活中的问题，值得我们学习。

诺琳写道：

一开始认识她的时候，总是看她在公园里转悠。我们会打个招呼之类的。不久之后，我就开始给她们家打扫卫生。这么多年来，我们有过很多欢笑——天南地北，我们无所不谈。她跟我谈起过她曾经经营和工作的疗养院。她很喜欢读书、看电视、整理花园。我一般会在她家里待两个小时。打扫完卫生后，我们就会坐下来喝喝茶，吃吃饼干。我发现她是一个很可爱的人，从来不说别人一句坏话。她会谈谈自己的家庭和朋友。虽然这些年经常这儿疼那儿疼的，但她的脸上始终挂着笑容。我很高兴认识苏珊。她的一举一动都会铭记在我心里。她是我的朋友。

最后一段要留给乔。他负责在当地送报，然后每周五上门收钱。我猜想，他应该是母亲生前最后见过的人。他写了有关母亲的几件事情：

第一次见面，苏珊不停地重复着说："我来自一个你不知道的小地方。"你不说我怎么知道！但很快也就习惯听她这么说了！接着，苏珊和我简单说了说她的过去，以及后来的困境。她跟我强调了很多次，说她做生意的水平和我不相上下，因为她曾经也经营过一家疗养院。

我每周五晚去家里收钱的时候，她总是会跟我开玩笑！她会说"你又来了！""让不让你进来呢？""我可没钱！""我没法付你钱，我找不到笔和支票簿了。"说完，她就会把早已填好的支票拿出来给我。

苏珊责怪我不该叫消防员去修她的防火警报器，说我搅了她的安宁；不该向地方议会提出在必要时给她一些帮助。但后来，她又向我道歉，说知道我一切都出于好意。她也经常会提醒我一些事情。

第三部分
孙如意的成长
我与英中了解的故事

第一章　与李约瑟的渊源

几乎在整个青少年时代，我都以为父亲已经去世了。我编了一个故事，说父亲在我小的时候得天花死了。说着说着，我自己也开始相信了。我母亲一直戴着婚戒，让大家以为她是个寡妇。虽然在我出生之前，她曾计划向我坦白身世，但真正到我问起的时候，她却什么也没有说。我觉得，那些收留过我的"阿姨"们曾经试着向我透露一些信息。比如，我记得弗雷达阿姨曾经和我有过一次谈话；在1961年3月我生日那天，弗雷德叔叔和格拉迪斯阿姨送给我一本玛利亚·格雷特写的《中国的孩子》。到我十几岁时，越来越讨厌别人问起我的中国血统——我发现大家都很好骗，当每次不可避免地被问及"你是哪里人？"时，我就会回答："瑞典。"于是，他们就不会再问了。

不过，我们一直和李约瑟夫妇保持着往来，而他们也善意地帮我寻根。多年来，他们给我和母亲寄过很多书作为生日或圣诞礼物。一般都会在里面题字，并写上日期和缘由。

我收到的第一本写着日期的书是吴承恩的《西游记》，英译者为阿瑟·韦理。那是1956年圣诞节时，李约瑟夫妇送给我的礼物。后来，每年的圣诞节我都会收到书，包括徐维理的《我在中国逗留的日子》（1968年圣诞节）和詹姆斯·贝特兰的《在今日中国的年轻旅行者》（1961年圣诞节）。1962年的圣诞节，我收到了中国出版的《中国民间故事》，而母亲则收到了路易·艾黎的《有办法！》。

1965年圣诞节，约瑟和大棐夫妇送给我们两本书——赵树理的《三里湾》，英译者为戴乃迭；柳青的《创业史》，英译者为沙博理。他们在书里附了一封信，说希望我们会喜欢这些书，而这些有趣的故事反映了中国农村正在发生的变化（信上特别指出，这些变化对中国意义重大）。信里还解释了李博士写在书上的这几个中文字。他给我起了个中文名字"李若金"，意为"像金子一样贵重"。李大棐在这封信里还提到，李约瑟让我和他们一样姓"李"，是因为中国人分不清"N"、"L"和"R"这几个音，"里德"和"尼达姆"都可以叫"李"。李约瑟还在信里夹了一小张纸（从一张大纸上裁下来的废纸，字写在背面——李约瑟从不浪费一点儿东西），上面写上了我的中文名字，再分别与我英文名字中的三个词一一对应。所以，"佐伊"等于"若"。在"里德"旁边，一开始写着"孙"（当然是我父亲的姓氏），后来涂掉了，写上了"李"字。我们当时并没在意这些，直到最近做研究，才发现它们的意义。李大棐还在信中写到，书的封面上写的其他几个字包括他们俩的中文名，以及"惠存"，意为"送给我这本书作为礼物"。信的最后，他们说想要买一辆新车，有机会开到"本思路疗养院"来看望我们，亲自跟我们解释一下给我起的中文名和其中每个字的含义。

接下来的每一年圣诞节，李约瑟夫妇都会寄书给我。1969年，他们寄给我一本李博士当年出版的《大滴定：东西方的科学与社会》，上面写道，"谨以此书献给鲁桂珍：她揭示、对比、体现并

这两本书的照片，上面有李约瑟写的中文字

李约瑟在纸上写了我的中文名（"孙"字被涂掉了）

李约瑟夫妇送给我的书，下方的绸布是他们送给我的结婚礼物

证实了东西方之间存在的密不可分的联系"。1979年3月21日，作为生日礼物，他们送给我一本李约瑟编著的《理解模型：一种自然哲学模式》以及李约瑟供稿的《中国与西方：人类的进化》。

如今我看着书橱上的这些书，心里却有一些遗憾和后悔。我意识到，如果小时候能全都拜读一遍的话，一定能够更深刻地了解中国。事实上，我当时和中国并没有任何联系，因此不觉得自己应该有中国情结，也不会想要了解中国。20世纪五六十年代长大的英国人有很强的种族观念，因此我每次见到不认识的人时都会被问及来历（鉴于我和母亲的生活经历，我小时候被问过很多次这样的问题）。谈话总是以"你是哪里人？"开场。我觉得，说自己有一半中国血统，又说不出在中国有任何亲人，就好像在骗人一样。所以对外我从不说自己有中国血统，因为我没法证明。

2004年6月1日，我和丈夫理查德前往剑桥大学图书馆查阅李约瑟博士资料时，提取了"佐伊·俊·里德"的文件。从中，我了解了自己的过去，弄明白了当时一直不懂的一些问题，知道自己小时候为什么很矛盾于承认自己的中国血统。文件中的第一封信是我在1973年11月11日写的，坦诚面对31年前的自己，这种感觉很奇妙。申请查阅时，我并没想到这封信会被放在李约瑟的文件里，就在剑桥这间小小的图书馆里！早在上大学时我就想了解自己与中国的渊源，通过写这本书，让我有机会在李博士的档案中找到答案。

"佐伊·俊·里德"档案中的第一封信是我在1973年11月11日手写的。信的开头写道："哦，约瑟叔叔和大斐阿姨——这几天，我总想找你们聊聊，私心里希望你们能帮我理一理头绪……"我接着说道，"几个月前，母亲终于和我说起父亲的事情。终于。其实我从来都不相信父亲在我小的时候病死了。我一直觉得他还活着，就在中国。我知道这话听起来很像事后诸葛，但这是真的。而且，很长时间以来我都有一个想法，那就是总有一天我会和父亲，或是了解他晚年生活的人见面。而这一切，都会发生在中国。"

这封信很长。信里接着说，我不知道听到父亲的消息该怎么办。是不是应该用我出生时李博士给母亲准备好的回邮信封给父亲写一封信？或者是不是应该给李博士写信，让他帮忙再找找我父亲？这也让我想到应该去读读家里的书——显然，当母亲告诉我父亲的事情时，她复印了一本当年李博士夫妇送给她的《有办法！》给我。在给李博士夫妇写这封信时，这本书我已经读完一部分了。我说，这个故事很励志，集体生活的想法也很有趣。

当时我正在学校读大四。大三时，我做过课题研究。我对研究人员做研究的动机和目的感到相当失望。科学和社会课也一样，老师总说"现实是由社会构筑的""现实是可以商量的",把学生弄得一头雾水。显然,我很难适应从硬科学到软科学的转变。所谓软科学,就是要审视科学在社会中发挥的作用,包括马克思主义。我记得,科学和社会课上曾经布置过一篇论文,题目是"为什么现代科学不能诞生在中国?",参考书目里就有《大滴定》。于是,我厚着脸皮给作者写了一封信,想获得一些有用的提示。在人口学课上,老师说要和我们探讨一下中国的人口控制问题,但我质疑西方获得的中国人口数据是不是有偏见的成分——于是我就请李博士帮我找一些公正的数据。

李博士总是喜欢先用手写,然后再把信打出来寄。所以在他的档案里,既有打印给我的回信,也有精心构思的手写稿。他在1973年11月24日给我的回信中说,他和大柴阿姨收到我的信,得知我已经了解到父亲孙光俊的事,并从中受到鼓舞,特别高兴。李博士说:"我可以负责任地告诉你,你父亲年轻时候非常有魅力。我相信如果他还健在的话,现在也一定是个很优秀的人(纺织工程师)。"但他也提醒我,跟父亲联系时要谨慎,因为"光俊可能根本就不知道苏珊发生了什么事情。他很可能早就在中国结婚了,有自己的家庭。如果是这样的话,他很可能从来就没有和他妻子谈起过在英国的这段恋情"。李博士还在信里说,只有一个人有可能帮忙联系光俊,这个人就是路易·艾黎,"现在时机差不多成熟了,或许可以通过艾黎私底下打听一下。"他还说,我在信里问到的其他事情最好面对面谈,信里说不清。他知道我在科学和社会学、绝对论和相对论之间感到无所适从,邀请我去剑桥和他们共度周末,再一起探讨。

文件里的下一封信是我写的。除了感谢他们的邀请,还确认会在2月16日去剑桥过周末。下一封信的日期是1974年2月25日，是李博士写给艾黎先生的。这封信同样也包括认真手写的初稿和最后寄出的打印稿。寒暄一番过后，李博士道出了此信的真实意图，希望艾黎先生可以打听一下孙光俊的下落，还提醒艾黎先生，说孙光俊就是1943年随他们一起去敦煌的两个男孩之一。信里还表示，自己非常喜欢这两个孩子，尤其是光俊。随后，李博士解释说，这两个孩子来了英国之后，"光俊和一个名叫苏珊·里德的护士相爱了，苏珊还在光俊回国后诞下了他们爱的结晶。苏珊勇敢、坚韧，品格优秀，她一个人养大了女儿。现在，我们跟她女儿佐伊也很熟。佐伊还来我们家住过一两个星期……光俊回国后就音信全无。苏珊试着给他写过几封信，但都石沉大海"。信里还说，"现在，苏珊（一直很专业、很能干，现在还当上了护士长）和佐伊（非常聪明，博学、上进、左派）都很优秀。直到一年前，苏珊才把佐伊的身世告诉了她。我也给她看了一些光俊的照片。她很为自己的父亲骄傲，并且由衷地希望能有机会去中国看看，了解革命的情况。如果可能的话，还想见见她的父亲，让他知道还有这么个女儿"。

李博士接着在信中说，之所以会找艾黎先生，是因为他是"世界上唯一能弄清情况的人"。他问艾黎先

父亲的相框照，李博士本来放在床头，后来送给了我

生光俊结婚了没有，有没有孩子，我有没有可能见他，并且说了让我去中国的计划——说他已经和我提过将由英中了解协会出面，并且可以给我一些资助。李博士说："中国当局还是很仁义的，我敢说，只要找对门路，中国方面应该会给他们做好安排。"信的结尾，李博士说："如果光俊知道苏珊这么优秀，也一定会很高兴。佐伊是个很有志向的年轻人，希望能为世界做出贡献，但在西方这个不道德的社会中，只能处处受阻。"

档案中的下一封信是艾黎先生在1974年3月16日写给李博士的。艾黎先生先说了一下自己的近况和身体状况，然后解释说，在他离开中国前，孙光俊和王万盛回学校来看过他很多次。光俊娶了山丹学校的一个女学生为妻，她的父亲和叔叔从双石铺起就在培黎学校工作。艾黎先生确实有一些担心，考虑到"之前光俊就因为

李约瑟写给路易·艾黎的信。
照片由李约瑟提供，转自李约瑟研究中心

跟我走得很近，给家里惹了不少麻烦"，他建议我们"最好不要找光俊，不要再让他解释什么。他的女儿来到中国，就自然知道这里是什么情况了。光俊很敏感，我不想让他再有负担"。信里还说，他很高兴未来有机会见到我，并且会尽可能为我在中国期间安排好一切。他劝我们"还是不要招惹麻烦"，并说"这也是我和孙光俊商量过后的意见"。

　　大柴阿姨一收到艾黎先生的信，就复印了一份寄给我。一个月后，李博士又给我寄了些父亲的照片。在1974年4月17日的回信中，我说："我自己也没有想到，艾黎先生的建议竟会让我如此失落。"在信的最后，我说我仔细想了想艾黎先生提出的"不要招惹麻烦"的建议，觉得他是对的。我希望有一天能去中国，不过要先

is a nurse in a county hospital. On the whole I think it
better if Sun is left alone, with no more explanations to make
and that his daughter just takes China as she finds it when
she comes. He is a sensitive person, and I would not like to
give him additional burdens. It is not easy for his daughter
to understand, I know, but that is how it is.

　　　　As for Wong, I last saw him in 1966, when he
came to Peking with the Red Guards. He is a teacher in the
textile college in Hsienyang near Sian. He could not find
lodgings so I lent him a big blanket.

　　　　I would be very pleased to meet Zoe and do
anything I could for her while she is around.

　　　　Last year, when I was in Lanchow, many Bailie
boys did call, but I was too rushed to see them all. But the
NW is the NW, and one must understand local problems. Best
sometimes to let sleeping dogs lie. Which is what I advise
with Sun. I did go to the woollen mill last summer, but
no one mentioned him. There have been many changes these
years and probably he has been transferred elsewhere.

　　　　Yes, I do remember with much pleasure our
journey to Tunhuang, and the gay company those two kids
gave. And all the discussion with you. I keep in touch
with Hungying, who expects to be able to come this year
sometime, if it is possible for her to see her relations.

　　　　Hope the spring is treating you well, and
that your work goes steadily on despite all.

　　　　　Love to all,

　　　　　　yours,

摘自1974年艾黎先生写给李博士的信。
照片由李约瑟提供，转自李约瑟研究中心

437

完成当年的教师培训课程。我还向李约瑟夫妇详细说明了自己参加艾塞克斯大学静坐示威、游行，警察拉起警戒线，以及逮捕"艾塞克斯90"的情形。被逮捕的都是些学生，其中还包括我当时的男朋友。那会儿，我只想和学联的代表一起支援被逮捕的学生，耽误学习也在所不惜！

文件里还有我结婚时和李约瑟夫妇互通的几封信件，以及母亲和李博士之间的信件。一直到20世纪80年代末，母亲仍在请教李博士，希望他给自己的生活提一些建议和指引。她说自己不开心，不知道未来究竟该往哪里走。李博士的建议总是体贴周到，很能理解别人的处境。

第二章　终于找到父亲

1992—1994年，母亲一直在照顾李博士。这两年间，因为探望母亲的缘故，我和李博士常常见面。他见到我总是很高兴，也会和我聊聊天。然而，在帕金森病的摧残下，李博士连交谈都困难了。我确实想问他有没有办法帮我跟我父亲联系，但当时的他已经十分虚弱，始终没能抽出精力来帮我们牵线。但这有点儿令人费解，因为其实当时我们就知道，父亲和李博士已经联系上了。

1993年2月，父亲给李博士写信，对鲁桂珍的故去表示吊慰，并再次感谢李博士在20世纪40年代给予自己的帮助。父亲还提到，他和王女士（他以前的老师，所以一直这么称呼她）正在商量要如何纪念那些过去支持过兰州培黎学校的外国友人。他说，从1992年起，他和王贤林（曾在兰州培黎学校工作）就时常见面，并从他那里得知了鲁桂珍去世的消息。1993年4月，李博士在我母亲的帮助下给父亲回了信。这样一来，母亲自然就有了父亲的住址。李博士在信中说，自己和第一任妻子大斐有过64年的"幸福婚姻"，但在最后5年里，妻子却患上了阿尔茨海默病。而他和桂珍在"分隔多年"后终于走到一起，虽然结婚仅两年桂珍便去世了，但她"至死仍神志清醒"。于是他告诉我父亲，自己现在正由我母亲照顾，他说"苏珊是最合适的人选，因为她人真的太好了"。

我在剑桥也见过黄兴宗博士。我第一次见到他是1992年5月在鲁桂珍的追悼会上。他是个很体贴的人，容易交流。我告诉他，我想去看看自己的父亲。等他离开李约瑟研究所，回到位于美国弗吉尼亚州亚历山德里亚市的家中后，我也和他通过信。他年轻时曾担任过李博士的秘书，并于1943年以"英中科学合作处主任"的身份陪同李博士一起游历了中国的大西北。当时同往的还有培黎学校的两个男同学，负责帮助李博士和艾黎先生处理途中的一些事务。我父亲孙光俊就是其中之一。1994年2月，黄博士写信给我，说他已经按照我母亲给他的地址写信给我父亲了，但无人回信。他打算等下次去中国时登门拜访，看看我父亲的情况。他还说，会提醒李博士给他孙光俊在中国的地址。

1995年，李约瑟博士去世。6月10日，我参加了他的追悼会。列席人员中也有黄博士。他前一天刚从美国华盛顿飞来，追悼会之前刚和朋友在大学俱乐部一起用了午餐，其中就包括我的母亲。能再见到黄博士，我非常高兴。我们讨论了一下接下来该怎么联系我父亲。黄博士认为最好的途径是先联系王女士。我们说好，如果我父亲拒绝，就再不提此事。母亲很支持我，虽然这段感情对她而言早已经是过去的事了。黄博士与王女士一直有联系，于是在1996年1月写信给她，提出我想联系父亲一事。他解释说，我并不想让父亲为难，并希望王女士找机会向我父亲提及此事。

1996年，王女士私下里和父亲见了两面，直到第二次时才终于告诉他，他有个远在英国的女儿。父亲回到家后，即向他的妻子凤云阿姨和女儿孙坤说明了我的存在，以及我想联系他的事情。她们都表示，父亲应该承担起自己的责任，并和我取得联系。其实父亲刚回国时，就向他的妻子和姐姐说过他和我母亲的关系。后来家里其他人也知道了，只是从未谈论过。

得到妻子和姐姐的同意后，父亲准备给我回信，表达他们这个中国家庭对我的热烈欢迎。于是在1996年2月，母亲和我收到了父亲的英文回信。他在信里表达了自己的喜悦，欢迎我们到他家里去。他对我母亲说，相隔近半个世纪后，这是他第一次提起"苏珊"这个名字，还在信里署下了我母亲熟悉的那个名字——Kim①。信的最后，他说希望给我起个中文名字叫"孙如意"（发音接近"佐伊"，意为"拥有希望得到的一切"）。他也希望我能同意做他的女儿。

1996年，我们保持着书信往来。父亲的信经常是写给我母亲的，但显然母亲还是希望由我来延续这段关系。他们互相说明了家里的情况。父亲如今已经退休了，和凤云阿姨住在兰州，就在工厂附近的家属楼里。儿子们也已经不在家住了。其中两个儿子已经成家，而小儿子在外打短工，很快也要回来了。他的女儿孙坤则带着丈夫和年幼的女儿住在附近，和老两口尤为亲近。父亲特别关心3个孙女的未来。

我告诉父亲，我已经有了一段幸福的婚姻，现在伦敦地方政府任高级职务。听说自己在英国还有一男一女两个外孙，他高兴极了。我们开始讨论见面的事宜，并做了详尽的规划。

我的丈夫理查德以及两个年幼的孩子凯特和赛梦都给了我莫大的支持，陪着我一起踏上这趟未知的旅程。虽然我们都有对方的照片，但我始终不确定他们是否真的会在约定的时间出现在约定的地点。我们到了北京后，住进了瑞士酒店。接着，在1997年3月，我46

---

① 此前，父亲孙光俊与母亲交往时常用此名。

岁生日那天，我们在天安门广场的国旗下见了面。那时，距离父亲离开英国，已经过去了47年。

1999—2007年，我又去中国看望过父亲5次。1999年，我和丈夫理查德第一次去了他的家乡兰州。他希望我们了解真实的他和他的家人。所以他举了个例子说，在我们去之前，他曾想过要在家里装一个西式的坐便器，但最后还是决定不这么做。

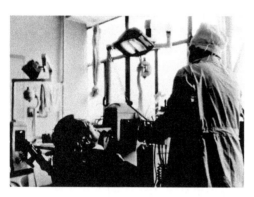

1999年，父亲在看牙医

我们住在父亲买的第二套房子里，这套房子就位于毛条厂的大院内。虽然已是3月，外面仍飘着雪，但暖气却已经停了。他指给我们看附近的诊所（中药西药都有）。因为他牙齿不好，我们陪他去当地的医院里看牙医。我们还去了培黎广场，这里是培黎学校的旧址，现在矗立着路易·艾黎的雕像。在兰州的这段时间里，我们参观了凤云阿姨退休前工作的病房。父亲还带我们参观了毛条厂，不过当时已是一副衰败的景象，他曾经酷爱摆弄的那些机器也只剩寥寥几台。我们还去了他外孙女娟娟的学校，站在65个活泼但又听话的孩子面前，用英语和他们简单地交谈，回答一些问题。

2001年，我们决定去中国的其他地方看看，于是一家四口就又出发了。这一次，我们和父亲、妹妹、妹夫和外甥女约在了山东省的省会济南见面（从北京往南坐火车两小时）。在济南，父亲的姐姐孙兰芬和她的一大家人热情地接待了我们，还在朋友开的饭店包

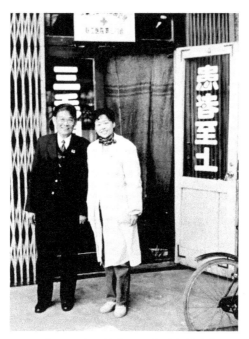

1999年，父亲和他的医生在诊所外合影

1999年，父亲、我和凤云阿姨在兰州的艾黎先生雕像前合影

间里设宴。孙兰芬姑姑的4个孩子都带来了各自的家人。席间，大家还唱了卡拉OK。他们留意着我们的每一句话，每一个举动和每一口食物。虽然桌上有些菜我们没有吃，饺子也没有吃完，不过真的全无恶意。

2003年，我决定独自回中国探望。父亲和他的家人觉得很奇怪，但我其实只是想找个机会和父亲独处，听听他的故事，了解他的人生。直到这时我才知道，我们每次来的时候，他都要花很多时间，费力地给大家从英文翻译成中文，再从中文翻译回英文。我们说的每一句话或做的每一个动作都会被大家所关注和讨论，所以每一句都必须要翻译！我提议单独和父亲乘一次火车，这样我们就可以坐下聊聊。我们从兰州乘火车向西，3小时后抵达西宁，最后在冷风中走去看了看佛寺。

2005年，我和理查德去看望外甥女娟娟。她当时正在四川省东南部的宜宾上大学。按照中国的标准来看，宜宾是个小城市，相对比较淳朴。娟娟好不容易才找到了整个小镇上唯一的供应咖啡的小店，让我解解馋。她尽力了解并满足我们的要求，虽然有些在她看来有点儿奇怪。但随着她英语说得越来越好，她终于可以向我们解释很多中国的习惯。在去兰州的路上，我们途经成都，不能免俗地去了熊猫研究基地，然后连夜坐火车赶去兰州。

我最后一次见到父亲是在2007年。当时我带着儿子赛梦去了成都，看了熊猫，然后在兰州住了一周。我们住在妹妹和妹夫家。他们刚刚搬入新房，美中不足的是房子位于7楼，却没有电梯。赛梦很喜欢和我最小的弟弟孙龙还有孙坤的丈夫晓虎在一起。他们俩都很爱玩闹，每次吃饭时都要让赛梦喝掉半杯以上的啤酒。我们逐渐感受到大家生活上的不同。通过学习中文，我更多地了解到中国文化和礼仪。因为文化上的差异，我们闹过各种笑话，好在我的中国家庭并不介意，逐渐明白我们并无恶意。举个例子，父亲不知如何跟家里人解释，为什么我大老远前来却只住一个星期，他们认为我应该多待几个月。我们也明白，当对方没有效仿我们所看重的文化礼节时，也绝不需要生气。在大家的共同努力下，我们很好地增进了中西方之间的共识。

2008年，父亲因白血病去世，享年82岁。他葬在兰州市郊一块风水福地。他去世后两个月，我带着家人和中国亲人一起去墓地看望他。按照传统，我和丈夫、孩子的名字同父亲的其他孩子和家人一起，都被刻在了碑上。这令我们非常感动。

父亲的墓，位于兰州市郊，摄于2008年8月

1997年，我们第一次去北京时的照片

1997年3月21日，我和父亲第一次见面

家人在天安门城楼前合影

家庭合影

欢乐的一家人

儿子赛梦在长城

父亲，1997年摄于北京

第三章 推动英中了解：个人层面 和政治层面

1997年3月21日，我终于寻到了自己在中国的根——我的生命中第一次出现了父亲的角色，还多了兄弟和一个妹妹。第一次见面时，父亲带来了他的妻子、女儿、女婿、外孙女，以及住在北京的侄子、侄媳和他们的宝宝。突然之间，我就有了一个大家庭——而且还是在中国！我还发现，这个国家里有很多很多的人都和我一样高，长得也跟我很像。这种感觉真是太奇特了！

这下，我终于有理由去做那个"中国人'如意'"了。早在去中国之前，我就已经开始学中文。很感谢我的第一位中文老师细心地教我准确地使用中文，就像教中国孩子一样。比如，让我大量地练习正确的书写笔画。我的中文水平目前还很差，所以我还在不停地学。不过，现在在伦敦地铁上听见中国人说几句奇怪的英语，我已经能够懂了，这也不失为一件妙事。我感觉到自己和中国是相通的。

从2000年起，我开始担任国家医疗服务体系（NHS）主任，在一家服务伦敦东南部的大型精神健康信托机构工作。工作中，我也努力抓住一切能与中国联系的机会，参与接待了很多从中国来的医疗专业人员，陪同他们考察国家医疗服务的管理体系和临床实践。通过与英国驻北京大使馆紧密配合，我们和山东省的一家精神病院达成了合作，中方派 6 名医生和护士到英国进行了为期一个月的培训和临床观摩。促成这样的合作需要坚持不懈的努力和决心，我之所以热爱这份工作，就是因为它促进中英之间的了解。

2009年，我成了英中了解协会的主席。我和母亲都曾是协会的会员。2000年左右，我自愿加入了协会的委员会。之后，我以普通委员的身份参加委员会会议。等到前主席退位后，我在大家的鼓励下申请了主席的职位。我猜就是从那时起，我和协会里的同事共同努力完成我们的使命，以此报答李约瑟博士对我的恩情。2013年，我带领英中了解协会团队，沿着我父亲1943年陪同李约瑟博士走过的路，前往中国西部。英中了解协会已经有相当长时间没有组织过这样的旅行了。我们从重庆到敦煌，途中停留兰州、山丹等地。当我们离开兰州，顺着他们70年前的足迹达到山丹，参观当地的培黎学校，然后再继续出发前往敦煌时，我感到无比的兴奋。

2015年，英中了解协会正式成立50周年。在5月30日晚的庆典上，中国驻英国大使刘晓明阁下致开幕词，他说道：

> 孔子说："五十而知天命。"今天，在庆祝英中了解协会成立50周年的特殊日子，我衷心希望英中了解协会矢志不渝于你们的"天命"，也是你们的使命——促进中英了解和友谊，在新时期继往开来，创新发展，担当桥梁，缔结纽带。

1965年，李约瑟博士和他的伙伴们成立了英中了解协会，在中英两国人民之间架起了一座桥梁。协会成立之初有数千名会员，也成为20世纪70年代，英国与中国沟通的唯一途径。在中国被国际社会孤立的那段岁月里，英中了解协会一直与中国保持着密切的联系。

现在的英中了解协会是一个小规模的志愿者组织，致力于与其他组织一道，朝着共同的使命迈进。英中了解协会的宗旨是让英国人了解中国，消除彼此分歧，澄清不实信息。我们已经发起了"英中了解协会2065"计划，向着未来50年的使命迈进——"在新时期继往开来，创新发展，担当桥梁，缔结纽带"。

2015年5月，英中了解协会成立50年庆典

2015年，我还受邀参加了中英学术基金会的年度颁奖典礼。我意外地发现，父亲和他的同事在1947年来到英国时也曾得到中英学术基金会的资助，并成为最早获得该项奖学金的中国学生。中英学术基金会的资金最早是由英国联合政府时期的掌玺大臣斯塔福德·克里普斯爵士负责筹集的。在他的说服下，他的妻子伊莎贝尔·克里普斯夫人也承担起了募集经费的重任。莫凤麟博士（当时名为"米勒夫人"）当时任组织秘书。

2015年，我在中英学术基金会年度颁奖典礼上领奖

THE SINO-BRITISH FELLOWSHIP TRUST
中英學術基金會

BRITISH
ACADEMY

THE
ROYAL
SOCIETY

THE TRUSTEES OF
THE SINO-BRITISH FELLOWSHIP TRUST

Look forward to the pleasure of the company of

Zoe Reed

AT THE ANNUAL RECEPTION AND CERTIFICATE PRESENTATION 2015

*Jointly hosted by the British Academy, Royal Society
and the Sino-British Fellowship Trust*

to honour scholars supported by

THE ROYAL SOCIETY/SBFT INTERNATIONAL FELLOWSHIP
THE SINO-BRITISH FELLOWSHIP TRUST
AND THE KATHERINE WHITAKER BEQUEST

To be held at

THE BRITISH ACADEMY,
10 CARLTON HOUSE TERRACE, LONDON SW1Y 5AH
ON THURSDAY 25TH JUNE 2015
12.30PM – 2.30PM

Please Note: The Presentation Will Begin At 12.30pm prompt

POUR MEMOIRE
*If you are **unable** to attend please contact
Debbie Haine, Trust Secretary, Sino-British Fellowship Trust
23 Bede House, Manor Fields, London SW15 3LT
email a.ely@btinternet.com*

2015年中英学术基金会颁奖典礼邀请函

他们发起了一项名为"英国联合援华"的全国性计划，募集了大约300万英镑的经费，向在战争苦难中挣扎的中国人伸出援手。当时的英国驻华大使薛穆爵士带头成立了一个专门委员会，将募集到的资金分发到中国各处。

1947年，培黎学校的学生抵达英国，受到莫凤麟博士
的迎接

这样的家庭关系成了我推动英中了解的动力。小时候，母亲很少对我提及父亲。但我记得她和我说过，父亲游泳游得很好。于是，我和所有孩子一样，给这个故事插上了想象的翅膀。最后在我

的脑海里，父亲竟然游过了英吉利海峡！母亲还说过，父亲是个出色的艺术家。但直到多年以后，她才给我看了父亲用蜡笔画的自画像。很显然，父亲是坐在厨房的桌子旁，对着镜子，很快完成了这幅画。母亲把这幅画卷起来收藏了很多年，直到我40多岁时才拿出来。画纸很粗糙，四边也不方正，想要裱起来也很困难。

1997年，"父亲"对我来说终于不再是一个虚构的称谓，而成了一个实实在在的人。他和他的家人都真实存在着。后来，我和家人还去中国看望过他们几次。我们逐渐意识到，两国的文化有着太多的不同，因为它们本就植根于两种不同的文明。虽然常常提醒自己不要"冒犯"，但这对于双方来说都是不可避免的。好在通过这么多年的磨合，我们已经完全理解和适应了。遗憾的是，2008年的

父亲的自画像

夏天，父亲还没能等得及我们8月去看他，就匆匆离世了。而他去世那天正是我母亲的生日。直到他走后，我才得知这个消息（这似乎也是中国的风俗），身体不住地颤抖，悲伤欲绝。他只当了我11年的父亲。不过，就像我曾经跟他说过的那样，如果他当年真的留在了英国，我恐怕不会像今天这么"富有"——现在，我有一个中国大家庭，包括一个"纯种"的中国妹妹和她的女儿。在他们身上，我感受到满满的温暖和亲情。

在英国时，我们跟中国家人的联系主要通过娟娟，有时候发邮件、用聊天软件，偶尔也会打网络电话。我的妹妹孙坤现在正在学英语，比我学中文的进步要大多了！这几年，我们仍然会去看望孙坤、晓虎和他们的女儿娟娟。2012年，我的儿子赛梦和凯莉结婚了。为此，孙坤和晓虎特地前来英国，和我们一起住了两周，还参

2012年参加赛梦和凯莉的婚礼

加了婚礼。此外，我表姐苏的女儿尼娜和克丽斯塔曾在2002年去过兰州。妹妹、妹夫此行也见到了这两个孩子，以及我的小姨伊莎贝尔。

2013年，娟娟和瞿德业（音译）喜结连理。我的女儿凯特去兰州待了10天，还给他们做了伴娘。2014年，作为新婚礼物，我们邀请这对幸福的小夫妻来英国玩了3个多星期。今年（2016年）6月，我和女儿凯特去了兰州，看望娟娟和德业的宝贝女儿悦悦。就像凯特说的，他们真的就像是我们的家人，我们是一家人。

2014年8月，瞿德业、娟娟和凯特在特威克纳姆区的圣玛格丽特，
于凯特的店门外合影

最后的想法

我的女儿凯特在我母亲去世后，写了以下几段文字：

    大家（也就是妈妈）总说，我喜欢颓废和奢华的东西，这一点绝对是遗传了外祖母的基因。我不知道这话说得对不对；我只知道，记忆里和外祖母在一起的每一寸光阴都是快乐的。我们在商场里喝过几次下午茶，有一次还打车从伦敦市中心直接回家；我们一起沉浸在芭比和瓷娃娃的童趣世界里；我们还一起探讨《ER》《聚散离合》和其他电视剧。恐怕真没几个大人会像外祖母这样，同一个9岁的孩子认真讨论电视剧，还能一起为宠物仓鼠制定每天的护理方案！

    我们绝不只是表面上的亲密而已。从很小开始，我就觉得自己和外祖母有着非常深厚的情谊。这种感觉我会永远记得。我们会聊天到深夜，她会告诉我在寄宿学校发生的糟糕经历，以及她那个有着种族歧视的家庭。我们也会谈到纳尔逊·曼德拉先生的奇事，还有祖父，以及那首名叫《在开往中国的慢船上》的歌。我想，我对于生命、死亡以及道德品行的思考，最早就来自外祖母。从本质上来说，我们一直在试图让世界变得更好。

祖母很善于与人交流，不会总说些俗套的老话。我猜想，这就是她最与众不同之处，成就她成为一个独一无二的灵魂。所以，成长的过程中能够有外祖母相伴，我真的觉得自己非常幸运。

母亲过世后，我的表姐苏回忆道：

我的姨妈苏珊·尤妮斯总是很善变，难以捉摸。今天在这儿，明天在那儿。精明、智慧、眼光敏锐，穿着时髦，内心强大，但同时又非常脆弱，独立、大胆、自立。她怎么想就怎么说，从不在意后果。她绝不是一个平凡或无趣的人。如今，一个光辉的灵魂离开了我们，整个世界也跟着黯淡下来。

我对母亲的想法很复杂。过去，我总觉得自己和她很亲密，并且对她负有很重的责任。而随着她日渐虚弱，我却常常苦恼，不知道究竟怎么做才是对的。她决意要死在自己的家里，直到生命的最后仍然顽强地想要自立——但我知道，她根本应付不来。她拒绝一切形式的帮助。2005年9月初，我对她实在放心不下。我决定不管她怎么想，都要定期安排一些人去家里照顾她，或者让她搬到更安全的地方去住。我给她打电话，她没有接，不过这在以前也发生过。我知道，必须得面对面地和她谈谈了。于是，我和好朋友黛安约在普雷斯顿火车站见面，让她开车送我去巴罗——就沿着世界上最长的那条死胡同。我们一边开，一边讨论该如何给我母亲说一个有说服力的例子，让她知道自己必须接受帮助和照顾。车驶向巴罗，我的心七上八下。因为我清楚，有可能她已经死了，可就算不是这样，她看到我这么坚持地要她接受帮助，也会中断和我的关系。结果，前一种可能性应验了。我很感激黛安一直支撑着我，否则我真的不知道自己该怎么挺过去。母亲从屋内把门反锁了，我用钥匙开不了门。我叫来了警察，他们破门而入……警察让我和黛安去宾馆等消息，再做下一步打算。我也很感激母亲锁住了门，以及警察对此事细致敏感的处理。

此刻回忆起我母亲一生的经历，发现她经常陷入事与愿违的境地。于是，我总算可以理解，她强烈地要求自立和对外界的攻击，都是因为她害怕伤害和失去。她本身就是一个巨大的矛盾体：她聪明、活泼，和很多了不起的人有交往，却又很脆弱；她一直想要规划一个更美好的未来，但却又始终无法将过去的不公放下；她希望我们不似母女，更似朋友，却又对我充满了慈母般的骄傲和爱；她不想被人看作一个传统的老祖母，但又像宝贝似的疼着自己的孙辈们。说到底，她很害怕社会上对老年人的歧视以及由此表现出来的各种行为和不公，却也因此不肯接纳生老病死的自然变化。

有趣的是，当我回想人生才发现，我的父亲和母亲都没有真正担起过家长的角色。父亲在世界的另一边，而母亲则经历了一世的苦难和考验。但他们都给了我很多力量和馈赠——我记得李约瑟博士曾多次表示，我有一些举止或言谈"很像中国人"，我听了非常骄傲。我确信自己身上也有很多母亲的影子和优点。我很高兴自己有很强的适应能力，这无疑是童年不断搬家的结果。从母亲的生活和我自己的童年经历中，我明白了什么才是最重要的。我一直非常清楚，我最想要的是稳固的家庭生活和爱，以及让我的孩子在一个地方长大；想要的是融入工作环境、社区和团体，与同事和朋友保持联系。现在我已经65岁了，要学会承认生老病死的自然法则。不过，我也和母亲一样独立，总是雄心勃勃，一旦确定目标就一定要实现！

父亲和母亲在一起度过的短暂时光，为他们留下了一笔宝贵的遗产，陪伴着他们走完了一世的人生。母亲去世后，我在她的遗物里找到了父亲在英国时送给她的一件纺织品。她把这件纺织品和她当时常戴的一条围巾，还有我的第一只鞋绑在一起。父亲去世后，我去看望过他的遗孀凤云阿姨，她把父亲的一些私人物品交给了我。根据中国的传统，凤云阿姨将父亲的大部分物品和所有的信件、文章都烧了，好让父亲带着上路，但却把他的几本中英词典留给了我。这几本词典是他的心爱之物，每天都在看。其中有一本还是在英国时使用的。她还把我母亲当年亲手织给父亲的毛背心也留给了我。很显然，父亲和母亲一生都保留着对那段珍贵时光的记忆。现在，我将这些物品放在一起，作为我对他们俩的纪念。

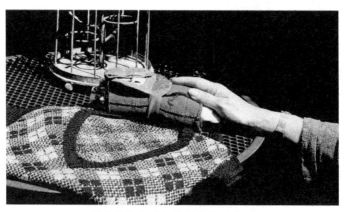

母亲当年亲手织给父亲的毛背心